Marriage beyond Black and White

Marriage beyond *Black and* White 0943

An Interracial Family Portrait

by *David Douglas* and *Barbara Douglas*

Bahá'í
PUBLISHING
Wilmette, Illinois

Bahá'í Publishing, 415 Linden Avenue, Wilmette, IL 60091-2886

05 04 03 02   4 3 2 1

Library of Congress Cataloging-in-Publication Data
Douglas, David (David Almerin), 1949–
      Marriage beyond Black and white : an interracial family portrait / by
   David Douglas and Barbara Douglas.
           p. cm.
         ISBN 1-931847-04-5 (softcover : alk. paper)
         1. Douglas, Barbara, d. 1995. 2. Douglas, Carlyle. 3. Douglas,
   David (David Almerin), 1949– 4. Interracial marriage—United
   States—Case studies. 5. Racially mixed people—United States—
   Biography. 6. Bahais—United States—Biography. 7. United States—
   Race relations. I. Douglas, Barbara, d. 1995. II. Title.
   HQ1031 .D68 2002
   306.84'6—dc21

                                    2002012478

Cover design by Suni D. Hannan

To my mother and father,
Barbara and Carlyle Douglas,
who bestowed upon me the gift of life,
instilled in me a love of reading,
and gave me a deep appreciation for
the family of humankind.

Contents

Acknowledgments

I am grateful to my sisters, Brigid Crantz and Linda Jones, for their encouragement and assistance in helping me recall many of the events in our family's story and to Brigid especially for her attention to dates and the chronology of events in this work. Linda added immensely to the heart and soul of our family chronicle by courageously sharing many of the more painful and difficult experiences of her life. I thank Theresa Haynes for her support and editing. I deeply appreciate the encouragement of my editor, Terry Cassiday, and her determined efforts to make my writing clearer and my book factually correct. She has a real gift for anticipating the questions readers might ask and, by pointing them out to me, helping me to answer them. I am profoundly grateful to my wife, Kim Douglas, for her patience with me in times when I paid more attention to the book than to her, for her constructive editorial comments, and for the love, understanding, and support she has given to me and to all of my family members throughout the process of writing this book. Finally, I am profoundly grateful to the National Spiritual Assembly of the Bahá'ís of the United States for its personal attention to this work, its spiritual guidance regarding some of the more troubling details, and for including this work as part of the Kingdom Project, thereby allowing me to share my family's story with the world.

—David Douglas

Marriage
beyond
Black
and
White

Introduction

My PARENTS BROKE ONE OF the strongest taboos in our society and thereby became outcasts in their native land. This is their story. Their transgression began in 1942 when, against conventional wisdom, they violated the unwritten rule that said Whites socialize with Whites and Blacks socialize with Blacks. When they first met, they felt an immediate attraction to each other. As they explored the nuances of each other's character and personality, their attraction grew into a love so strong that it lasted a lifetime. It was a love forbidden in our society. It resulted in a marriage that was outlawed in many of our American states at the time and was regarded as anathema in the rest.

Despite this opposition, throughout some fifty years of marriage their relationship retained the freshness of teenage puppy love, the romantic spark of newlyweds, and the intimacy of best friends. It was wonderful to watch them even in their seventies, holding hands and flirting with each other while they laughed and joked like kids. They loved to play chess and Scrabble together and enjoyed an intensely passionate private relationship. My mother once confided in me, at a time when I was experiencing some difficulties in my first marriage, that they had made love every day of their marriage except when they were physically separated or ill. Each found in the other a confidant and trusted companion with whom they shared their deepest concerns and feelings. While they had their share of typical marital problems, the deep love they held for each other endured for over fifty years. As a couple they were physically attractive, charming, witty, and intellectually engaging. And yet because he was Black and she was White, they were ostracized.

When they got married, interracial marriage was illegal in twenty-seven states of the union. In states such as Indiana police stopped and either harassed or arrested interracial couples. My parents dared not travel through the South because Black men were lynched for the slightest hint of association with White women. In the two Northern cities of Detroit and Chicago, where they spent most of their married life, they were not permitted to rent hotel or motel rooms except in red-light districts. Racist thugs in Chicago verbally harassed them. In Woodstock, Illinois, one of the windows in their home was shattered by gunfire, their canary was killed, and their fellow townspeople eventually chased them from their home. In Detroit they were socially isolated for more than forty years. Their professional coworkers shunned them as soon as they discovered the interracial nature of their marriage.

While interracial marriages have always been part of the fabric of American society, they have nevertheless been rare. I am not talking about the sexual liaisons common between White slave owners and their Black slaves. Nor am I talking about the illicit unions between mixed couples neither willing nor able to become legally married. Legal marriages between Blacks and Whites have been forbidden and discouraged for most of our nation's history. While increasingly common, interracial marriages of all kinds comprise only about 2.6 percent of all marriages in the United States, according to the year 2000 U.S. Census figures. Such marriages are still frowned upon by many Whites, Blacks, and other ethnic groups in this country. According to a survey reported by the *Washington Post Online* on 5 July 2001, 52 percent of interracial couples reported being mistreated because of their relationship. According to the same survey 46 percent of Whites considered it better to marry someone of their own race, while only 21 percent of Blacks considered it preferable to marry someone of their own race. Thirty-five percent of Whites reported that it would bother them if a member of their family were to marry someone of a different race, and an additional 9 percent said they simply could not accept it. Only 9 percent of Blacks surveyed said they would be bothered if someone in their family were to marry a White person, with an additional 4 percent saying it would be unacceptable.

Because such marriages were extremely rare in the 1940s, my parents attracted attention wherever they went. When they were out in public as a couple, people stopped and stared at them, often with disapproving or hostile looks, sometimes worse. Our family attracted as much attention as a traveling menagerie while we engaged in ordinary activities such as shopping, visiting amusement parks or museums, or going to the movies or the public library. Although people seldom made comments, they turned their heads as they walked down the street or drove past us in their cars.

My parents taught us to respond to these situations with humor and a sense of personal pride. After such excursions, we laughed and joked about the events of the day in the safety and security of our home. Mom and Dad always let us know that the attention we received was not our problem. It was the problem of those who were ignorant and rude enough to stare. They taught us that there was one race: the human race. We learned that racial distinctions are arbitrary and illogical. Racial prejudice was born out of ignorance and greed and had been encouraged by corrupt plantation owners, politicians, and others in positions of power who stood to benefit by perpetuating racism.

While my parents shielded us in our early years from their personal experiences with racial discrimination, they taught us about the heroic struggle of Blacks against the forces of racism in this country. We learned Black history from our parents in the fifties, long before Black pride became popular in the African American community during the sixties and seventies. They consciously planned to help us take pride in our African, as well as our European, heritage.

My parents took pride not only in their heritage but in their marriage itself. They knew they were breaking the paradigm of ethnic isolation most Americans follow. They knew they were pioneers in establishing a new paradigm in race relations. They believed that if other Americans saw how well an interracial marriage could work, it would lessen the fear of—and the prejudice against—such marriages. They hoped that in some small way their marriage would help to bridge the gap between Blacks and Whites in this country. That was, in fact, part of my mother's purpose in setting out to write this book.

Marriage beyond Black and White was started some fifty years ago when my parents decided to share their story with a fascinated yet profoundly ignorant public. Together they drafted an outline of their proposed book and wrote the first chapter—alternating voices—each giving his or her personal perspective. In that preliminary work, written in 1952 after nearly a decade of marriage, my father wrote that this book was

> a sincere attempt to place before the American public the problems which face us and others like us in the hope that we can dispel some of the myths surrounding interracial marriage and create some measure of understanding toward it. . . . We believed that society would, in time, take a marriage such as ours in stride. We did not know, but we believed.

About the same time, describing the purpose of the book, my mother wrote,

We are not alone in our situation—interracial marriages are increasing in number. Perhaps such a book as we propose will help to bring about a greater understanding of and sympathy toward such marriages. We hope so. Anyone who has ever found himself on the wrong side of a wall will know what the feeling is that Carlyle and I have sometimes. But we know where the wall is, and we know what there is on the other side that is worth getting.

Although my parents were committed to each other and believed there was nothing wrong with interracial marriage, the constant struggle to survive in a racist culture took its toll over the decades. My parents began their marriage with bright hopes, buoyant and full of optimism about their union. They dreamed of achieving success in their careers. They hoped that society would gradually learn to accept interracial marriages. While their optimism concerning their own marriage proved to be well founded, over the years they became bitterly disillusioned by the degree of racism in America. My father elaborated on his career struggles:

> Now began two years of disillusionment. When I applied for positions ranging from clerical to minor executive in the business world, I was told that although my education and personality were well suited to such work my color made me unacceptable. Eventually I took a part-time clerical job with a research organization, but the pay was inadequate. This was followed by substitute teaching (two calls a week). Then through the state civil service I received an appointment as a social worker, but I was unable to support six people on two hundred dollars a month. Once more I became a janitor. Full circle! Had the struggle for education been a waste of time and effort and hope?

At the age of thirty-two and after four years of college, the best-paying job my father could find was a janitorial position, which was no better than the jobs he had held before college.

My mother entered the marriage with deep feelings about the brotherhood of all humanity. Though she was White, she came to hate White people because of the contempt and hatred so many of them displayed toward her and her interracial family. She came to hate her own race even more as she delved into African American history and learned of the depth of the brutality and constant indignities that African Americans

8

have faced throughout their history in this country. She was stunned and enraged by the torture, mutilation, and murder of Emmett Till.* She realized that the same fate might overtake her husband or her children. Finally, the shock of her demotion from first-class citizenship as the respected daughter of an established family in a university town to second-class citizenship as the wife of a "Negro"—caused her to see the stark reality of racism more clearly than many Black people can. Typically, American Blacks can only dream of having the advantages that the majority of Whites hold as their birthright. She enjoyed those advantages for the first three decades of her life and then lost them overnight. Only in her eighties, after decades of reflection and healing, was she finally able again to accept White people as individuals.

For my father, the effect of the lifelong struggle with racism was less obvious but equally devastating. In the early years of his marriage, he dreamed of becoming a college professor. That dream was dashed when a perfectionist advisor rejected his proposal for a master's thesis. Although my father was a brilliant man, he never believed in himself enough to overcome that obstacle and other similar obstacles. He was accepted at the University of Chicago but never completed his degree. He wrote beautiful poetry in the early years of his marriage, yet his pen was suddenly stilled and his poetic voice silenced forever well before he reached the age of thirty. He never explained why. I never knew he was capable of writing such exquisite poetry until after his death. It was then that my mother shared with the family a much-cherished collection of his poems that she had kept hidden away, like buried treasure, with other family heirlooms. Although his poetry clearly demonstrates his command of the written word, he never believed his work was special. My mother, a published author, often said he could write better than she could, but he was never convinced of the value or quality of his work.

My mother described him as a courageous man who proudly stood against society on the issue of interracial marriage. He was able to maintain that audacious stance well into their marriage. However, after decades of rejection by a world of cold, staring strangers, he no longer enjoyed going out in public with his family—the price was too high. For

---

* Emmett Till, a fourteen-year-old Black boy from Chicago, was savagely brutalized and murdered in Money, Mississippi, in the summer of 1955 simply for saying "Bye, baby" to a White woman.

much of his adult life, he was plagued by nightmares of mobs of White men who hunted him down like an animal. My mother said he often awoke terrified in a cold sweat from these nightmares. Although at some deep level he experienced absolute terror of Whites, he never displayed his fears to his family or others. He always projected an image of dignity and intellectual detachment that concealed the fear, anger, and frustration that lay beneath the calm surface.

While I cannot prove that any of these difficulties in my father's life were due to racism, there is no doubt in my heart or mind that racism was one of the root causes. The tragedy of my father's life is that he was a great man who never realized his greatness. He was a nightingale convinced that he was a sparrow, so he hid in the bushes and stopped singing. Only his mate and a few of his friends knew the quality of his voice and the beauty of his soul. The world never knew and will never know the charm and elegance of the melodies it missed. It is my hope that a small measure of his wonderful qualities will be revealed in this book.

Although my parents began this book as a joint effort during the 1950s, the struggles of living soon overwhelmed them, making it difficult to write. While my mother later continued writing and enjoyed the publication of a novel, my father never mustered the psychic energy to write again. When my wife, Kim, encouraged him to write his story, he replied, "It would be like taking a razor to my wrist." He could not bear to relive the years of pain, turmoil, hate, rejection, and failure.

Unfortunately, my mother felt that the story of their marriage would not be complete without his perspective. She wrote about her adventures in China. She created a novel about Detroit's race riots. She even wrote about the tragedy of Native Americans. But she would not write about their marriage. Not without him. Not until after his death. Until that time, it was her steadfast hope that he would join her in sharing their story.

When my father died at home of cancer on February 17, 1995, I thought my mother would immediately follow. They had always said they could not live without each other. Even though she was grief stricken by the loss of the man to whom she had devoted more than fifty years of her life—her best friend, her lover, her close companion and confidant— she was energized by her determination to complete the book they had started together in the fifties. In 1995, from February until July, she wrote furiously, sleeping little and working late into the night. She said openly that her only reason for living was to complete this book. She wanted the world to know the story of her marriage. She hoped that by sharing her pain and her struggles, White people in particular would come to understand the damaging and long-lasting effects of racism. She also wanted the world to know that she had experienced great happiness in marriage and that interracial marriages were not automatically destined for failure.

Writing their story after my father's death gave continuing purpose and meaning to her life. It also tormented her. While she enjoyed memories of the ebb and flow of her love relationship with Carlyle, remembering the good times only made her miss him more dearly. Sometimes she couldn't sleep because of the emptiness she felt without him. She often awoke crying in the middle of the night, aching for the gentle touch of his hand or longing for the soothing tones of his deeply resonant voice. When she remembered the bad times, the pain and anger resulting from the racism she experienced flared up as strongly as ever. When she recalled the murder of Emmett Till, she struggled in vain to control her tears as she cried out, "How could they do this to another human being? He was just a child . . . just a child." When these troubling memories overcame her, she needed my father's comfort and support, and he was no longer there.

In the end she never finished the book—the pain of writing her story was too much for her. She could not endure the acute loneliness of living without her husband while daily reliving the intimacies of their life together. She could not stand the pain of their struggles without his supportive presence. She called my wife, Kim, almost daily in tears. She said repeatedly, "This book is breaking my heart. It's killing me to write this book." Although she spoke figuratively, I believe that writing this memorable account literally killed her. She suffered a heart attack in late July and died during the month of August 1995 as her systems shut down one by one. The doctors say that she died of multiple systems failure, but it's clear that she really died of a broken heart.

Ironically, while she would not finish the book when my father was alive because she felt his input was necessary, she could not finish it after his death because she needed his emotional support to endure the painful memories.

As my mother lay dying in the hospital, unable to speak because of the ventilator in her mouth and unable to write because of a stroke that had paralyzed half of her body, we struggled to communicate with her. Through voice and touch, eye contact and notes, we tried to convey our love for her. Three generations of our family—my sisters and I, our spouses, our children, and their children—maintained an almost constant vigil at the hospital during the last month of her life. The doctors told us she had only days to live, yet she proved them wrong. She struggled to regain the ability to complete her memoir. The will to live, however, was not enough to heal her damaged brain and heart.

As Mom slowly crossed the chasm from life to death, we held on to her as long as we could. Unable to stop the inevitable journey, we watched as the gleam of light gradually faded from her eye. Sometime during those agonizing hours, I promised that I would finish her book.

Though she had written furiously during the last sixth months, churning out thirteen well-written chapters, she had only covered the first fifteen years of our family biography. The bulk of her story was untold.

Taking up the story where she left off, I have attempted to finish the chronicle of our family life. While understandably my work cannot reflect the same detail and charm she brought to her composition, I want the reader to know the entire story of their marriage. In addition, I hope that the added perspective of an interracial child who was a product of their union will enrich the reader's understanding of the dynamics of our family life and broaden his or her insight into the disease of racism. I also hope the reader will come to appreciate the depth and beauty of the spiritual teachings of the Bahá'í Faith, especially on the subject of race relations. While this memoir is not about the Bahá'í Faith, it would not be complete if it did not explore the profoundly positive effects that the teachings of the Bahá'í Faith and members of the Bahá'í community have had upon my life as an adult.

Finally, to fulfill my mother's wish that my father's voice be included in this memoir, I've inserted some of his poetry. Each poem was selected because its theme reflects one of the themes in the chapter it precedes. While the poems do not add to the details of the history of my parents' marriage, they reveal the depths of my father's feelings on a variety of subjects—particularly his deep love for my mother. I hope the reader will appreciate them.

In my struggle to blend my mother's writing and my work into a coherent and meaningful memoir, one of the challenges I faced was the use of language when referring to Americans of African descent. My mother wrote in the language of the forties and fifties, often referring to Americans with African lineage as "Black" but also occasionally as "colored" or "Negro." Although this language is dated, I have retained it in some places in an effort to maintain the authenticity of her voice and to give the memoir historical accuracy. Similarly, when I write about my experiences with people of color during the sixties and seventies, I use the terminology that was most natural to me at the time, referring to people of color as "Blacks." Toward the end of the book I use the terms "Black" and "African American" almost interchangeably, reflecting the fact that both terms are common in today's dialogues and literature and that I use both terms in my conversations. In all cases I use capital letters because I strongly believe that capital letters should be used to denote respect for the group of people being named, just as we show respect for people of all ethnic groups and nations by capitalizing the first letter of their ethnic or national names. I might add that philosophically, I prefer the term "African American" to "Black" for a variety of reasons. The terms "Black" and "White" as applied to people have their origins in our country's history of racism. They are a purely social construct with no scientific meaning and have been used to separate people legally, socially, and politically. If we are to overcome racism completely, I believe we will have to transcend or go beyond the use of the terms "Black" and "White" to denote groups of people. Paradoxically, it's impossible to talk about racism in this country without using these very terms that in some measure help to perpetuate separation and division. The terms "African American" and "European American," while awkward to some, are both more comfortable and meaningful to me. They refer to our ethnic and cultural heritage without invoking the false construct of race. Nevertheless, I have used the terms "Black" and "White" liberally in this work in the interest of using language that is understandable and comfortable to the average reader.

Another struggle I faced arose from the tension that exists between my desire to be truthful about the events of our family history and my desire to protect the privacy of my family members and others who have crossed our path. While I have consulted with them liberally to the extent possible, the final copy of this work has not been edited or approved by any of them. In the final analysis, this work is a combination of my mom's memoir and my purely subjective interpretation of the events of my family's history. I offer my humble apologies to any and all family members whom I may offend by sharing my interpretation of their personal struggles and by offering very limited and inadequate descriptions of them as people.

Finally, in order to protect the reputation of people whose behaviors are mentioned in this work in a less than positive light, I have changed some names and, in some cases, locations while stating my memory of the related events as accurately as possible. I sincerely hope that these minor changes will not undermine the reader's understanding of the truths that I mean to convey in this work.

—*David Douglas*

Part 1

Barbara's Story
Personae Non Gratae

1

The Last Flaming Ray

TWILIGHT

At twilight when the air is clear,
Old memories hold sway;
Shades from out the past appear.
Why, why can they not stay?

The setting sun's last flaming ray
Retouches nostalgia with cheer;
But the heart is unmoved by this golden display
At twilight when the air is clear.

For the present with its stifled fear
Of time to come, the untried day,
Fades in dreams of a bygone year;
Old memories hold sway.

As mellow twilight fades away
And softly, swiftly, night draws near,
With equal softness through the gray
Shades from out the past appear.

But no sounds reach the eager ear.
What can a memory say?
Their message is for the heart to hear.
Why, why can they not stay?

When hearts are young and life is gay
The musings of age are queer
And age itself does not betray
Why memories are so dear
At twilight.

—*Carlyle Douglas, May 16, 1944*

PERHAPS AS WE GROW OLDER, all of us, at one time or another, undertake a bittersweet journey through the past, searching for the milestones, the secret impulses, the dimly remembered encounters that have shaped the course of our lives.

For more than five decades I have been estranged from White America, so I find it extraordinarily difficult and unexpectedly painful to think back to the time when middle-class White America was the only world I knew and the mores, values, and laws dictated by the Caucasian majority circumscribed my life. At that time, I was quite contented that it should be so. How could I have felt otherwise? Had I not been born into the greatest democracy the world had ever known? Did I not, with my classmates, learn the Declaration of Independence and thrill to the words of Patrick Henry, "Give me liberty, or give me death"?

I had learned nothing of the inequities and injustices that had corroded and continue to corrode our democracy. Both teachers and textbooks discreetly avoided discussing slavery or somehow made it seem an advantageous way of life for the poor African, who was presumably only one step removed from primitive man. As for the destruction of the American Indians and their way of life—well, they were savages and dangerous. Also, if this democracy of ours was to flourish, we must acquire their tribal lands by whatever means necessary in order to accommodate the expansion of our fast developing country. This was God's will, America's manifest destiny.

We knew how our White ancestors had fought for freedom in the Revolutionary War, but no one had ever told us about Crispus Attucks's heroic role in the Boston Massacre or about the gallant Blacks who had fought at Bunker Hill. We learned with pride about the Civil War and about how bravely the Boys in Blue had fought to free the slaves, but no one had told us that Black soldiers—ex-slaves and freedmen—had fought side by side with those Northern White men. No one ever told us that Lincoln said it would have been impossible for the North to win without the help of the colored troops.* And, most shameful of all, our history teachers had never spoken of the legendary all-Black 369th Regiment, which had fought in World War I and each of whose members had received from France the Croix de Guerre.†

We did not know that the heroes of American history George Washington and Thomas Jefferson had been slave owners. We had never heard of Frederick Douglass. Like my peers, I accepted without question the myths interwoven with facts that comprised our history books. So you see, from kindergarten through high school, in our predominantly White classrooms, we saluted the flag each morning, sang "America the Beautiful," and sincerely believed that all was well with our world. This was the Promised Land.

How, then, did I get from there to where I am now?

I am seeking now for the events, the signposts if you like, which led me from that smug, comfortable way of life into a bewildering kind of no-man's-land not unlike a dark and sinister bog. In that murky bog, one moves with utmost caution, wary of a fatal misstep, dogged by fear as tangible as the chill sweat in the palms of your hands or the nausea seething in your stomach. Yet all the time there was, and is, a bitter, self-destructive rage growing in my heart against my countrymen who have permitted and even indulged in acts of violence and insidious repression against Blacks. These acts of violence and repression have the potential

---

* Lincoln wrote in a letter dated August 1864 to John T. Mills, "The slightest knowledge of arithmetic will prove to any man that the rebel armies cannot be destroyed by Democratic strategy. It would sacrifice all the white men of the North to do it. There are now in the service of the United States nearly 150,000 colored men, most of them under arms, defending and acquiring Union territory. . . . Abandon all posts now garrisoned by black men, take the 150,000 from our side and put them in the battlefield or cornfield against us and we would be compelled to abandon the war in three weeks." J. A. Rogers indicates that "178,975 Negro soldiers fought in the Union Army between 1861–1865," placing the total number of Black men aiding the Union Army at "perhaps twice that number" (*100 Amazing facts about the Negro with complete proof,* pp. 39, 14). Henrietta Buckmaster explains, "The famous Fifty-fourth Massachusetts swung [into action] on its way in February, and the Fifty-fifth followed soon on its heels, some of those two hundred thousand Negro troops who were, by Lincoln's testimony to turn the tide for the Union" (*Let My People Go: The Story of the Underground Railroad and the Growth of the Abolitionist Movement* [Harper & Brothers, 1941], p. 306).—D. D.

† The Croix de Guerre is a French military decoration that was awarded to individuals and groups for feats of bravery in the course of the two World Wars.—D. D

to destroy our ancestors' dream of a world where all men, women, and children would be free. But worst of all was the sickening sense of guilt—the realization that I, too, had stood by passively, whether because of inexcusable ignorance or inertia, and done nothing to make amends.

Though bewildered and frightened during those early years of my new life, I fought side by side with my husband, who, brave beyond belief, stood steadfast. Although knowing better than I the consequences of flouting the rules of society, he, too, was determined not to let racism destroy what we both believed to be a viable marriage, even though he could very well have lost his life in the process. Melodramatic? Not at all. In those days, Black men had been killed for so much as smiling at a White woman.

I look back upon those long ago days of my childhood and adolescence with overwhelming gratitude for the great good fortune that allowed me to be born to a mother and father who, it seems to me, typified the very best America has to offer. They believed in the Declaration of Independence, the Constitution, and the Bill of Rights, and in their own quiet, gentle way, they lived what they believed without self-righteousness or ostentation. As parents, they were equally remarkable—particularly since they came to parenthood in the early years of the twentieth century, when Victorian methods of child rearing were still approved. The prevailing philosophy of the day toward parenting was typified by the adage "Spare the rod and spoil the child." Yet I was never physically punished, never spanked, never shaken or slapped. Disciplined, certainly, for my parents were no pushovers. One must abide by the house rules or lose privileges. Fortunately, they were not only kind and just but extraordinarily understanding and good-humored.

I was born and raised in the Midwestern university town of Ann Arbor, Michigan, where as an only child I was sheltered, if not indulged, and enjoyed the usual quota of birthday parties and Christmas trees.* My mother, Ethel Louise Tinker, was the daughter of a doctor and a schoolteacher. She had not gone to college, but because her brothers and sisters were professors, doctors, or professionals of one sort or another, she straddled the social line between "town and gown." Although she hobnobbed with professors and their wives, she never put on airs or acted superior to the "townies." My father, Almerin David Tinker, quiet and

---

* Barbara's younger sister, Ruth, died of peritonitis at the age of three.—D. D.

unassuming, was well liked by faculty and townspeople. He, too, had been unable to go to college because a lack of money had forced him into his father's haberdashery business. Despite the pressures of his business and the demands of his young family, he continued his research in ornithology until he achieved recognition as an authority in the field.*

My mother was active in the university church and organized a club for students. Her closest friends were faculty wives, a snobbish group of unenlightened conservatives to whom my mother's liberalism was anathema and a constant source of irritation. Nevertheless, her personality and charm won their loyalty and affection.

Although my parents were far from well-to-do, it was a foregone conclusion that I would attend the university, since the professional family members had ordained that I become a teacher. With the help of these relatives and an income of sorts derived from babysitting, waiting on tables, and helping in the children's ward of the university hospital, I managed eventually to gain a degree. My first radically independent decision was to get a degree in oriental civilization rather than teaching† My second was to go to China.‡ My third was to marry Carlyle Douglas. I regret none of these decisions.

---

* Barbara's father, A. D. Tinker, wrote a monograph entitled "The Birds of School Girl's Glen Region. Ann Arbor, Michigan: A Study in Local Ornithology," which was published in the Michigan Geological and Biological Survey. The State Geologist R. C. Allen included this study in the survey as a model to both students and teachers, saying that the work was "an illustration to teachers and students of the results to be obtained in an intensive study of a small area."—D. D.

† Barbara received a bachelor of arts degree in English from the University of Michigan in February 1933; she received a master of arts degree in oriental civilization from the University of Michigan in June 1934.—D. D.

‡ Barbara left for China on October 2, 1936. According to letters she wrote, she arrived in Shanghai on October 20, after a short visit to Japan. Her purpose was to study oriental textiles. Her first few months were spent in the home of Y. S. Chi, a former provincial governor. During her stay in China she was arrested because she was suspected of spying for the Russians. On another occasion she was accused of having a stolen passport. Her three-year stay in China provided opportunities for her to spend time in Shanghai, Beijing, and Chengdu to study Chinese textiles. She returned to the United States early in 1939 and wrote an account of her journey, which she submitted to the University of Michigan's annual Hopwood essay competition. Her entry, titled "The Height of a Mountain," earned her the top award of $1,500. According to a local newspaper article, judges described her work as "an amazing picture of the common people of China as they are touched or left untouched by the war." The judges also

In retrospect, I realize that my parents were indeed "color-blind," to use Margaret Haley's apt expression;* I never heard either of my parents use the words "nigger," "chink," "Jap," or any other derogatory name based on race, color, or religion. I recall that when the Daughters of the American Revolution refused to allow Marian Anderson† to give a concert in Washington, D.C.'s Constitution Hall, my mother and her sisters resigned from the organization, as did Eleanor Roosevelt.

I remember, too, that Mrs. Benjamin, a leader in the local Black church, came to my mother for help when she and other members of her church decided to open a boarding house for Black female students who found it well-nigh impossible to rent decent rooms in Ann Arbor. My mother went into action, and within a month she and Mrs. Benjamin were able to raise—through bake sales, rummage sales, donations, and money they borrowed from the bank—enough to rent a house on a pleasant, shady street in a nice neighborhood. They then furnished it and hired a cook and housekeeper, thus providing a home away from home for eight Black female students.

I also remember that when Mrs. Benjamin's two sons graduated from law school cum laude and no merchant of men's clothing would sell clothes to them, it was my father who ordered the tailored suits for their graduation ceremony.

These are small things, perhaps, but they are indicative of the liberal background in which I grew up, totally unaware that my parents were in any way different from those of my friends. Because I felt no prejudice, I was unable to measure its strength in those about me. Therefore I brought to my marriage an appalling social naïveté, which cost me dearly.

During the years of our marriage I gradually learned how to cope with racism. But it has taken the better part of five decades to achieve even a modicum of the objectivity necessary to survive in this predominantly Caucasian society, whose values and laws shape all of our lives whether

---

found her essay to be the most outstanding literary effort in several years of essay competition. Throughout her life she retained a love for China and its people; one of her greatest unfulfilled wishes was to return to China to once again to live among the people in the culture she loved most.—D. D.

* (1861–1939) An American educator and strong proponent and organizer of labor unions for Chicago public school teachers.—ED.

† (1897–1993) An African American singer, one of the finest contraltos of her time.—ED.

we subscribe to or rebel against them. I now find it possible to distance myself for the most part from the fear, the pain, the rage, and the bitterness that so warped my perspective that I began to perceive every White person who came within the periphery of my life as a possible enemy. Even now, much to the amusement of my children and grandchildren, when one of them recounts to me an unpleasant encounter with someone, I say, "Well, was he Black or White?" The wounds have healed, but the scars are still there. How much worse is it, then, for the members of my husband's race? Is it ever possible to forgive or forget?

In the early years of our marriage, to protect myself against ostracism, I erected an inner barricade, which enabled me to remove myself emotionally from White people. I avoided, as much as possible, all but the most casual contact with them. I learned the rules of the game from my mother-in-law: First and foremost, you must divorce yourself from prejudice. View it objectively as a malignant illness springing from ignorance, insecurity, fear, greed, and guilt. Second, tears and rage are self-destructive. Channel them into constructive action like the Civil Rights movement. Third, when dealing with White people one-to-one, never make the first advance socially. If they appear to be friendly, return whatever courtesy they offer, but remain aloof. Fourth, ignore as best you can hostility or rudeness—that is a no-win situation. And, finally, my mother-in-law said that in time I would develop a sixth sense—an instinct that would enable me to detect insincerity beneath a seemingly cordial facade.

My mother-in-law's advice stood me in good stead. Although on the one hand I overcompensated and was unduly suspicious of encounters with White people, yet on the other hand I was cushioned against hostility and snubs that I might otherwise have had to endure had I not followed my mother-in-law's advice.

During Carlyle's furloughs from the United States Army Air Corps, however, I gained some firsthand knowledge. I discovered what it was like to be denied admittance to a hotel, to be threatened with mob violence, and to be driven out of a community. The picture was not all bleak, however. There were gentle people who, with a smile, a nod, and a pleasant word, made us realize that we were not outcasts from all of society, but only from a part of it. And there were others, those who went out of their way to demonstrate their belief in the brotherhood of man.

In the years since World War II, society has slowly begun to change. It has become more tolerant and people have learned in general to accept the fact that minority citizens are entitled to the full rights of citizenship, though society has not always been willing to treat them as social equals.

I, too, have changed. From the lofty pinnacle of my eighty-five years, I find that it is now possible for me to interact gracefully with White people. I can be sincerely and spontaneously friendly with the people I meet on elevators, in the halls, or in the lobby of the building where I live.

I remember, you see, that in the past such casual encounters have occasionally revealed a treasure—a man or a woman who was truly without prejudice, who saw beyond race and color and judged you simply as a human being. This has not happened more than two dozen times in my life. However, on each occasion it was as though the heavens opened to send a warm, golden ray of hope—a promise, perhaps, that one day our children's children's children will be born into a world where neither race nor color is of any moment.

2

A Man of Integrity

To Barbara

To one who is my life's most joyous part,
In whom are wrapped nobility and grace,
Whose inner beauty time cannot erase,
I dedicate these verses and my heart.
All nature cannot match the careless art
With which she binds her hair; her gentle face
Reveals deep purity; in her embrace
The glory and the good of living start.

A woman only, she has all the might,
The courage, and the Spartan strength of mind
That men unwisely claim for their sole right.
The heritage of intellect combined
With passion from the sultry, southern night
Make her a rarity—the prize of all her kind.

—Carlyle Douglas, October 6, 1944

I HAD BEEN IN CHINA visiting a Chinese family in Peking when the Second Sino-Japanese War broke out in 1937.* Since it had been my intention to also go to West China University in Chengdu in south central China, I started overland rather than going straight home as most foreigners had already done. As a result of this unwise decision, I was caught behind the battlefront. For me the only way out of China was to leave through Southeast Asia. To do this I had to flee more than 1,500 miles before the advancing Japanese Army. It took me over a year's travel by boat, rickshaw, mule, and foot to reach Hanoi in Vietnam. I then had to go by gunboat to Hong Kong, where the American consulate general generously offered to ship me home.

Exhausted and penniless, I returned to Ann Arbor in 1939. Immediately I went to stay with my parents on a farm they had just purchased not too far from Ann Arbor. I needed time not only to regain my health but also to somehow come to grips with the harrowing experience of those war years. I began writing the story of my experience in China and in June won the prestigious Hopwood Award from the University of Michigan. The $1,500 prize helped me to feel a little more self-sufficient while I continued to live with my parents.

The peace and quiet of farm life hastened the healing process of both mind and body. By the time Christmas came, I began to think once again about resuming a normal life, perhaps getting a job with the University of Michigan.

Early in February 1942 I received a call from a Mr. McNeal, the director of a National Youth Administration camp at Cassidy Lake, not too far from my parents' farm.† He had heard that I was a graduate of the

---

* The Second Sino-Japanese War (1937–1945) was the conflict between Japanese and Chinese forces for control of the Chinese mainland.—ED.

† The National Youth Administration (NYA) was a former U.S. government agency established in 1935 under the sponsorship of the Works Progress Administration; it was

University of Michigan and that I was looking for a job. He asked to see me about a position that was open at the camp. I agreed.

The position bore the impressive title of Social Director. However, so far as I could determine from Mr. McNeal's vague description of the job, it was a hodgepodge of unrelated duties such as librarian, English teacher, manager of social events, and so forth. The salary was adequate and the work seemed simple enough, so I agreed to take the job for the spring and summer of 1942.

The camp was situated on the slopes above a pretty lake not far from the village of Chelsea and within a half-hour's drive of my family's farm. The campus, as it was called, consisted of a number of newly erected wooden buildings that served as dormitories for students and those of the faculty who chose to live there. There were also a dining hall, a gym, a variety of shops where trades were taught, and, of course, the library, which was my domain.

Except for cooks and clerical workers in the office, I was the only female on the grounds. It was not surprising, therefore, that my English class was quite popular. Most of the young men, as a matter of fact, seemed truly earnest in their efforts to improve their reading and writing skills. I was fairly successful in this area, but the library was an entirely different matter. During my first week there, many young men came in asking for books or magazines and seeking help in finding them on the shelves. I later learned from Carlyle that I was the talk of the camp— they came to the library just to get a glimpse of the pretty new librarian.

It soon became apparent that my first task was to put the books in some sort of order. Having never done this before, and with only a vague memory of the Dewey decimal system residing in some dark corner of my mind, I sat at my desk, pen in hand and a blank sheet of paper in front of me, trying to think of some practical approach to the problem.

The door to the library was open, for it was a beautiful spring day outside. The trees were turning green, the sky was a soft blue, and I saw

---

transferred in 1939 to the Federal Security Agency and was placed in 1942 under the War Manpower Commission. Created in a period of widespread unemployment as part of the New Deal program of President Franklin Delano Roosevelt, the NYA at first engaged in obtaining part-time work for unemployed youths. As unemployment decreased and war approached, emphasis was gradually shifted to training youths for war work until, early in 1942, all NYA activities that did not contribute to the war effort were dropped. Its activities ceased in 1943.—ED.

robins and sparrows flitting from bush to bush. Someone was coming up the walk to the library. I can still see him standing there as clearly now as I first saw him then. A tall, slender, brown-skinned man who walked with the carriage and dignity of a college president on his way to the podium.

"Good morning," I said. "It's a beautiful day, isn't it?"

His face lit up with a charming smile. "You're new here, aren't you?" he said.

"Yes," I replied, "and I haven't the faintest idea what I'm doing. I'm supposed to be the librarian," I added ruefully.

"Dewey got you down?" he laughed. "Perhaps I can help." This was the first intimation of his quick wit and jovial sense of humor. What's more, he not only walked like a university president, he talked like one.

"I certainly hope so," I replied. "Sit down, won't you?"

He smiled and took the chair beside the desk. His name was Carlyle Douglas. He was twenty-two years old and worked at Cassidy Lake teaching a class in radio repair. There was no sense of strangeness between us. It was as though we had known each other forever.

Years later, I asked Carlyle about that first encounter. By then, of course, I was no longer a naive newcomer to the tangible and intangible ghetto walls that both limited and affected every phase of our lives.

"How come you even spoke to me at all?" I asked. Carlyle paused for a moment or so and then looked at me in a special way that made my heart leap.

"First of all, the sun was in your hair and you were very pretty, but it was more than that, and I don't quite know how to explain it to you." He paused while he searched for words.

"You see, if you had been any other White woman, you would have said something like 'Yes, how can I help you?' or 'What do you want?' in a particular tone of voice. But instead you said, 'Good morning. It's a beautiful day, isn't it?' You smiled and your voice was warm and friendly."

Carlyle knew as well as I how we measure, almost subconsciously, tones of voice and demeanors before responding to people. Black people, especially in the South, are particularly sensitive to the nonverbal cues of Whites because their survival depends on it.

He continued, "Well, you see, there was nothing in your voice or behavior that sent out warning signals. Never before had I in my entire life spoken to a White woman without trepidation, let alone laughed and joked with one. I avoided contact with any of them. In the South, you don't take chances like that."

He leaned forward and touched my cheek. "But you, my love, were different!"

So on that spring morning in 1942, so long ago in time yet only yesterday in memory, he sat down in a chair beside the desk, and we talked for over an hour, wonderfully at ease with each other. He came back every day thereafter when he had a break from the radio shop where he supervised the trainees. Ostensibly, he was there helping me put the library in order, and, indeed, we did do that. But we also talked endlessly about books, music, people, politics, and ideas. In the process we discovered a great similarity in our interests, tastes, attitudes, and outlooks—even our senses of humor seemed to be completely attuned. Oddly enough, we never once spoke about race, not because it was a delicate or distasteful subject, but because it simply did not seem to matter to either of us.

During this time I learned a little about how different our lives had been. While I had had a stable childhood with both of my parents in a middle-class neighborhood and had enjoyed all of the attendant privileges of being White, Carlyle had come from the chaotic background of a broken home, poverty, and prejudice. He had been born in New Orleans, the son of a man who described himself as "just an old carpenter" and a woman who, in striving to better herself, became a schoolteacher. Carlyle's father, William Riley Douglas, was, in fact, skilled in all aspects of construction and built several impressive churches in Atlanta and Detroit. His mother, Lucille Hoffman, was strong-willed, beautiful, and talented. Before entering the teaching profession she had traveled as a pianist with the Chautauqua, a traveling cultural performance company. She had high educational aspirations for her husband and left him when it became apparent that he wouldn't give up the construction business to further his education. Carlyle was eight years old when they were divorced. Both his mother and father had lost their first spouses in death, and they each later married two more times.

Carlyle's early life had been spent moving from one city in the South to another. His first move came at the age of four, when he, his mom, and his half-brother, Willie, son from his mother's first marriage, left New Orleans and went to Nashville, Tennessee. They left Carlyle's father, William, behind. After a few years there, the three of them moved to Knoxville. The only times Carlyle saw his father were during his occasional visits to New Orleans.

When Carlyle took his last trip to New Orleans at age fourteen, he stayed a year and a half. By this time Lucille had married her third husband, Mr. Hoffman. In Carlyle's absence his mother and new stepfather moved to Salisbury, North Carolina, where Mr. Hoffman was to teach.

Abandoned by his mother, Carlyle lived with his father in New Orleans for a time. His father was too busy with his construction business to care for him, so Carlyle was sent to an Episcopal boarding school, where he remained for a year on the strength of his father's promises to pay the school's tuition. However, things went badly in the construction business, and his father was unable to pay his school debt. This was during the Great Depression. Work was scarce and the pay inadequate. While the time between jobs was never long, the time between drinks was all too short, and the time between meals an eternity.

When Carlyle left the boarding school for financial reasons, he went to live with his father's older sister, Louise Alain. That fall he started in one of the public high schools, only to find himself being shipped back to his mother a scant two months later because of an altercation with a cousin who also lived with Aunt Louise. It seemed that no one wanted him.

Carlyle was sixteen years old by this time. His mother carefully explained to him that he was not his stepfather's responsibility. Mr. Hoffman would only support him until he got a job and could pay his own way. Three months later Carlyle finally landed a job hauling freight on a hand truck at a freight point called Spencer Transfer. The work was strenuous enough to more than compensate for the meager pay. A five-cent raise brought his wages up to thirty-nine cents an hour. It was 1936, the middle of the depression, and he was lucky to have a job. Sometimes there was plenty of work for all; at other times not enough. When he would arrive at the work site and there wasn't enough work, he would be sent home.

While his mother and stepfather remained in Salisbury, it mattered little that work was not steady. But when they left for Chicago and Carlyle was on his own, he soon ran into debt and resolved to visit his mother to borrow some money. When he arrived in Chicago, however, he unfortunately learned that she had left his stepfather and was living alone in Detroit. So Carlyle purchased a railroad pass and went to Detroit, but he found her in no position to help him.

Since he could live with his mother while looking for employment, Carlyle chose to stay in Detroit rather than return to the South. However, work was not easy to find. He searched in vain. Eager to return to school and wanting to avoid idleness, he followed his mother's suggestion and enrolled in high school. In addition to going to school, he worked afternoons and weekends at his mother's place of employment whenever the opportunity arose.

A few months before his high school graduation in 1942, Carlyle landed a job with the National Youth Administration (NYA), which, after graduation, led to a placement in the NYA resident project where we met.

He later wrote of our first meeting:

> Love, a poet has said, is a weather in the heart. It's rather like the first day of spring. Not the day the calendar says is Spring, but the day you first notice that the buds are popping and the birds have returned and the wind has a more gentle touch. Late or early, you know it is spring.
>
> I liked Barbara from the first. She was good company. We talked of books and music, of people and ideas. We discovered in the process a great similarity in our interests, tastes, attitudes and outlook. The more we learned about each other, the more time we spent together; the more time we spent together, the more we learned about each other.

It seemed to me at this point that it was quite natural for me to ask Carlyle to come to dinner and meet my parents. He accepted the invitation and several days later came home with me after work. The evening was a pleasant one for all of us. There were no awkward moments, and I could tell that my parents really enjoyed his company. My father drove him back to the camp, and after the two of them left, my mother told me that Carlyle was not only charming but a perfect gentleman. This was the highest praise she ever bestowed on any man.

While I did not consciously refrain from telling my parents that I was attracted to Carlyle, the fact remains that I said nothing to them, nor did I say anything to Carlyle. I know now, of course, that he was as deeply troubled as I was by the depth of our feelings for each other. In any case, we managed somehow to keep our relationship, overtly at least, on a friendship basis.

Since Carlyle had met my parents, he asked if I would care to meet his mother and other relatives. I said I would, and we arranged to meet in Detroit the following weekend.

The next weekend, as promised, he was waiting for me in the lobby of the hotel where I had registered for the night. For the first time, I felt vaguely ill at ease. I was suddenly conscious of the fact that we, as an interracial couple, were attracting attention. Carlyle greeted me some-what stiffly, and I sensed the same uneasiness in him. Somewhat self-consciously we walked out of the hotel, a prudent distance apart, trying to bridge an uncomfortable gap with commonplace chitchat.

Once we were in the car he had rented for the occasion, we recovered the better part of our equilibrium. Still, nothing was quite the same until, having reached a side street, Carlyle stopped the car and, turning to me, took my hand in his and smiled at me wryly, saying, "This isn't easy is it?" He was referring to the awful discomfort we had felt because of the attention we were attracting as an interracial couple. I was close to tears. I could only shake my head wordlessly, but at the same time I felt a current coursing through our linked hands—call it love, or empathy, or whatever. I knew then that I did not want to lose Carlyle. Later he revealed that he felt the same way. He knew as I did that, at whatever cost, we belonged together.

We drove silently, our hands still linked, all the way to his mother's house. Still somewhat demoralized, I was not at all sure Carlyle's mother would approve of me. A wide-eyed younger cousin let us in and told us that Carlyle's mother was in the living room. When I entered, the first and only thing I saw was the armchair by the window. In it, regally poised, sat an incredibly beautiful White woman.

"Mom," Carlyle said, going across the room to kiss her, "this is Barbara."

She held out her hand and smiled.

"I'm glad to meet you, my dear," she said. "Carlyle has told me all about you."

I recall saying all the proper things and going through all the proper motions but remember little else. We stayed no more than an hour, though it seemed like an eternity. She was polite, but in a stiff, formal way. I felt, even though she didn't say it, that she was judging me and that there was something about me she didn't like. We had tea and little cakes, and once when I looked up at her I saw a twinkle of amusement in her eyes.

I think she enjoyed the fact that I was squirming under her gaze. I felt uncomfortable, ill at ease, and relieved beyond words when we finally said our good-byes.

Carlyle and I drove from his mother's house to Belle Isle, an island park in the Detroit River, where we stopped beside the river to talk.

"Your mother doesn't like me," I said bleakly.

"What makes you think that?" he asked, turning in the seat to look at me.

"I can tell," I insisted, sitting stiffly in my corner of the front seat. "And it has nothing to do with race, because she is the same race as I."

"Look at me," Carlyle said, swinging me around to face him. There was a faint, humorous twitch to his mouth, but his eyes were tender.

"Listen, Love, my mother isn't White. On her birth certificate, her father is identified as the son of a White shopkeeper and a slave girl, and her mother as the daughter of a plantation owner and a slave girl. It was common practice in the South in those days. So you see, she really is mixed, half-and-half."

"I'm sorry," I said. "I feel like a fool. But then why is it she seemed so distant and aloof?"

"It isn't you as an individual. It's your race. She feels that if I enter into a relationship with you, I'll be in danger."

To this day I do not know why, but the words "I'll be in danger," uttered by Carlyle at that moment with what seemed unbearable force, triggered a distant memory in me that was so terrifying, so hideous that I had been unable to deal with it as a five-year-old child and had repressed it. I had buried the memory so deep that until that evening there had never been the slightest trace of it, no sign it had ever happened.

At that moment, I remembered that in 1914 I had been on an outing with my parents in our touring car. We were coming home at dusk over a bridge above the Huron River, and we drove up Hill Road to the courthouse square when suddenly traffic began to slow down. People were carrying lighted torches and screaming words I did not understand as they streamed by us on either side, all moving toward the courthouse square. We were swept along in the crowd and unable to turn either way. My father, his face white and grim, held firmly to the wheel while my mother, tears streaming down her face, held me close and said, "Don't look, Baby. Don't look."

But I did look. I saw the square full of people waving torches, scream-ing wildly with fierce expressions on their faces. Down the long steps of the courthouse came a cordon of policemen swinging batons and shoul-dering guns. In their midst was a young Black man—his hands cuffed behind him, his clothes hanging in shreds, his hair standing on end, with a look of such anguish and terror on his face that even now I cannot bear to think about it.

Many years later, long after Carlyle and I were married, I asked my mother about this incident. She said the young man had been accused of raping a White woman and stealing her car. That night in the square the police were moving him to another county, where he would be safe until his trial.

Sitting with Carlyle in the car that evening after meeting his mother, I understood exactly why his mother was afraid of me. I cried so hard that I could not see Carlyle's face. He held me tight and said he loved me, and the more he said it the more I cried. Then, as abruptly as I had started crying, I stopped. I couldn't find my handkerchief, so I asked him for one. He provided one wordlessly, and when I regained my composure he asked me to tell him what was wrong. I explained as best I could and then sat silent and exhausted.

"That was a long time ago, Honey," he said, trying to reassure me. "Things aren't that bad anymore. Not in the North, anyway." He leaned over and kissed me. "I love you," he said.

Without another word he turned on the ignition and drove me back to my hotel.

For a week thereafter, day in and day out, every hour we spent to-gether was devoted entirely to the problem of whether or not we should continue our relationship. On the one hand, it was clear to both of us that we were unusually compatible and that if we had been of the same race (White or Black), we would have a happy, successful marriage. But here we were, I obviously White and he obviously Black, and there was no way in the world to change that.

Carlyle wrote of our discussions during that time:

I realized one day that I loved her, and was troubled. When she asked what was on my mind I told her. She was troubled too. After a long talk in the afternoon and a restless night, we talked more. Our decision: that the happiness we would find together would be greater than either of us could find separately; that this happiness would more than compensate for the inevitable pain we would encounter.

We believed violence would be unlikely so long as we stayed away from the South and its bordering states and refrained from living or traveling in states where interracial marriage was illegal. Neither Carlyle nor I were sure how many states had such laws, but we later discovered that half of the states in the Union had declared interracial marriages illegal. Fortunately for us, Illinois and Michigan were not among them.

We also agreed that in all probability we would stand a better chance of succeeding if we lived in a university town, where the population would be more educated and therefore, we thought, more liberal.

We agreed on all of this but came to grief over the manner in which prejudice reveals itself in daily living. Carlyle tried to make me understand how it insidiously destroys self-esteem and engenders bitterness and rage. I, with no prejudice of my own and never having been exposed to it, could neither understand its power nor grasp the meaning of its ghetto walls—the sense of being caged and belittled.

After long discussions, day after day, weary to the point of exhaustion, we still had not arrived at a solution. Then, quite suddenly, Carlyle's military orders came through. In a few weeks' time he was to report to the Signal Corps Training Center in Chicago. From there he would go into the U.S. Army Air Corps. This galvanized us into action. Within twenty-four hours we came to the decision that we would never be happy without each other. Therefore we would have to try our luck with the future, believing that our love was strong enough to conquer any problems that might arise.

Having made this decision, Carlyle went to Detroit to tell his mother. She was not surprised, but she warned him that this was a feckless and dangerous course to pursue.

We then went to tell my mother. Much to my confusion and distress, she, who was so liberal, burst into tears and protested, wailing, "Oh, those poor little mongrel babies you will have!"

Carlyle, as stunned as I, went back to the camp. Unable to say anything at all, I stormed to my room, where I wept, imagining how hurtful my mother's insensitive remarks must have been to Carlyle. I could not understand how my gentle, tolerant mother could be so cruel. Exhausted, I fell across the bed.

Sometime later my father entered my room and sat down next to me. I sat red-eyed and forlorn. He put his arm around me.

"He's a good man, Barbara," my father said. "I trust him, but it looks like a hard way to go. It's your life, Honey. Whatever you decide, I am with you all the way. Your mother will come around. She always does. Don't be too hard on her."

The next morning I told Carlyle what my father had said, expecting him to be overwhelmed with gratitude as I was. His reaction was understated. Rather than showing gratitude, he smiled at me warmly and said, "I like him. Don't worry about your mother. It was just a shock. She'll take it in stride. Wait and see."

I suddenly began to understand why I had been drawn to Carlyle and why I had come to love him so much. He was very much like my father: a man of integrity, gentle for the most part, understanding, and kind. Yet he was strong enough to overcome the almost insurmountable problems that faced him with the same wry sense of humor, the same twinkle in his eye.

3

Whither Thou Goest . . .

PASSION
SONNET TWO

When shadows touch the fevered brow of earth
And deepen as the sun withdraws its light,
The cooling darkness quietly gives birth
To jeweled skies and crowns the princess, Night.
The moon half hides her radiance from sight
As if too shy to fully show her face,
And then, just as an impish maiden might,
She whisks away her veil of cloud-knit lace.

But Night with her serenity and grace
Is powerless to lull the leaping flame
Of mad desire whose vigor grows apace;
This conflagration you alone can tame.
The white heat of this blaze which you inspire
Cools only when combined with your sweet fire.

—Carlyle Douglas, June 15–16, 1944

BECAUSE CARLYLE WAS LEAVING IN two weeks for the Signal Corps Training Center in Chicago, I decided to look for a job there so that I could be near him. When I told my parents what I planned to do, my mother accepted it without a murmur, just as my father and Carlyle had believed she would. I was extraordinarily lucky; an employment agency immediately found a job for me as a correspondent with the American Hospital Supply Company. After a half-hour interview with the manager, I was hired and told to begin work the following week.

I spent the rest of that day, newspaper in hand, trying to find a suitable apartment. Two days later I found a studio apartment on the northeast side, close enough to work and cheap enough to suit my salary. Located in an ordinary and rather shabby building facing Lake Michigan, the apartment was clean and adequately furnished but had no amenities. A single telephone in the hall and a single bathroom served the whole floor. There was an intercom in the vestibule but no elevator. It was the best I could afford. Several months later I inadvertently learned through a coworker who knew the area that the building's residents were prostitutes, but by that time nothing surprised me.

I returned to the farm near Ann Arbor over the weekend to collect my belongings and to reassure my parents that everything was going well and that I was reasonably content. Indeed, I really was happy and excited at the prospect of a new and interesting job and the knowledge that for the next few months, while Carlyle was in training, I would be close to him.

He called to tell me how pleased he was to know that we would be near each other, even if only for a short while, and to say he wanted me to know how much he loved me. He would be stationed in Chicago until July of the following year, when Signal Corps training would be finished. He would be staying with his aunt and uncle on the South Side of Chicago on weekends. After completing his training he would be transferred to the Army Air Corps and stationed at Biggs Army Airfield in Fort Bliss, near El Paso, Texas.

I was not naive enough to suppose that I could go with him to Texas. I had learned by then that his life would be in jeopardy if he were seen with me anywhere in the South. We both knew this year in Chicago would be the only time we had together, except for occasional furloughs, as long as the war lasted. We also knew, though we never put it into words, that, given the uncertainty of war, the separation might be forever. Now, when Carlyle told me that he would be living on the South Side of Chicago, I thought that merely meant that it would be quite a long distance for him to travel to visit me. I had not the faintest clue as to the meaning or significance of living on either the north or south side of the Chicago River. In those days, when segregation was in full flower, the north and northeast sides of the Chicago River were lily White, and as far as I know, no Black families lived along State Street or in the western suburbs. However, on the near south side of the river from the Loop to the small neighborhood of Roseland, a corridor of streets housed the Black ghetto, while along the lakefront lived middle-class professionals. It took me months to realize how brave Carlyle had been and how much he must have cared for me to cross that hostile land to see me every weekend.

I remember that first visit with an ache of nostalgia. He called me the night before to let me know he had arrived at his aunt's home and that he would come to see me the following afternoon. I spent hours choosing the right dress, applying my makeup just so, and fixing my hair exactly as I knew he liked it.

My heart pounded and my body trembled when the intercom buzzed and I heard his voice. When he reached the top of the stairs and turned toward the door where I stood waiting, I managed a trembling "Hello." I don't remember what, or even if, he said anything, but as we stepped inside the door, he put his arms around me, and whatever doubts I may have had were gone. I felt safe and sheltered and at home.

During the early months of our relationship we rarely ventured out in public together. It was too painful and frightening. Neither of us was prepared to face the unconcealed hostility, the sneers and stares that followed us everywhere, when we rode the buses, sat in the park or theater, or just walked down the street. The most crushing blow of all was the reaction of Black people, who looked at us askance and with almost as much hostility as White people.

On one particularly frightening occasion when two young White men dogged our footsteps, calling us names and laughing at our obvious discomfort. Afterward, we faced each other across the little dining room table in my apartment.

"Is it always going to be like this?" I asked, ashamed that my voice was shaking.

"I don't know," Carlyle replied slowly, his eyes full of tenderness and compassion. "You see now what I meant when I tried to warn you."

I nodded, blinking back the tears.

"Is there nothing we can do?"

"Maybe," he said. "Kind of a stopgap. If we lived among my people I don't think it would be so difficult once they came to know us. The problem is that you might not ever be welcome among your own people. Could you bear that?"

I felt the heat rising in my cheeks, and my heart was pounding like that of a marathon runner.

"My people! Your people! What are you talking about? You sound as though we came from different countries. It's a wonder we speak the same language."

Carlyle looked at me wide-eyed and obviously startled. Then he laughed.

"Anger is very becoming to you," he said.

In no mood for teasing, I glared at him across the table and threw my purse at him.

"Either we have something that is worth fighting for," I said, "or we don't. Make up your mind!"

He reached across the table and took my hand. "If you are willing, we'll keep trying. I believe we can do it."

I loved him. I could not, would not stop trying. I told him so, and from that moment on we grimly fought together to keep society from walling us into a ghetto or tearing us apart. From my husband, my mother-in-law, and from all of the dear friends who through the years have shared their wisdom, their strength, their love, and their laughter with us, I learned how to cope with prejudice.

After our talk that afternoon, Carlyle and I seemed to have reached some sort of unity or oneness that shielded us from the hostility. We were still in the process of bonding, sharing quite frankly our fears and misgivings so that eventually we reached a point where we presented a solid front to the outside world.

By the fall of 1942, I had moved to the Gold Coast, a section of Chicago just north of the river and within walking distance of the lake.

This small section had its own identity. It housed artists of every sort. There were galleries and small theaters, boutiques, ethnic restaurants, and antique shops. Every stratum of society was represented here.

I lived in an inexpensive basement apartment whose bay windows gave me an intriguing view of the footgear of passersby. It had a private entrance, which enabled Carlyle to come and go as he pleased. He was still only able to see me on weekends, but we did not separate ourselves from society. We strolled along the beach, went to theaters and occasional art shows, attended the nearby foreign movie house, and dined at smaller, less expensive ethnic restaurants.

We were learning the art of walling people out instead of letting them wall us in. Because we were happy, time passed quickly. With Christmas approaching, we knew that Carlyle would soon be leaving for the Signal Corps training program in Chicago, and after that he would be stationed at Biggs Army Airfield in Texas. We decided it was time to make more concrete marriage plans. Like many other wartime couples faced by separation imposed by military service, we chose to form a permanent bond. Plans for marriage gave us mutual reassurance that our relationship would not dissolve in the sea of uncertainty imposed by the war.

On Christmas Eve of 1942 we attended a Russian Orthodox church just a few blocks away, where as part of their midnight ceremony, an orchestra played Beethoven's Ninth Symphony, followed by a choir that sang the "Hallelujah Chorus." It was a beautiful evening; the sky was clear and the moon shone on the glistening snow. We walked to the church arm in arm and sat in the back pew, listening to the music. When it came time for the "Hallelujah Chorus," Carlyle took from his pocket a jeweler's box of carved ivory. He opened it and, smiling down at me, slipped the engagement ring he had chosen on my finger. It was a fire opal (we were both born in October) surrounded by garnets, not in any way ostentatious, but in its simplicity the most beautiful ring I have ever seen either then or now.

"I love you more than I can ever put into words," he whispered with tears in his eyes. "Will you marry me?"

"Yes," I whispered back, kissing his cheek.

The music stopped. Quietly we left the back pew and, hand in hand, walked out into the night.

It was snowing big, soft flakes like flower petals floating through the night. We strolled slowly down Elm Street toward a gazebo. It was on the beach, one of our favorite places. We sat down on the stone bench, his arm around me, watching the snowflakes drifting gradually, enclosing the gazebo and screening us from the world. We kissed, gently at first and then passionately. I experienced a closeness with Carlyle that I had never felt with anyone else in my entire life. I hoped with all of my heart that our wondrous union would last forever. At the same time I began to fear the awesome challenges our fragile union might face in a world that both feared and despised us.

The bells in the cathedral nearby were playing Christmas carols, and my fears melted away in the beauty of the music and the warmth of Carlyle's arms. We sat in silence listening to the music, happier in that moment and more at peace than we had ever been before. Gently he turned my face to his and said, "It's going to be all right, my darling. I promise you."

A few days later Carlyle called to say that he had received his orders and would be on his way to Signal Corps training within a week's time. Numb and dazed, we wondered what we should do. Were we really ready for an interracial marriage? We knew we were committed to each other, but what about our families? And the rest of America? Should we get married now? Or should we wait until Carlyle came home on furlough?

We went through the necessary procedures—first the blood tests and then the license bureau. Afterward neither of us could recall much of the procedure beyond a vague awareness of staring eyes and the embarrassed confusion of the clerk who filled out the marriage license, misspelling our names and putting down the wrong date. Red-faced, the clerk hurried through the corrections without once looking at us. After his first startled glance he directed us to a bishop at a South Side church who was licensed to conduct marriage ceremonies.

By the time we left the building, we were nearly hysterical and giddy with relief at having that ordeal behind us. As directed, we took a cab to an address on South State Street. The driver looked askance at us as Carlyle gave him the address. We fully understood why when he pulled up in front of a dilapidated two-story brick building, which stood forlorn next to a vacant lot heaped with debris that appeared to have been there since Mrs. O'Leary's cow tipped over the lantern.*

---

* Legend has it that a cow belonging to Mrs. Kate O'Leary started the Great Chicago Fire of 1871 by kicking over a lantern in the family barn.—D. D.

"Are you sure this is the right place?" Carlyle asked, his face a study of dismay and ill-concealed amusement.

"Yes, sir," the cabby said impatiently, pointing to the lopsided gilded cross that was nailed to the door. "That'll be five dollars and eighty cents." His tone of voice brooked no argument.

Carlyle gave him the money and helped me out of the cab. We stood on the curb, silently watching the cabby wheel his cab around and speed back to the Loop.

"Well," Carlyle said, "here we are. Shall we give it a try?"

I nodded, speechless. There, standing on the curb in front of the paint-flaked door and the crooked cross, we laughed until we ached. He took my arm and we cautiously approached the door. Carlyle pushed a button just under the cross, and there was a faint, faraway clang. Almost immediately a child's voice shouted down, "Come up!"

We obeyed and slowly climbed an enclosed flight of stairs, emerging into a shabby living room. The room was decorated with vases of artificial flowers placed on either side of a large table, which appeared to be a makeshift altar. A gilded cross on the wall behind it was festooned with more artificial flowers. On one side of the room was a long pew, and scattered along the other walls were some folding chairs.

As we stood in the doorway an elderly man in a minister's gown appeared through a side door. He beamed at us cordially and introduced himself as Bishop Hamilton. He carefully examined the license that Carlyle had handed him. He beamed at me again, seemingly not at all disturbed by the fact that I was White.

"Everything seems to be in order," he said. "If you will wait a moment, I'll call my wife and children as witnesses." He smiled apologetically and continued, "No music. I'm afraid my daughter who plays the piano is not here today."

We stood awkwardly near the door, neither of us knowing quite what was expected of us. At that moment a very large woman in a crisp housedress that rustled as she moved entered the room. Five children ranging from ages two to fourteen followed her. All of them smiled at us as they arranged themselves around the room in the pews and on the folding chairs.

"This is my family," the bishop said and introduced them one by one. They nodded politely and looked at us round-eyed. The bishop motioned us toward the table. He stood behind it, a Bible open before him.

He had barely begun to intone the beginning lines of the ceremony when the telephone suddenly shrilled in the hallway. The bishop frowned and waved the oldest girl to the phone. We all stood immobile, waiting. The girl came to the door and said in an audible whisper, "It's for you, Dad— the police."

The silence in that room was electric. Carlyle's hand tightened over mine. My heart was pounding in my ears. Without a word the bishop strode across the room, took the telephone from his daughter, and went into the next room and shut the door.

We were motionless, and for the first time in my life, I felt an overpowering fear of the police. After what seemed a lifetime, the bishop returned, walked briskly behind the table, smiled benignly at all of us, and said, "Let us continue. It was nothing much . . . an interracial couple whom I married was jailed in Indiana. Nice people, but it's against the law in that state. However, they were released on my say-so, provided they get out of there immediately."

Without even taking a deep breath, he intoned the ceremony and pronounced us man and wife. Both of us moved through that last half-hour like sleepwalkers. I cannot recall how we got down the stairs and into the street. I remember only a cold weight in my stomach and the pounding of my heart as I kept stride with the tall, rigid, silent man at my side. It seemed to me that our world had collapsed around us. I did not understand then as I do now that he already knew the fear that I was experiencing, had known it from childhood, and was now bracing himself to do battle with this new challenge and conquer it, not only for his own sake, but for mine.

4

Poor Little Mongrel Baby

PARTING
SONNET 3

The night is filled with laughter while my heart
Is busied with the labor of good-bye;
Your eyes and lips are smiling as we part,
But still I sense the sorrow in your sigh.
Should this, our parting, last eternally,
The memory of the past will ease the strain
And dreams of moments spent in ecstasy
Will touch our grief with beauty, dull its pain.
Our golden days together were replete
With joys whose equal man has never known;
We scaled Olympian heights with eager feet
And for a space claimed Eden for our own.
Because the past contained such rich delights,
I'll have rich dreams to fill the lonely nights.

—*Carlyle Douglas, June 20–24, 1944*

THE NIGHT BEFORE CARLYLE LEFT for Signal Corps training we lay side by side on the daybed in the basement apartment, watching the shadows of passersby marching across the ceiling. There seemed to be nothing to say. No words could express the emptiness, the loneliness already creeping in upon us. It was small comfort that all across the country hundreds of other men and women were feeling the same devastating sense of loss. I think we only spoke three times to each other during that long, agonizing night.

"I'll write as soon as I get there."

"Yes, I know."

"I'll be back."

"Yes. I'll be here."

"I love you."

"I love you, too."

He left at seven in the morning, and I could not bear to watch him walk away down the street, so tall and straight with that wonderful, dignified walk of his.

I went to work early that day and all the days thereafter. I ate out, went to movies and concerts, and toured the museums—anything and everything to keep busy. I wrote to him every day, trying to make my letters cheerful and interesting. I felt as though I were sending messages to the man on the moon. Carlyle's commanding officers gave him little time to himself during training, so letters from him were few and far between. I constantly fought off a feeling of abandonment even though I understood why he could only manage to write a few words now and then.

I was beginning to feel very tired and a little sick. I went to see the company doctor and learned, to my dismay, that I was pregnant. The baby was due in October, about eight months away. I sat down on a bench in the park outside the doctor's office. Wild thoughts were tumbling about in my head. I knew the time would come when my condition would force me to stop working. Where would I get the money to live on? Carlyle's allotment had not even started yet, and my health insurance didn't cover pregnancy.

Luckily, in Chicago there were free prenatal clinics for indigent women, and these same clinics provided doctors and nurses who came to your home to deliver the baby. I would have to get a leave of absence from my job. All of these thoughts went through my head with a certain degree of calmness, but all the time underneath lurked a hidden fear that I could not, dared not face: I was going to have a Black baby, and I was going to have it all alone, since by then Carlyle would be stationed in Texas.

I thought of my mother's anguished cry, "Those poor little mongrel babies!" I thought of all the suffering Carlyle had endured as a child, the intimidation and humiliations that had scarred him forever. I was far beyond tears. I pulled myself up from the bench and walked slowly across Elm Street and then went home, thinking all the time of one "what-if" after another.

What if Carlyle did not want the baby? What if my father and mother disowned me? What if? What if? What if? How was I going to bring up a Black baby by myself?

I sat on the daybed glooming for a while, and then, disgusted with myself, my husband, and the world at large, I tossed a shawl around my shoulders and walked down to sit in the gazebo on the beach.

First of all, whether it was Black, White, or purple, it was my baby, and it was growing inside my body, and it had the right to be a healthy baby without any physical flaws, and that was up to me. Never mind anything else. This was what was important: a flawless, healthy baby. Therefore I needed to find a good pediatrician for the baby, and I also needed to take good care of myself.

So step-by-step I began to overcome the fears that were causing me to spin around in space, flapping my wings and crying, "What if?" I concentrated only on the baby and me. I wrote to Carlyle and informed him that we were going to have a baby. He responded that he was overjoyed and expressed the hope that we would have a close and loving family—one more like my family of origin than his. I responded with a series of long, loving, chatty letters that helped to relieve my aching emptiness.

I told my office manager about my pregnancy, and he said I could work up to my seventh month of pregnancy as long as I felt like it. That was a godsend. Now I could pay my rent, buy food, and put the army allotment in the bank until the time when the baby arrived. I concentrated entirely on the baby. I did not allow myself to think about prejudice, segregation, racism, or anything but giving birth to a healthy baby. Subconsciously, I knew that I would never be able to get through this by myself if I really stopped to think about it.

I asked Carlyle by letter if there were any way that he could be there for the birth. He wrote back to say he would try to get emergency leave near our baby's due date, the last week in October 1943. I was pleased, certainly, but all my attention was focused on the baby, who they told me was a girl. By then she had been kicking for some time and had become very real to me.

When I went into labor in the early morning hours of October 23, 1943, I asked my landlady to call the doctor and wire Carlyle. Carlyle wired back that he was on his way. A nurse arrived to help with the delivery. The labor seemed long and hard, although objectively it was under twelve hours. Fortunately, there were no complications, especially since Linda was born in my apartment.

She arrived at about eleven o'clock in the morning of October 23, 1943—the same month in which her father and I had been born. When the nurse held her up for me to see, I was both enchanted and relieved. Her skin was cream colored. Her hair was a thick, straight, silky black, and her eyes a lovely deep brown. "She'll be able to pass," I thought. "Life won't be as difficult for her."

Carlyle had explained to me that in the Black community "passing" meant the ability to pass for White. Carlyle's mother, Lucille, had been able to pass, and as a consequence, she landed jobs and was socially accepted in places were Blacks were not welcome. At this point, you see, I was thinking as many Black mothers did at the time. I realized that if my daughter were accepted as White, she would have all of the advantages that my skin color brought me and none of the disadvantages that Carlyle's skin color brought him. I did not realize then that passing has its price. I did not realize that passing meant denying your heritage and your real identity. I did not realize that passing meant living a lie by pretending to be something you are not. All I knew was that life would be easier for my daughter if White America accepted her as one of their own.

Having a Black child changed me forever. I had crossed the border into my husband's and daughter's world. I was no longer a visitor or a voyeur in this harsh new land—I was a part of it. I would never again be able to stand aloof or retreat into the old, familiar world of my youth. I left the protection and the advantages afforded by my skin color behind me and never looked back.

Less than two hours after Linda's birth, my landlady came running down the stairs to tell me that my mother had called. It must have been her mother's instinct, that special connection between mothers and their children, that set off an alarm in her. When she learned from the landlady that I had given birth to a child, my mother responded that she was on her way to Chicago to take me home. This was the last thing I needed, but there was little I could do about it. When my mother arrived about five hours later, she took charge of the baby, the nurse, the landlady, and me with her usual efficiency. I protested feebly but was too exhausted to care what happened. I tried to make my mother understand that Carlyle was on his way, but she paid no attention. My baby and I were loaded into an ambulance and whisked off to a drawing room on an eastbound train. It seemed to me that before I had even finished nursing Linda we had pulled into the station in Ann Arbor.

Carlyle and his mother arrived at my Chicago apartment no more than an hour after we had gone. I had left word with the landlady to tell him I was with my mother, but she never passed on the message. I don't believe that her failure to let Carlyle know my whereabouts was accidental. She must have decided that I would be better off without him. Her meddling decision caused us both a great deal of anguish. He had only twenty-four hours of leave, and there was little he could do since he did not have the farm's telephone number or address. He asked his mother to try to locate me and, deeply troubled, returned to the Signal Corps Training Center.

Within two days I realized that something had gone wrong. I called my old landlady, and she said that Carlyle had come and gone. I did not have his mother's phone number, and she was not listed in the book. Restless and uneasy, I went through all the motions of being a good mother and a thoughtful daughter. It wasn't that my mother and father were not kind and loving. I just didn't belong with them anymore, and I didn't know how to tell them so. I was afraid Carlyle would think I didn't want to see him, and I was afraid I had lost him.

I wrote to him, but there was no response. After two agonizing months of this, I told my parents that I had to go to Chicago. They wonderfully understood my situation and my mother came with me to support me and to help me find an apartment. Linda, an unusually happy baby, seemed not to mind in the least traveling around in her buggy as we looked for an apartment. Finally, at the end of a week, we found one— again, on the North Side in a far-from-elegant neighborhood. My mother protested, but I was desperate and adamant. The apartment was at the back of a building overlooking an alley. It had its own two flights of back steps and a little porch. There was a small kitchen, a foldaway bed, a chest of drawers, and two armchairs.

Shortly after my mother left, I managed to get in touch with Virginia, a cousin of Carlyle's in Detroit. I told her my plight, and she said she would contact Carlyle's mother. Not more than half an hour later the phone rang. It was Carlyle's mother. She said not to worry and that she would be there the following day. I had mixed feelings about her coming, remembering how cold she had seemed before. But when I opened the door the following afternoon and saw her standing there, I was so over- whelmed with relief that I couldn't say a word. "It's all right, Child," she said, putting her arms around me. "Now, where's my granddaughter?"

She went over to the pram, picked Linda up, cuddled her, remarked about what a beautiful child she was, put her back down, hung up her own coat, and washed her hands. Her direct approach was exactly like my mother's: "Do you need any groceries?" Before I could answer she opened the door to the refrigerator, took a quick look at the nearly empty shelves, and said, "Where is the nearest grocery store?" It didn't seem possible that this was the same woman who had seemed so aloof, remote, and queenly a few months earlier. She telegraphed Carlyle and stayed long enough to be assured that he was on his way home. When she left she kissed me and said she would return whenever I needed her.

A week later Carlyle called from Texas to say he would be arriving in two days. Oddly enough, the news did not exhilarate me. On the con- trary, I was suddenly apprehensive. I had not seen him in ten months, and I was not the same person he had known. My whole life seemed to have spun out of control. I loved my daughter, but that love caused me to worry constantly about her present and future well-being. How could I make her happy when there was so much against her? The responsibil- ity weighed me down like a stone around my neck.

Physically, I was worn out with nursing, bathing, washing diapers, worrying about getting Linda to the pediatrician for shots, and wonder- ing where the money would come from to buy her clothes and the solid foods she would soon need.

The morning Carlyle was to arrive, I dressed Linda in a pretty embroidered dress my mother had given her and brushed her silky hair. As she lay there smiling up at me, I thought about how beautiful she was and hoped she would always be as safe and happy as she was then. It was almost time for Carlyle to come, and with each passing moment I became more uneasy and uncomfortable. I put on the blue dress he liked so much, but it was too big now and looked baggy and shabby.

I stood before the mirror, remembering how he had spoken about the sun shining on my hair and my pretty face. My hair seemed drab and dull now. There were shadows under my eyes and hollows in my cheeks. I hardly had any makeup, just some powder, and no lipstick. I didn't even have any perfume. Dispirited and pessimistic, I went into the kitchen and looked out the porch window. There was Carlyle, walking down the alley, tall and graceful as always, looking more handsome than ever in his uniform. I watched him coming down the alley, and it crossed my mind like a dark shadow that he always had to use the back stairs.

I opened the door for him, managing a smile of sorts. It was the best I could do. He put down his overnight bag and stood looking at me with an expression I could not fathom, certainly not joy, but not disappointment either. Without saying anything at all he put his arms around me and held me tightly against him. I don't remember much about the next few minutes or what either of us said, except that it was as though we were trying to reach across an abyss to find each other, looking for some sign of the intimacy we had once known. He walked over and looked at Linda, remarking on how pretty she was. He touched her cheek with his finger but made no effort to pick her up.

"You must be hungry," I said. "Would you like a sandwich or something to drink?" I sounded like a polite hostess talking to a guest.

"I'll wash up, if you don't mind," he replied equally politely. I showed him to the bathroom and then sat down to wait for him. When he returned he pulled the remaining armchair closer to me and sat looking at me. He didn't touch me. He simply looked at me gravely.

"You've had a rotten time of it, haven't you?" he said. He sounded both worried and guilty.

"Well, it wasn't my idea of Oktoberfest," I replied. He looked startled and amused. We both laughed.

"That's why you are the joy of my life," he said, reaching across to kiss me. "You have the most wonderful gift of humor."

It was all right then; everything was just as it had been, except that we were now parents and none too sure of what that entailed. As though he had read my mind, he went to pick up our daughter and, cuddling her, came again to sit beside me.

"You know," he said, "ever since I have known you I have envied you for your family—the closeness and the fellowship." There was something so wistful and sad in the tone of his voice that I wanted to reach out and comfort him.

"Well," I said, "we're a family now—you and me and Linda—and we have a lot more at stake than my mother and father did. We somehow have to make the world right for our child."

In my heart I knew that I was not only talking about Linda but about Carlyle as well. He also needed the safety and comfort of belonging to help heal the wounds he had suffered in his childhood. This I could try to do, but it was not all one-sided, for I, too, was forlorn, adrift in a sea of dark, uncharted waters and frightened at the prospect of having to live in exile because I had chosen to break society's rules. I needed Carlyle's strength, his love and understanding, as much as he needed mine. Hesitantly groping for words, not quite sure of myself, I told him what I thought. Somehow we had to create space for our child and for ourselves without regard for the boundaries that society dictated—a kind of fortress to keep us safe from racism and all of the painful damage it could do.

Carlyle listened quietly, still holding the baby. "How do you propose to do this?" he asked.

"I haven't the faintest idea," I replied, "but that's the way strong families are built, isn't it? One for all and all for one? What chance do we have without something like that? We have to try."

"It's not going to be easy," he said, "with me in Texas and you here, but you're right. We have to make a place for ourselves."

We spent the night talking, trying to put together a plan for ourselves. Though I can no longer recall the context, I suddenly remembered something my mother had said many years earlier: "You can't have a strong family without knowing its roots." I think she must have been defending her sister's interest in the genealogy of her family, the Wilsons.

"A family has to have roots," I said aloud. "Wilsons, Tinkers, Carters, and Douglases—they're all part of us."

"What are you talking about?" Carlyle asked, looking at me as though I had lost my mind.

"Just as I said—all those people are our roots. They are what we've got to build on. I've never really thought about it before, but it is comforting to know about your grandparents and all the others from way back when."

"Supposing you found out that your great, great grandfather was Jack the Ripper. What then?" The corner of his mouth was twitching. Sitting on the side of the bed, I rocked with laughter, and temporarily, at least, we abandoned the ancestors.

Carlyle was due to leave the next evening, so we had very little time left to discuss anything that was not of immediate importance. We agreed, however, that from now on we would write to each other at least once a week, even if it were only a postcard. We also decided that I should immediately begin looking for another apartment on the South Side, near the University of Chicago and Jackson Park, and that I should use part of the money from his Liberty bonds to buy some decent furniture. We really had made no progress at all toward building a fortress, but still I had the feeling that we were more secure than we had been twenty-four hours before.

I had nursed Linda and tucked her into her buggy and we were lying side by side in bed, half asleep, when Carlyle suddenly sat up, propped his head against a pillow, and turned to look down at me.

"It's a good thing to know something about your ancestors," he said without preamble, "but I think it is far more important to give a child security. He has to know that you're going to be there when he needs you, no matter what, and that you are always going to love him. It really doesn't matter a damn, does it, whether your grandfather was president of the United States or a ditchdigger, as long as he was a good, caring person who was always there for his family—somebody you can depend upon, who never switched horses in the middle of the stream.

"Look at your own family. On the one hand you have the Wilsons, descended from James Wilson, who signed the Declaration of Independence and helped draft the Constitution and the Bill of Rights. Very impressive. I'm not saying they weren't good people, the Wilsons—but who meant the most to you? Who was always there for you no matter what you did? Granted, your mother was a Wilson, but she outgrew that. And next to your parents, who was the person you loved most, maybe even more? Grandmother Tinker, right? And who were the Tinkers? Gypsies, your father said. Menders of pots and pans who traveled around Ireland in covered wagons."

Carlyle stopped abruptly and was silent for so long that I began to wonder what was wrong.

"You know," he resumed slowly, "I hope I can be as good a father as yours is."

We talked about parenting and parenthood many more times after that. We planned to expose our children to as much art, literature, and music as we could within our limited resources. We would plaster our walls with affordable fine art prints. Carlyle and I would get a Victrola and begin collecting records so that our children would be raised with classical music and jazz. We would read to our children daily and take them on regular cultural expeditions to the city—to the art museum, the Field Museum, the library, the aquarium, and the zoo—to absorb everything that Chicago had to offer. We enjoyed dreaming of the things that we would do for our children. We agreed that we would raise them to take pride in both their African and European ancestors. The conversation captured Carlyle's excitement in a way that I had not seen before and have not seen since. Never again did Carlyle reveal himself to me with such frankness and passion as he did that night.

I believe that, despite the wounds inflicted by his shattered childhood and the constant battle to achieve self-esteem in a racist world, Carlyle did indeed fulfill his wish to raise educated children, and I know beyond doubt that his children and his grandchildren believe it, too.

Carlyle left the following afternoon. The parting was not as painful as it had been before, primarily because our long discussion the previous evening had brought us closer together and made our future more secure.

I was eager to begin putting into effect all the things we had planned, but I also still believed that some knowledge of one's roots was important. I realized, of course, that it would be impossible for Carlyle to trace his ancestors much beyond his grandparents, but even that seemed important to me, and I was sure his mother would be able to help.

Furthermore, I was convinced that any Black child born in this country—facing as he inevitably would the humiliation, contempt, and other manifestations of racism that destroy self-esteem—needed to know the accomplishments of both slaves and freedmen and the invaluable contributions they had made to this country. With that knowledge, the child, whether boy or girl, could stand tall and fight off the attempts of his Caucasian peers to reduce him to a second-class citizen.

I also remembered the many conversations Carlyle and I had had at the National Youth Administration camp when we discussed music, art, and literature. Were not these things also important? Were they not a means both of escape and enrichment in the battle for self-esteem?

As a first step in my plan, I asked my landlord to direct me to the nearest branch of the public library and learned that fortunately there was one only three blocks away. That same afternoon, I tucked Linda into her buggy and started off to find the library. I stopped at the curb to wait for a light to change, and a well-dressed, pleasant-faced White woman stopped beside me.

"What a beautiful baby you have," she said.

I thanked her politely, and she continued, "But isn't she dark?"

Completely taken aback, I replied, "Yes, isn't she?"

I caught a glimpse of the woman's startled expression as the light changed and I crossed the street. Thereafter, when anyone made a similar remark, and it happened now and then, I always smiled and gave the same answer, wickedly pleased by the puzzled expression it engendered. I was learning to play the game.

When I reached the library, I asked the librarian where I could find books about Negro history. She appeared nonplussed. She shook her head and said she did not believe they had anything like that. A young Black woman standing some distance away who heard my query beckoned to me, and together we went to the rear of the library, where books by and about Blacks were stored—histories, fiction, biographies, poetry—enough to keep me busy for months. From then on I read omnivorously, and the more I read the more excited I became. It was as though I had unearthed a gold mine.

I learned that Africans who had been kidnapped and enslaved were brought to Virginia as early as 1619 and that it was their blood, sweat, and tears that had brought to fruition the whole South. As freedmen, they had fought in the Revolutionary War and in the Civil War. In fact, the Fighting 54th Massachusetts Volunteer Infantry, a Black regiment that fought in the Civil War, is now famous for its heroism. In World War I, four entire Black regiments—the 369th, 370th, 371st, and 372nd—received the Croix de Guerre en masse.*

---

* See Lerone Bennett, Jr., *Before the Mayflower: A History of Black America* (Chicago: Johnson Publishing, 1987), p. 29; see Gail Buckley, *American Patriots* (New York: Random House, 2001), pp. 3–40; see J. A. Rogers, *100 amazing facts about the Negro with complete proof* (New York: Helga M. Rogers, 1957), pp. 13–14.—D. D.

The names of Harriet Tubman, Nat Turner, and Frederick Douglass became as familiar to me as those of Ulysses S. Grant or Abraham Lincoln. I read about the Black men who had invented such necessities as refrigerated railroad cars, steam engines, better light bulbs, and ways to process and store blood plasma. I learned about George Washington Carver, who found an amazing number of uses for the lowly peanut. I read the poetry of Langston Hughes, the fiction of Richard Wright, and the essays of William Edward Burghart Du Bois.

I stumbled upon a thin little book entitled *Little Known Facts about the Negro*. I was amazed and delighted to learn that the Queen of Sheba was Black; so were the Russian author Aleksandr Pushkin and Alexandre Dumas, the author of *The Three Musketeers*. I found that Napoleon's Josephine, as well as Beethoven, apparently had Black ancestry, which, of course, was the same thing as being all Black.*

I came to the conclusion that no Black American need ever step back or give way to his White compatriot. For better or for worse they had built this country together, and together they would shape the future.

I realized that our daughter had no reason to feel that because of her race she was a lesser being, but it was up to us as her parents to reinforce the concept of equality by all those methods we had agreed upon.

---

* In an exhaustive search I have been unable to locate *Little Known Facts about the Negro*. Due to the vagaries of memory and the passage of time, it is quite possible that Barbara's memory of the title is incorrect. A similar title supports some of the assertions she made about African Americans: J. A. Rogers, *100 Amazing facts about the Negro with complete proof*, 23rd ed. (New York: Helga M. Rogers, 1957). While there is clear documentation from a variety of sources that Pushkin and Dumas had Black ancestry, it should be noted that there is no clear consensus that the Queen of Sheba, Beethoven, or Josephine Bonaparte had Black ancestry.—D. D.

5

No Room at the Inn

FREEDOM

He is a slave who would be free:
>The dream of freedom conquers all.
What nobler mastery can there be?
>He is a slave who would be free—
A slave because he cannot flee
>The voiceless lash of freedom's call.
He is a slave who would be free;
>The dream of freedom conquers all.

—*Carlyle Douglas, May 10, 1944*

ON THE WAY TO THE LIBRARY, I often passed a shabby little secondhand furniture store. The owner and his wife, Mr. and Mrs. Gillespie, a middle-aged couple, frequently sat on chairs just inside the door, talking to each other and to the occasional passerby who stopped to speak to them. One day I saw in the windows a Chinese lacquer secretary with bookcase, desk, and drawers. It was truly a beautiful piece of furniture with delicate little garden and temple scenes painted on the desktop. I found it irresistible and inquired about the price. Much to my amazement and delight, Mr. Gillespie said it was only fifty dollars.

I was sorely tempted, but as yet I had no place to put it. My apartment was just too small. As I stood looking longingly at it, Mrs. Gillespie, smiling, said in a coaxing voice, "Missus, you and the baby come in for a cup of tea and a cookie, maybe . . . Yes?" I could not resist her friendly offer.

I joined them for a glass of iced tea and cookies and stayed for a while, basking in the warmth of their friendly hospitality. We seemed to have very little in common except, perhaps, that we were strangers in a strange land, all of us having moved from somewhere outside of Chicago into the city. We slowly developed a friendship. Nearly every day thereafter I stopped to say "hello" and lingered for a bit to gossip. When they learned that I was looking for an apartment in the Jackson Park area, they offered to drive me in their panel truck to look around.

Because of them I finally found exactly the place I wanted. The building was only a few blocks from the park. The two-story building stood on a corner, and there was a small grocery store on the first floor. When I saw the For Rent sign in the window, I asked the Gillespies to stop, and I went inside to inquire about the place. The shop owner had the keys and took me to see the apartment, which was at the front of the second floor. When he opened the door I could scarcely believe my good fortune. Sunshine flooded in from a bay window in the large living room. To the left, I saw a kitchen with more windows facing the side street, a refrigerator, a sink, enough room for a kitchen table and chairs, and beyond that was a small bathroom. There was also a sunny bedroom big enough for a double bed, a chest of drawers, and a crib.

Barely able to conceal my excitement, I asked the price. "Thirty-five a month," he said. "You pay the electricity and gas for the stove." It was just within my means if I scrimped a little here and there. Never mind that I didn't have a stick of furniture of my own.

"I'll take it," I said. "How much do you want in advance?"

"You come tomorrow about nine. I'll hold it for you until then. The landlord comes in about then." I was so excited that I nearly danced out to the truck. The Gillespies agreed to bring me back the next day. The following day, I signed the lease and gave the landlord the rent and the deposit—seventy dollars in all—which left me with about a hundred in the strongbox under the bed.

Within two weeks, the Gillespies unearthed a stout double bed, a mattress, a crib, a chest of drawers, a kitchen table with two chairs, and a very nice tapestry armchair with only one dingy spot, which could be covered with a doily. They also brought along the Chinese secretary. I was totally broke but very happy.

After moving in and installing a telephone, I called my mother. Almost overnight, she shipped my grandmother's heirloom chest of drawers along with some bed linens, pots and pans, dishes, curtains, four heirloom rosewood chairs, my Victrola and records, my books, and a reproduction of the Lebrun painting *Mother and Child*, which had hung over my family's fireplace for as long as I could remember. For Linda, my mother shipped some children's books, a cardboard circus, a ball, a rag doll, and a playpen.

I was overwhelmed by her generosity. Now, with all of these riches in place, the apartment was not only comfortable but utterly charming.

All this time, of course, Carlyle and I wrote to each other. I had not known before that he was a poet, but now he began to send me a poem almost every time he wrote. Somehow the poems seemed to bridge the distance between us. His love poems helped me to feel his deep love for me. I in turn wrote to him with news about our daughter and the new apartment, and I also began to put together scrapbooks full of items from *The New Yorker* and *Atlantic Monthly*, often jokes I thought might amuse or interest him along with comments of my own. The distance between us seemed much smaller than it had in the past.

Days passed more quickly than they ever had before. I read to Linda, and we listened to music and went, each pleasant day, to the park. I was teaching her colors, and she could tell the names of the animals in her toy circus when I pointed to them.

In October of 1944, Carlyle telegraphed to say he was getting a two-week furlough. I called his mother. She came immediately and seemed nearly as excited as I at the thought of seeing him. His train was to arrive at Union Station about ten o'clock in the morning, which meant that if it were on time he would reach us about an hour later. His mother and I sat at the bay window, watching for either a cab or a streetcar, but neither came. Hour after hour went by. I became alarmed, but Mom said, "Don't worry. If anything goes wrong with either of my boys I would know it right away. That's the way it's always been."

I wasn't too sure about that, but I settled back to wait. The next streetcar to appear stopped at our corner, and there was Carlyle. This time I was prepared. I had a new dress, my hair was washed, and I not only had makeup, I had perfume as well.

I stood at the top of the stairs waiting for him, barely able to resist rushing headlong down to the vestibule. The door opened. Carlyle looked up at me and took the steps two at a time. His mom was waiting inside with Linda in her arms. Carlyle kissed them both and held me in a heavenly embrace. He then went to bathe and change. I was deliriously happy: I had a pretty, bubbly baby, my husband was home, and I had an extremely nice, though modest, apartment.

For the next two days we stayed at home talking and playing with the baby. Carlyle's mother tactfully disappeared for most of the time, reappearing just long enough to prepare meals or to take Linda for a walk.

At the end of that time she said she had to return to Detroit and suggested that we go with her, at her expense, since her sister Edna and her daughters, Carlyle's cousins, hadn't seen Carlyle for nearly two years. We were not particularly enthusiastic, but there seemed to be no way around it since Mom had done so much for us. So we agreed to go.

The next afternoon we took the train with Mom to Detroit. She had called ahead to a hotel—one of the newer establishments in Detroit. We arrived at dark, and when we got out of the cab in front of the hotel, Mom turned to me and, to my surprise, told me to go on ahead. The room had been engaged and would be ready for us. I was puzzled. A bellhop took my bag, and with Linda in my arms, I went into the hotel. The man at the desk was pleasant enough, and the bellhop escorted me to the elevator and up to my room. The room was all right, but I was uneasy. Somehow this whole thing didn't seem to make sense. Why did she tell me to go in alone?

The telephone rang, and a pleasant male voice said, "This is the manager, Mrs. Douglas, would you be kind enough to come downstairs?"

With butterflies in my stomach and becoming more apprehensive every moment, I picked up Linda and went down. When the elevator opened I saw Carlyle and his mother standing at the desk. I wasn't sure there was anything really wrong until I saw the bellhop crossing the lobby with my bag. I stopped halfway to the desk and just stood there.

The manager was talking to Carlyle. "Sir," he said in dulcet tones, "I am sorry, but it is not the policy of this hotel to rent to colored."

Before I could do anything, Mom turned and said to me, "Go up to the ladies' room and wait." She motioned toward the stairway, and I fled. I felt guilty and ashamed as I did so, but I kept going. I was puzzled then but later understood that she wanted to spare me from the ugliness of the racial discrimination they were experiencing.

When I reached the ladies' room, a hotel maid—a middle-aged Black woman who was standing in the doorway—took one look at my face and hurried to get a chair for me. I sat down, still clutching Linda. I was scared and miserable—feeling worse than ever before because I had let my husband down. I had run away and left him to face the problem alone. I didn't realize that his mom, with her strength of character, intelligence, and years of experience in dealing with racism, more than made up for my absence. I felt the tears running down my face and began to rock back and forth. I felt powerless to do anything else.

"Hey now," the maid said. "Ain't no use to cry, Honey. Ain't nothing you can do. Let them fix it up." She offered me a tissue and patted my hand.

Within a few minutes Mom came upstairs to the ladies' room and beckoned to me. I followed her meekly down to the lobby where Carlyle was waiting for us, his face closed and grim.

The manager, still apologizing, suggested another hotel. Carlyle, emasculated by the humiliating experience, gave me a lopsided smile, took Linda's and my bag, and started for the door. Mom and I trailed him. He hailed a cab. We stopped at some other hotel, but it was the same story again: no room at the inn. Not for Blacks. Not for an interracial family like us. We tried a local motel with the same results. The entire experience was a rude awakening to the pervasiveness of racism. I had had no idea that Blacks faced this kind of discrimination every day of their lives.

The driver suggested that he take us to a nice place he knew of that would surely have room. It was indeed a very respectable looking house. It looked residential from the outside, perhaps a boarding house. The hall was clean. A well-dressed lady politely greeted us from behind a desk. I stood, looking around while Carlyle explained our plight to her. A double door opened into a large living room sumptuously furnished with an overstuffed sofa and a number of armchairs with what appeared to be a small bar at the far end. The room was occupied for the most part by a number of very pretty Black and White women in elegant dresses.

Mom and Carlyle were still talking to the clerk at the desk, so I took a good look at the ladies, and I knew immediately that we were in what was delicately known as a "house of love." I was too tired to react one way or the other but dared not look at Carlyle. I was too embarrassed. I waited patiently while Carlyle talked first with the woman at the desk and then with a fashionably dressed man who seemed to be in charge.

Finally Mom motioned to me, and we walked up two flights of stairs to the third floor, which we had to ourselves. There were two bedrooms, sparsely furnished but clean, and a bathroom.

Carlyle and I took the larger room and made a bed of sorts in the bureau drawer for Linda. Mom said good night and retired to her room. When she was gone Carlyle rolled his eyes heavenward. "You know where we are, of course?" he asked.

"Of course," I replied, "where else?" We smothered our laughter to avoid waking Linda.

"What in heaven's name happened?" I asked as we undressed.

"Mom made a mistake," he said in his usual terse style.

"I'll say," I said and buried my face in a pillow.

"What now?" I asked when I could talk again.

"Well, we'll stay here tonight and tomorrow," he said, watching my face. "They're really quite nice," he added.

"I'm sure," I said and buried my face in the pillow again. In fact, the room and bed linens were very clean, and the bed was comfortable. Little or no noise came from downstairs, and we slept soundly until Mom woke us in the morning to pick up Linda.

Mom offered to watch Linda while we went to see Carlyle's cousins and had dinner with his Aunt Virginia and Aunt Edna. I looked forward to getting away from the tawdry world of prostitution. It was a real treat to visit Carlyle's family. They were warm and accepted me like family. We stayed much longer than we had planned. When we returned to the house where we were staying, I apologized to Mom for staying away so long. She seemed unconcerned and told us that she had enjoyed taking care of Linda and had a pleasant, quiet day. We planned to take an early train back to Chicago, so we went to bed almost immediately. Mom called a cab for us in the morning, kissed us good-bye, and, I assumed, went on back to her sister's house. In all the years that followed, Mom never once mentioned the hotel fiasco to either Carlyle or me.

Although in many ways the experience remains a mystery to me, I have since figured out that Mom just wanted us all to stay in a nice hotel, and while there were no signs that said it, all the nice hotels were for Whites only. Mom must have known it would be difficult, but she probably thought that since I was White and she could pass, somehow we could slip Carlyle in. She had miscalculated. Even in a Northern city the forces of racism were just too strong.

We reached the station just a few minutes before departure time, and as we stood in line side by side with Carlyle holding Linda, a well-dressed White man standing behind us leaned forward and said, "You have a beautiful little girl there." He chatted with us for a few minutes and, as we reached the gate, smiled pleasantly and said, "Have a good trip."

He was one of those whom I mentioned before. That brief encounter brightened the world around us and helped to soften the memory of that disastrous trip, which we dubbed the hotel fiasco.

Not more than an hour later another incident occurred, which even today remains a highlight of those early years. We took seats in the coach section, just in front of two middle-aged White ladies who had brought their lunches with them and spread the food out neatly on the seat between them. Shortly after the train started and the conductor came through to punch our tickets, one of the ladies leaned forward and almost apologetically tapped Carlyle on the shoulder.

"Sir," she said, "my sister and I have brought far too big a lunch. We were wondering if you and your wife would care to share it with us."

Carlyle, looking first at me and searching for a clue, saw that I was pleased and accepted the offer. Indeed, we were very hungry. We spent a pleasant hour with them engaging in the usual sort of conversation that is customary between amiable strangers bridging the gap. A quite ordinary encounter you might say, and yet to us, this experience and the earlier incident when the man in line spoke to us were the highlights of our trip. Even after all these years, when I recall those three friendly people, I experience the same exhilarating glow I did then. Their act of kindness helped to heal the pain of the hotel fiasco, yet even now, after more than fifty years, the scars from the incident are still there.

Once we were back in Chicago, we spent the last few days of Carlyle's furlough at home, quietly listening to records, playing with Linda, and enjoying each other's company. I dreaded his departure but had to resign myself to the inevitable.

That winter was a long one for me, for it was nearly impossible to take Linda outside. It was bitterly cold, and the snow never seemed to stop. Neither my mother nor Carlyle's was able to visit me. Although I talked to them now and then by phone, I was very lonely, so much so that when the postman occasionally failed to bring a letter from Carlyle, I was devastated.

The one bright spot was that Carlyle was still at Biggs Field, and it did not seem likely that he would go overseas. Like everyone else, I listened to the radio, every day hoping to hear that the war was over. By this time, Germany was tottering on the verge of collapse, and it would be only a matter of months before it surrendered.

It was becoming more and more difficult to write cheerful, gossipy letters to Carlyle, and his letters to me were becoming briefer and more despondent.

Despite the gifts my mother and father sent, the little Christmas tree in the window, and the carols on the radio, it felt more like doomsday than Christmas.

Sometime after New Year's Day of 1945, life began to improve. Carlyle's older brother, Willie, whom I had heard about but had never seen, wrote me a very nice letter. He had only just heard of our marriage and wanted to welcome me into the family. He also sent a photograph of himself. He had a light complexion, a charming smile, and looked very much like his mother. He was stationed in Okinawa, where he was waiting to be discharged from the Army and sent home. He wanted to stop over in Chicago and see me. We corresponded for a while, and I was pleased to be developing a good relationship with yet another member of Carlyle's family. Meanwhile, in May Germany surrendered, and it began to appear that Carlyle might soon be discharged too.

6

Banished

CHILDREN OF BONDAGE

Children of bondage from over the sea,
Strike for your fathers now in the grave;
Time now to rise, become men who are free.

Remember the suffering you seldom could flee;
The horrors endured and the lives that you gave.
Children of bondage from over the sea.

Remember black bodies destroyed wantonly;
The floggings, the lynchings, all deeds of the knave;
Time now to rise, become men who are free.

Strike so your sons may know liberty;
Strike for the freedom deserved by the brave,
Children of bondage from over the sea.

Time now to heed your forefathers' plea;
Cast off the shackles that mark you a slave;
Time now to rise, become men who are free.

In the fierce fight for freedom to be,
Your conduct shall show how the valiant behave;
Children of bondage from over the sea
Time now to rise, become men who are free.

—*Carlyle Douglas, May 30, 1945*

ANTICIPATING CARLYLE'S RETURN FROM Biggs Army Airfield, I began to think of a more permanent residence for our family. The winter had been particularly severe, and the late spring went to my head like wine. The smell of newly turned earth and growing things, the sight of jewel-bright tulips, of curled, rosy maple buds, and of young green grass made me homesick for a small town. With feelings of eagerness and excitement, I searched the real estate ads of the *Chicago Tribune*. By great good luck, or so I thought, a small house was for rent in Woodstock, Illinois, a town well removed from the metropolitan area yet readily accessible. I invited Ann, a good friend from the office, to come with Linda and me by train to Woodstock the next day. I fell in love with the town, the center of a thriving farming community. Its charm lay in the gently sloping hills on which it was built, in the broad, quiet streets overhung with tall elms and oaks, and in the old houses set widely apart on lawns with carefully tended gardens.

The house that a genial real estate agent showed us was on a little side street where others of like modesty were to be found. The house itself was not prepossessing, but it was comfortable. A huge old tree grew in the front yard, and a lilac bush was in bloom. Apple trees were misted with white blossoms in the fenced area at the back. We discovered a grape arbor and a bed of lilies of the valley.

I signed the lease without a qualm, for I believed that once the neighbors came to know the baby and me, they would soon realize that we were just ordinary people, not queer or strange. And when Carlyle came home, having accepted me, they would also accept him. Such were the abysmal depths of my naïveté! I hadn't learned from our experience with Detroit's hotels. Perhaps because I had grown up in a small town I thought the experience in Woodstock would be different from that of the city.

Carlyle was completely against the move, but I overrode all of his objections, believing that his pessimistic and apprehensive letters were based only on his past experiences in the South. As I embarked on my summer idyll, a reluctant Carlyle was in tow.

Late in June of 1945, Ann and I moved to Woodstock. We got along very well, so I invited her to stay with me until the Army discharged Carlyle. We agreed to share expenses, making it a good deal for both of us.

The move itself was a hilarious adventure. I could not afford professional movers, but a cousin of the janitor in our building volunteered his services and that of his somewhat antiquated truck. He was a pleasant-spoken, friendly individual with whom I felt completely at ease, mostly because of his personality but partly because he was Negro. By this time I had had so many negative experiences with members of my own race that I was beginning to feel more relaxed with Negroes than Caucasians. His only fault lay in being overly fond of beer, a fault that he shared with the two friends whom he engaged to help with the move.

It was a hot day, and my furniture had to be moved down three flights of stairs. This called for refreshment. A quart of beer shared among the three friends served the purpose, and soon we were ready to start on our journey. In a prudent attempt to save money, we decided to ride on the truck. Since the men were unfamiliar with the road leading to Woodstock, Ann and I, who had been poring over the map for a week, felt fully qualified to act as guides.

When the furniture was finally piled in and tied on the truck, a space about two feet deep remained to accommodate me, the baby, Ann, her canary, and her two dalmatians. The owner of the truck and one of his helpers, together with several quarts of beer, rode inside the cab. The other friend, plus his supply of beer, were perched precariously on the cab's roof, where he was to act as the liaison between the driver and us, relaying directions.

With the throttle wide open and no hint of a muffler, we roared and rattled through the streets of Chicago. The man in the cab waved his bottle in friendly greeting to all and sundry. The dalmatians barked, and we shouted directions that were either misinterpreted or ignored. Somehow we managed to escape arrest for disturbing the peace and arrived on the city's outskirts without incident.

It is impossible to follow a road map when your view of the surrounding landscape is backward, and twice we lost our way. On the second occasion we found ourselves in a narrow lane winding through deep woods. An overhanging branch caught one of my mother's rosewood chairs, an heirloom she had entrusted to me, and sent it crashing to splinters in the wake of the truck. This totally dampened my ardor for the whole venture, but it was too late to turn back.

We arrived in Woodstock just as the soft, quiet summer dusk was descending and split it asunder with the roar of the truck, the barking of our dogs, and the happy singing of the beer-soaked men. Keenly aware that this was scarcely an auspicious beginning, Ann and I worked furiously to help to unload the furniture. After an agonizing hour or two, we saw the last of the men and their truck roaring gaily off into the night.

We quickly settled into the neighborhood, and the pattern of our days assumed a delightful, leisurely sameness. The young couple who lived in a small, modern house on one side of us had two young daughters about Linda's age, and the three of them played together all day long. The mother and I fell into the pleasant habit of chatting over the fence as we hung out our washing. On the other side of us lived an elderly Polish lady who had never quite mastered the intricacies of the English language. She and I had a mutual interest in gardening, and we, too, developed a friendship.

Across the street was a small bakery. Every morning the summer breeze would bring us the satisfying odor of freshly baked bread. The bakers, an older couple, proved to be as unaffectedly wholesome as their bread. They often sent over cookies for Linda. The grocer down the block was friendly, too. He knew I was living on a military allotment and helped me stretch my food money.

I had been in Woodstock nearly two months when I received a letter from Carlyle saying he was coming home on leave. The very next day my brother-in-law, Willie, telephoned me from San Francisco. After four years of overseas service he was being discharged from the Army and had just arrived from Okinawa. He would reach Chicago within a few hours of Carlyle's arrival and intended to stay with us for a while. I had not seen Carlyle for a year and was so exhilarated at the thought of his coming that I ran to tell my neighbors the news. They shared my happiness.

The baby and I went into Chicago to meet Willie and Carlyle. All the way out to Woodstock on the suburban train, I sang the praises of our new home. Carlyle and Willie did not completely share my enthusiasm or my faith in the democratic attitude of the townspeople.

The day was warm and sunny. The trees overhead formed pools of cool, green shade, the scent of roses filled the air, and all the garden flowers were in bloom. Walking three abreast from the station down the main street, we passed the bakery and the grocery store. It was a proud moment for me. Willie and Carlyle looked so splendid—tall and straight in their uniforms. Willie wore the battle ribbons of the European and Pacific theaters together with the Purple Heart. Linda, beautiful in a little pink dress with pink bows in her hair, rode laughing on her father's shoulder.

I was too engrossed in my own happiness to notice the reactions of passersby, but I do remember that the grocer came to his door. He smiled, waved, and called, "Welcome home." I shall never forget that. Later when I went to the store to buy groceries for dinner, he gave me a huge steak—so difficult to obtain during the war—to celebrate the homecoming.

I did not see either of my immediate neighbors until the following day when Grandmother Pulaski smiled at me in her usual friendly fashion and asked if I were not happy now. The young mother next door came to invite Linda to her daughter's birthday party and offered to get us fresh eggs and a chicken from her father's farm.

It is only in retrospect that I understand the full significance of these incidents. At the time, I took them as matter of course, for I did not realize that these kind people with their simple, friendly gestures had thrown a lifeline into a dark and turbulent sea.

Now, it is not to be inferred that because some people were well disposed toward us as a couple they approved of intermarriage. The only inference to be drawn is that they found nothing wrong with our particular intermarriage because they found us acceptable both as individuals and as a pair. It is a singular fact that people who consider themselves liberal on every count often are unable to accept the idea of marriage between a White person and a Black person. This was true in the case of my own mother. It took her many months after our wedding to rediscover the virtues she had discerned in Carlyle before she learned that we intended to marry each other.

For the first day or two after they arrived in Woodstock, Carlyle and Willie did not venture far from the house—a brief trip to the store or the bakery was all—but as time passed, the unease and doubt that they had brought with them disappeared. They took Linda for walks and even went shopping on Main Street. Woodstock was not one of those towns with ordinances prohibiting the presence of Negroes after sundown; in fact, it boasted of the presence of a Negro family among its population.

Then the first blow fell. The real estate agent came to see us. He was flushed and ill at ease, for his was not an easy task. He began by assuring us that he was not prejudiced. To Willie and Carlyle this was an all too familiar refrain, but I took him at his word, not suspecting what was to follow. The woman from whom we had leased the house did not wish to rent to Blacks, and we were told to leave at the end of the month.

My brain was numb, nausea clogged my throat, and, despite the warmth of the day, my hands were icy. I have no recollection of the conversation that followed, if indeed there was any. The real estate agent took his leave, and we began to pick up the pieces.

The hard, cold facts of the matter were these: In three days Carlyle would have to return to his base, we had no money with which to defray the cost of moving back to Chicago, and we had no place to move into. As a first step Carlyle and I went to Chicago to look for an apartment in the city streets shimmering with August heat. For three days we walked and rode buses, rental ads in hand, from early morning until long after dark. It was always the same: Either the apartments had already been rented, they were too expensive, or the landlords did not rent to Blacks.

The anesthesia of shock had begun to wear off. I felt the wall of the ghetto closing in around me. Overnight I had lost my rights as an American citizen and had become an undesirable alien, yet I was no different than I had ever been. What had changed? I had married the man of my choice, and he happened to be Black. It was as simple as that.

We returned to Woodstock. Carlyle was now AWOL (absent without leave), but he refused to leave until he found us someplace to stay. Ann gallantly stood by Carlyle, Willie, and me throughout the entire ordeal. Carlyle and I now spent the long evening trying to work out a solution. We found none and finally went wearily to bed.

Ann, sleeping in a bedroom just off the dining room, was awakened toward morning by a sound she could not identify. She drifted back to sleep without bothering to investigate. In the morning when we gathered for breakfast, the canary that normally swung in his cage at the sunny front window did not greet us with his usual liquid trill. He lay in the bottom of his cage, a pathetic huddle of feathers. In the window a star-shaped series of cracks radiated from a small hole. The sound Ann had heard in the middle of the night had been a gunshot.

We ate nothing that morning but sat in stony silence over endless cups of coffee, each isolated from the others by our own thoughts.

In the end both Carlyle and I went to the Red Cross. Fearing that my presence would only cause further trouble, I remained in the lobby, but only briefly, for Carlyle, with hope in his voice, called me to join him. The lady with whom he had talked—a Mrs. Landis*— was one of those rare individuals who has room for everyone in her heart. She instantly made our problem her own. From the moment I walked into the room where she sat I felt the rapport between us, and I loved her.

Mrs. Landis patted my hand comfortingly. She was on the telephone trying to reach Carlyle's commanding officer with the intention of asking that his leave be extended, but the circuits were overloaded and she was told it would be several hours before her call could be completed. Meanwhile, as gently as possible, she told us what had been happening in Woodstock. Like any other small community, it had an extremely efficient grapevine. Within twenty-four hours of Carlyle's arrival everyone in town knew about us. Many, like our immediate neighbors, had been inclined to accept us. But others, factory workers from the South and from Chicago, who had taken up residence in Woodstock to work in the newly built war plant, were bitterly opposed to our staying.

According to Mrs. Landis, a number of town meetings had been held about us in which the more sober elements of the population were trying to prevent the more radical from resorting to violence. She told us that the chief of police was prepared to assign special guards if the need arose, but somehow this was little consolation.

To have a landlord decide that she did not want to rent to us is not a very bad thing. It was inconveniencing, and it was disturbing and irritating, but not earthshaking or even heartbreaking. The case was somewhat different, however, when half a town arose in arms to shout that we could not live there and most of the other half tacitly agreed. This was democracy in action, and the people were not to be denied. The still, small voice of the tiny minority who were not opposed to our staying was unheard in the clamor.

Because the townspeople were not to be denied, we had to go. No matter that we had nowhere to go; no matter that we had no money with

---

* A pseudonym.

which to go; no matter that Carlyle was a soldier in the uniform of our country, fighting for it and for them. Their presumed right to an all-White neighborhood was not to be denied, no matter what happened to our family or our constitutional rights. Having our rights trampled in this manner hurt very deeply.

We went back to our house to await word from Mrs. Landis. Some hours later she came, bringing with her Mrs. Hill, a very gracious resident of the town. Mrs. Hill invited us to her home in the countryside outside of Woodstock for tea, thus giving us an opportunity to relax. Before we left she offered us shelter for as long as we might need it. Our faith in humanity began to revive.

We returned home with the pressure relieved, but early that evening Mrs. Landis came again, and as I opened the door for her I saw tears in her eyes. She told us the request for an extension of Carlyle's leave had been denied and that the military police from Fort Sheridan were on their way to pick him up. They were, however, to come first to her house, so if Carlyle would leave immediately for Chicago and from there take the next train to Texas, he would arrive at Biggs Field of his own volition and thus escape the severe penalties that might obtain if he were to arrive under escort.

I packed Carlyle's bag, and he kissed the baby good-bye. Leaving Linda with Willie and Ann, I went with Carlyle to Chicago. No train left Woodstock in time to help us, so we took a cab to a town seven miles farther south, and from there caught a suburban transit to Chicago. We did no talking; we just held hands. After an hour's wait in Union Station, Carlyle boarded the transcontinental train, and I returned to Woodstock.

When I reached the little house, which we could no longer call home, Willie told me the military police had been there and that they had been sent, not to arrest Carlyle, but to protect him. Before I could assimilate this information, Mrs. Landis called to inform me that Carlyle was indeed safely on his way to Texas. She also told me that the townspeople, after a long and heated meeting, had agreed to give me twenty-four hours in which to leave Woodstock, even though some of the newer residents wanted to burn down the house and violently evict me. She assured me, however, that a police cordon had been drawn around the block and temporarily, at least, we were safe. A few minutes later the chief of police called to say that he would be by his telephone all night and that if any trouble developed I was to call him immediately.

I moved through this nightmare with a calm engendered by despair. At my request Willie took Linda to Chicago, where they would stay with friends until I could come for her. Ann refused to leave me. After Willie left, we dragged a mattress under the living-room windows (remembering what had happened to the canary) and lay there fully clothed, wide awake and watching the moving shadows of the trees on the wall. Every creak of a floorboard or squeak of a branch against a window or sound of footsteps outside induced abject terror, but we remained rigid and quiet on the floor. Somehow the night passed.

The following morning we placed an ad in the *Woodstock Gazette* advertising household effects for sale. Since we had no money and no place to go, we hoped to raise enough money from the sale of our furniture to rent an apartment in Chicago. By late afternoon the house was crowded with people. To me they were a blur of cold eyes in White faces. All the things I had so lovingly and thoughtfully gathered for our home were carried out the door, one by one—the Chinese lacquer cabinet that I had found in a dusty corner of a secondhand shop, the graceful gateleg table, the tapestry wing chair, and, finally, Linda's crib. I saw them all go. A few things, however, remained: my grandmother's chest, the rosewood chairs, our books, and the phonograph. These Grandma Pulaski had offered to store in her basement. It was she who brought over sandwiches and cake and lemonade for our lunch, and the young mother next door came in ever so quietly to help me pack the books in boxes for storage. Mrs. Landis came too, along with her good friend Mrs. Hill, who had offered the shelter of her home. They did what they could. Late in the evening my mother and father arrived. Mrs. Landis had called them, and they had driven all night to reach me. Wordlessly I watched them as they packed my bags and gathered the few pitiful remnants of my belongings. Somehow I managed my good-byes to all these kind people, and with my parents and Ann, we drove out of Woodstock in the warm, scented dusk.

This was Woodstock—made up of the cruel and the weak, the kind and the courageous, the stupid and the intelligent. It might have been any American town. It happened in 1945. It could happen again tomorrow.

7

Dusty Road to Peace

SORROW
SONNET 1

The lovely music I enjoyed so well
Rings false, discordant; I no longer care
For strains whose magic wove a dreamy spell;
My bitter soul lies trampled by despair.
All joy is gone from life; my heart is bare
Of all the homely things that made it gay;
A grief too deep for words or tears dwells there
And Laughter sighs to see the heart decay.

Although the gloom of heartache rules today
Some bright tomorrow sadness will be gone:
The gloom that fills my soul shall drift away
As quietly as darkness flees the dawn.

Tranquillity and courage shall conceal
The hurts that lie too deep for time to heal.

—Carlyle Douglas, May 28–June 4, 1944

ON THAT LONG DRIVE FROM CHICAGO to the family farm near Ann Arbor, I had nothing to say. It was without doubt the lowest point in my life. I had allowed a selfish, juvenile whim to destroy not only my own life but that of all those close and dear to me. I had caused my parents an infinite amount of anxiety and a loss of money as well. My husband might easily have been killed because of me, and I had unnecessarily exposed my child, my brother-in-law, and my friends to danger.

Not only was I a slow learner with tunnel vision, but I had deliberately brushed aside my husband's justifiable concern as though what he thought or felt were of no importance. It would be a wonder if he ever spoke to me again.

Hunched in a corner of the backseat of my parents' car, I wallowed in a pool of guilt, apprehension, disillusion, and self-pity.

When we reached the farm, Mother went to fix something to eat, and my father began to unpack the trailer he had rented. Linda was overly tired and fractious. She fussed over her supper, unhappily protested the strange bathtub, and objected loudly to the room in which she was to sleep. Ordinarily, she was easy to manage, but I could do nothing with her that evening. She cried and fussed and swayed back and forth against the bars of her crib until finally she fell asleep from sheer exhaustion. I went to bed tired and miserable.

The next morning I went to face my parents, who greeted me over the breakfast table as though nothing had happened, but I could not let it go at that, so I just plunged in and told them what I had told myself. They listened without comment until I had finished. Then my father said, "It was a bummer, no doubt about that, but it doesn't necessarily mean the end of the world. You can't just say to hell with it and walk away. I know you better than that. You're a fighter, Barbara. So go to it."

He paused a minute and then smiled at me.

"Your husband called late last night. The lady at the Red Cross had called him. She told him what happened. He wanted to be sure you were all right. He said to tell you he loves you. You're a lucky girl. You'd better begin to pick up the pieces."

And so I did with the help of my husband, my father and mother, and Mrs. Landis of the Red Cross.

Within a few days of our arrival, I received a pamphlet of information and a letter from Mrs. Landis saying that she and Mrs. Hill had talked to the head of a project on the far South Side of Chicago that was being financed by the United States government. It was to be a low-income housing project built on about a thousand acres of reclaimed land next to the Calumet River. It was to be self-governed, but at the same time the city of Chicago was to provide maintenance and transportation. The project was to house several thousand families in individual units, two stories high, ranging in size from one to three bedrooms on the second floor, with a living room and dining-kitchen arrangement on the first. There also were a few studio apartments available. The buildings were to be arranged in thirteen blocks around parking lots, courtyards, play-grounds, and an area of lawns and flower beds. Each building was to elect a leader to represent block residents in monthly council meetings. There was to be a mall with a grocery store, drugstore, beauty salon, barbershop, laundromats, and two small shops for other businesses. It was to be an independent community with its own churches, schools, medical clinic, library, auditorium, and day care center. The project was nearly completed now, and the first occupants were to be veterans. They were hopeful that it would be an integrated community, and they were looking for interracial couples.

Needless to say, I immediately sent the pamphlet by special delivery to Carlyle and put in a call to Mrs. Landis. She asked that I meet her and Mrs. Hill at the office of Mr. Underwood, the man in charge of the housing project. Two days later, I had not, of course, had time to hear from Carlyle. I did not want to make the mistake I had before of going ahead without his consent. Fortunately, Mrs. Phiney, a Red Cross worker, took matters into her own hands. She had called the Red Cross chaplain at Biggs Army Airfield, and he, in turn, passed the information to Carlyle, who immediately telegraphed both Mrs. Landis and me. Fortunately, the telegram came the following day, and I was able to reach Chicago in time to meet with Mrs. Landis and Mrs. Hill. Mr. Underwood met us in his office. He was obviously impressed with the fact that I fit all the qualifications: I was a veteran's wife, I was interracially married, and I had a small child. That was, as far as I can remember, the only occasion when being interracially married proved to be a distinct advantage.

Mr. Underwood graciously shook my hand and declared himself delighted to assign us to an apartment at Altgeld Gardens. We were going to be one of the first families to move in and could come within the month. Our apartment was to be in block 1, not too far from the center of the project and close to both the clinic and the mall. I signed all the papers, thanked Mrs. Landis and Mrs. Hill, who were as delighted as I, and took the first bus back to Ann Arbor.

On the way back to the farm I speculated about the future. We had completely failed in an all-White community, so what assurance did we have that we would succeed in a nearly all-Black one? Yet we had no alternative, really, short of going to live on a desert island.

I knew we would never make it through another disaster like Woodstock, and despite the glowing description of Altgeld, I could not quite believe that it was all that perfect. So what was I to do? I did the same thing I always did—held my nose, plunged in the water, and hoped it wasn't too deep.

As soon as I arrived home, my father handed me another telegram from Carlyle. It read, "Home in March."

I knew that demobilization had begun, but Carlyle had pessimistically predicted that in all probability it might be as much as a year before they reached him. March was little more than six months away!

I had seen a plan of our apartment, which consisted of only three rooms—a living room, a kitchen with a dining alcove, a bathroom, and a bedroom. The rooms looked small, which was just as well because I had only my monthly allotment to invest in furniture. I took nothing from home this time except, of course, Linda's crib and high chair. I went to a small secondhand shop in Chelsea, bought a double bed, a chest of drawers, three straight chairs, a stuffed armchair, a daybed, and a small bookcase. We loaded them into the trailer, and Mother, Linda, and I drove to Chicago. It was treacherous driving, with snow blowing and ice forming on the pavement. It seemed to take forever. We arrived late in the afternoon, first stopping at a grocery store for some supplies. We then went to pick up the keys from the night watchman and drove back to the unit where I was to live.

BARBARA'S STORY

I shall never forget my first sight of Altgeld: the broad, tree-lined streets, the rows of sparkling new buildings, the lighted windows of the large grocery store, and the bright holiday lights strung around the plaza. Everything I had been told about the place seemed to be true, except for one thing: Among people shopping or moving across the plaza, I saw not a single White face. For a fleeting second, I felt a tremor of fear. Was this going to be Woodstock in reverse?

Our apartment was in block 1, and we parked the car and trailer in the lot nearest to it. As we parked, two young men in work clothes emerged from a truck and said they had been assigned to help us unload. They turned on the lights, showed me where the outlets were and how the stove worked. Then they unloaded the truck and put all our furniture into place. They adjusted the heat, went around to the windows and doors to be sure they were locked, and then refused any sort of remuneration and went on their way. My mother spent the night, helped me unpack and put everything away the next morning, and then left for home shortly after noon.

I loved it all. Never mind that the refrigerator was actually an icebox and the bathroom had no shower. I spent the first few days unpacking—putting away books, dishes, and toys—and hanging curtains in the windows and clothes in the closet. I had met none of my neighbors, but one morning there was a knock at the back door. A young boy stood there smiling shyly, holding a covered dish in his hands.

"Mama says would you maybe like some biscuits and honey?" He thrust the dish into my hands and ran back across the court. I watched him go, pleased, surprised, and touched by this friendly gesture. I remembered what Carlyle had said about our being happier with his people, and I knew he was right and that we had made the right decision. While several people in Woodstock had made similar friendly gestures, my recent experience there had completely undermined my trust in White people. In Woodstock I had learned how quickly "nice" people can turn into hate-mongering demons when they are faced with an interracial marriage. In contrast, I discovered in Altgeld Gardens an entire community that would accept my husband, my family, and me.

The biscuits were delicious, and we ate them with relish. After we had finished them I bundled Linda in her snowsuit and went across the courtyard to the apartment into which the little boy had disappeared. I knocked at the door, and the young woman who opened it smiled at me warmly. I introduced myself and thanked her for the biscuits.

"I'm Doris Washington," she said. "Come on in. I saw you just moving in, and I thought you might like something hot."

We talked for a while, totally at ease with each other. Afterwards, feeling happy and peaceful, I took Linda home for her nap.

It was through Doris that I met Mary and her mother, whom I came to call affectionately "Mama." Through all our years in Altgeld Gardens it was to Mary and Mama that I turned when I was in trouble. Mary, who was not much older than I, was a thin, dark woman whose face was already worn with the cares and concerns of life. For years she and her son and mother had lived in a tenement basement on welfare, fighting hunger, bedbugs, and roaches. They had been on Altgeld's waiting list for almost three years, and only the month before had received a notice that they could move in. I could not then, nor can I now, explain why we became such close friends. We seemed to have nothing in common, yet the rapport between us was as strong as if we were twins. As for Mama, she was the Rock of Gibraltar, a tall, gaunt old woman with a deeply furrowed face and almost no teeth. She always wore a turban, and I rarely saw her without her corncob pipe. She might very well have been as old as Methuselah, but she walked with her head high and with a stride that had a youthful spring to it. There was something about her, an innate dignity, that commanded our respect. Occasionally she babysat our children, and no matter their age, they behaved like saints in her presence.

One day shortly after settling in, I found tucked in the front door a flyer announcing a meeting the following afternoon. It was to take place in a social room located in the basement at the far end of the block. Now I, who usually stayed to myself and had done so most of my life, suddenly decided I had better take another step toward integration. I put Linda, who was asleep, in her buggy and walked to the social room. There were about a dozen people already seated around the room. One man helped me get the buggy down the steps. Others nodded and smiled at me and introduced themselves. A few ignored me completely. A middle-aged woman sitting on the couch moved over and motioned for me to sit beside her. I did so, and the couch collapsed. In a tangle of legs and arms, laughing hysterically, we helped each other up, righted the couch, and gingerly sat down, vainly trying to retain what few shreds of dignity we had left. This was my introduction to Helen Young, who, with her husband, became our close friends, beginning a friendship that endured for more than forty years.

Already, then, in the space of a couple of weeks, I had met Doris, Mary and her mother, and the Youngs. Furthermore, I was on speaking terms with all of the neighbors in our block. Word had gone out that my husband was being discharged from the Army the following month. When I saw neighbors in the courtyard, they would say, "Not too long now!" or "How many days?" I felt comfortable with all of them.

As the day of Carlyle's arrival approached, I began to feel more and more nervous. Heretofore he had only come home for visits, a week or two at most, but this time it would be forever. Of course I loved him. Of course I couldn't live without him. But what did we really know about each other? I mean little mundane things, habits that can irritate or exasperate one over a period of time. Did he like to go to bed late or early? What kind of food did he like? Was he a homebody, or did he want to party all the time? The more I thought about it the more nervous I became. The last week before he arrived, I was so restless and uneasy that I could scarcely get through the routine tasks of the day. Both Mary and Helen knew what was bothering me, but neither of them seemed able to assuage my anxiety. It was Mama who gave me the answer.

I was sitting in Mary's living room, silent and shifting position from time to time, unable to relax. Mama sat in her chair, rocking, seemingly unaware that anything was wrong.

"When's your husband coming home?" she asked, looking at me intently.

"Five more days."

"You been married a long time?"

"Nearly three years."

She just sat, rocking, looking and looking at me. "In the Army all that time, was he?" Her eyes were still on my face.

"How come you to marry him?"

"I loved him."

"Changed, has he?" Still rocking, still looking right at me.

I hesitated. "I don't think so." I couldn't very well say I didn't know which side of the bed he liked to sleep on or whether he wanted his eggs scrambled or poached. So I said nothing.

She rocked in silence for a little and then spoke out again. "You're probably not the only one feeling uneasy. Maybe he's out there worrying about all this and that, too."

She paused to light her pipe. "Chances are, Child, it's going to be all right. Stop borrowing trouble. Be glad he's coming home, and make him glad, too."

I was still a little uneasy, but when the day of his homecoming arrived, I dressed Linda in her prettiest rompers and put on my most becoming skirt and blouse. I made sure the house was in perfect order, and with one eye on the clock, I paced the floor. As I had it figured out, Carlyle's train would come into Union Station about noon. He would then have to take a cab or a bus to the bus terminal and then maybe an hour after that he would be in Altgeld Gardens. I had a casserole ready to put in the oven and a salad waiting in the refrigerator. Doris sent over some of her biscuits. Helen contributed a lemon pie, and Mary baked a loaf of raisin-nut bread.

I was so nervous I couldn't sit still for more than five minutes at a time. I paced from door to window and back again. It was a beautiful day—a little cold, but the sun was shining. If my calculations were right, he would arrive on the 4:10 bus. It was a quarter after four when I looked out the kitchen window and saw him walking across the parking lot into the courtyard. As I watched him come, his duffel bag slung over his shoulder, striding along, tall and erect as always, I remembered what Mama had said: "Just be glad he's coming home, and make him glad, too."

I pulled open the back door and stepped outside. There in the middle of the courtyard he put down his duffel bag and opened his arms as I ran to meet him. I knew that every eye in the block was on us, but it made no difference, nor did it matter which side of the bed he slept on or how he liked his eggs. For all I cared he could have slept on the floor and eaten his eggs raw. This was Carlyle, and no matter what, we belonged to each other.

Among His People

HOMECOMING
SONNET 4

No more the tramp of weary feet along
The dusty road to peace. The fight is won,
And strife and death by violence are done;
Tired men of war rejoin the aimless throng.
From crowds who greet them gaily and with song,
Forgetful of the course these men have run,
The warriors turn aside, as if to shun
Reminders of the war and its grave wrong.

They wonder, as they leave their last parade,
How long the peace they fought for will endure;
And pray that all the sacrifices made
Shall have been made for peace that is secure.
They fear that theirs was one more vain crusade;
For peace, though sweet, has never yet been sure.

—*Carlyle Douglas, October 1, 1944*

DURING THE NEXT WEEK CARLYLE and I were dined, if not wined, by Doris Washington, Helen and Ted Young, and Mary and Mama. By Saturday night Carlyle was complaining that he had been at home so little he couldn't find his way around the bathroom. Over Sunday breakfast he looked across the table quizzically and asked me how I had managed to become belle of the ball in such a short space of time.

I told him that everyone had been so kind and helpful that I was now sure he had been right when he had said we would be happier living with his people.

"If I'm not mistaken," he replied, "you were incensed with me when I talked about *my* people and *your* people. What changed your mind?"

"Woodstock and Altgeld Gardens."

"You have to be fair," he said. "There were good people in Woodstock. We wouldn't be here today if it weren't for Mrs. Landis and Mrs. Hill. Remember the Polish lady next door and the girl on the other side? The grocer and the baker? They did what they could to help."

He was right, of course, and yet there was a difference somehow. I could not yet put my finger on it.

"Well," I said, "for whatever reason, I don't want to live anyplace else, at least not for the time being. Remember what your mother always says when she goes from the White part of town into the section where Blacks live, 'It's good to be home'? Well that's the way I feel about Altgeld." He sat for a moment, sober and silent. Then, with an odd little smile, he reached across the table and held my hand.

"I don't know how it happened," he said, "but what we have is very special."

The thirteen years we spent in Altgeld Gardens were the most crucial years of our marriage, for it was during that time that we built the foundation of the fortress which was to keep our family secure.

It is well-nigh impossible for me to explain how it came about that, although we were confronted with one crisis or disaster after another, we still were happier than either of us had ever been in the past. How could that be?

I have puzzled over this enigma many times, worrying about it as a puppy worries an old shoe, but to no avail. Now, as I write down our breakfast conversation of long ago, I have the key. It lay in the simple phrase "It's good to be home." I realized that ever since I had left the white clapboard house on the hill in Ann Arbor where I had spent my childhood and had come of age, I had not known the comfort, ease, and safety of a secure harbor. As for Carlyle, never before, not even once in his childhood, had he experienced security. This, then, is what Altgeld had bestowed upon us.

There were no high walls topped by barbed wire to seal us off from a hostile world, yet the moment the bus we took from the city turned into the Gardens, we were home and felt safe. Not that Altgeld was free of all the problems with which small towns must deal—petty thefts, housewives quarreling over space on the clotheslines, drunks rousing the whole neighborhood on their way home from an all-night spree, children fighting over toys. Except for the Fourth of July, we rarely heard gunshots, and few, if any, cars sped through our streets. We had a comfortable feeling of physical safety. Each block even had its own playground equipped with swings and teeter-totters so that a mother could do her housework and still keep an eye on her small children.

The amenities were such as might be found in any village during the forties. The milkman came by twice a week with milk, eggs, butter, and cottage cheese, sometimes offering the treat of homemade cookies or cake. Most of us had iceboxes, so the iceman, his wagon piled high with blocks of ice covered with canvas against the sun, came by every day. Then there were the vegetable men who, from spring to late autumn, came through the project with their horse-drawn wagons piled high with melons, potatoes, and all kinds of fruits and vegetables, depending upon the season, of course. As they came down our streets they advertised their produce with beautiful improvised chants.

The bane of every mother's existence, however, was the ubiquitous candy lady. Every block seemed to have one. There wasn't a child in the unit who, from the time he could toddle until he became a teenager, didn't beat a path to the candy lady's door, clutching the pennies he had earned, begged, or hooked from his mother. I gave birth to three additional children in Altgeld. When they were older, it seemed to me that I spent my day trying to fend off the pathetic, sad-eyed pleading of my children, who, self-diagnosed as martyrs, trailed me from one room to another until I either gave in or sweetly suggested that they ask their father for a donation.

We fully appreciated all the advantages that Altgeld offered—neat lawns, well-tended flower beds, playgrounds, clean streets, yards where we could plant gardens, shops, schools, a clinic—all of these. But what really mattered was that, at least within our own block, we were never regarded as outright enemies, intruders, or mere curiosities. We were permitted to build our own niche and became a part of the whole.

Occasionally, when some child was at odds with one of ours, he or she would announce to all that I was a "yellow nigger." Other than that we never saw any sign of hostility or resentment, except, perhaps, from Mrs. Stewart down the block, who partly because of her enormous size and foghorn voice, intimidated not only her frail little husband and her children, but all the rest of our block as well. To the best of my recollection, whenever the cry "Here she comes!" was passed down the row of clothes-lines, we all fled to the safety of our homes or dodged behind the sheets on the line.

Not long after Carlyle's discharge from the Army, my mother and father came for a visit. We took them on a tour of the Gardens, and they were properly impressed. We had dinner at home and spent the evening talking and playing with Linda. Carlyle seemed entirely at ease, and I could see that both of my parents liked him. Before they left a day later, my father told Carlyle that if he could help in any way, he should just let him know. The rapport that seemed to have been established between them pleased me a great deal.

A few days after they left, Carlyle received a letter from my father—a letter we still have among our family heirlooms—in which my father said how pleased he was to have him as a son-in-law and how honored he would be if Carlyle would call him "Dad." There were tears in Carlyle's eyes as he read it; I understood why he was so deeply moved, because I knew how much he admired my father.

Shortly after my parents' visit, Ted Young came to tell Carlyle that he could get him on the landscape crew for the summer. Carlyle would drive the truck that carried plants, fertilizer, and tools for the landscapers. Naturally, we were delighted because our allotment check from the government no longer came. We were now on our own.

About the same time, one of the doctors at the clinic set up an office in the empty apartment next to ours and hired me as his receptionist. We enrolled Linda in nursery school and began following a daily routine.

Sometime before this, Carlyle learned about the University of Chicago's unique program for World War II veterans who had a valid high school diploma but who had never gone to college. If they passed a comprehensive test devised by members of various university departments, they could skip the bachelor's program and enter a master's program of their choice. Carlyle took the examination and scored among the top third of applicants. This meant that in the fall he could enter the graduate school of political science (his first choice) as a legitimate candidate for a master of arts degree in that field. He was also told that married GIs who entered the program would receive a monthly allotment to help defray their expenses.

The news was so exhilarating that our feet didn't touch the ground for a week. This meant Carlyle would have a chance to earn the degree he had always wanted and also might find an academic position at a college or university. If he did well enough in his master's program, he might even qualify for a scholarship or fellowship in a doctoral program. The world was an oyster, no doubt about it. Life was very good and getting better every day.

One afternoon a few days later, Carlyle stopped in the drugstore to pick up some vitamins for Linda. Maurice Haynes, the young Black man who waited on him, was the assistant manager, and they introduced themselves. Maurice, who had heard about us through the grapevine, mentioned that his wife, Theresa, was also White. Maurice and Carlyle exchanged telephone numbers. When Carlyle returned later that day he suggested I call Theresa. It is amazing to me that Carlyle and I, who had never found it easy to make social advances and frequently avoided them at any cost, suddenly found ourselves becoming social butterflies—and enjoying it. At Carlyle's urging, I reluctantly called Theresa and asked her to come for tea. Tea yet! Imagine that! My mother would have been overcome with joy! Theresa accepted and asked if she might bring a friend. Although I was nervous about the prospect of meeting an additional stranger, I felt I could not get out of the situation gracefully. What was I to say? When I told Carlyle that I was going to have to entertain two strangers instead of one, he struggled to conceal his amusement. Then, seeing how upset and insecure I really was, he put his arms around me and soothed my uneasiness with all the flattery at his command.

Fortunately, I only worked half-days for the doctor and could arrange for Linda to stay at the day care center until Carlyle could pick her up after work. So I had the apartment to myself. It didn't look too bad, and I was wearing an attractive dress. Actually, I didn't have to wait more than a few minutes before there was a knock at the door. There they stood, two young White women: one tall and blond and the other smaller and broader with dark hair and brown eyes. I found them both so friendly that I began to relax. The tall blond introduced herself as Theresa Haynes, and the dark-haired lady was her friend Elsa.

We went through the customary opening ceremonies that occur whenever interracial couples, specifically wives, meet for the first time. Where did you meet? How did it happen? How does your family feel about it? Have you had any bad experiences? Are you going to stick it out?

By the time we had asked and answered all of these questions, we were perfectly at ease with each other and well on the way to becoming friends. Although Elsa's family had disowned her, her husband's family had welcomed her. Theresa and Elsa were both astonished to learn that Carlyle's mother and my parents had accepted us almost from the beginning. Theresa said very little about herself or Maurice, but it made no difference at all to me, for this was the beginning of a friendship that has lasted for over fifty years and is still as exhilarating and viable as it was when we lived in the Gardens. We fit together as perfectly as interlocking pieces of a puzzle. Even though we rarely see each other now, the ties between us are so strong that neither time nor distance has any relevance.

It is noteworthy to me that Carlyle and I, who were not socially inclined and rarely allowed a casual relationship to develop into a true friendship, blossomed in Altgeld. It was as though a cornucopia of sparkling relationships had spilled upon a holiday table. Through Theresa and Elsa we met Marie and Johnny, the third interracial couple. Marie, a pretty Italian girl, had been disowned by her family, but unlike Elsa she had not been accepted by her husband's relatives either. In an effort to establish a new life, she and her husband had left New York and had eventually come to Altgeld. Our circle of friends expanded even more. It now included Rossie Williams and her husband and children, who were neighbors of the Hayneses, along with Barbara and Leonard Jones, who were friends of Rossie. And there was Emile Breda, whose presence was overpowering. Physically, he towered and filled any room with his bulk. His laughter shook the windows, and when he played the piano and sang, he was so good at both that we danced or wept as his mood dictated. We loved him dearly, and his heart was big enough to encompass all of us.

During our years in Altgeld we lived in three different units, moving always to accommodate our growing family. We always found some of our neighbors to be friendly and willing to welcome us into the block activities. We rarely went outside of Altgeld for entertainment, yet I cannot ever remember being bored or lonely.

Looking back now, I recall with amusement that indeed we never had time to be either bored or lonely. During that summer of Carlyle's return and nearly every summer thereafter, sometimes on weeknights but almost always on weekends, our calendar was filled with social activities. We played pinochle with Helen and Ted, had picnics and other outings with Theresa and Maurice, and all-night weekend sessions with the Harpers, playing Liverpool while their children slept in our beds or ours slept in theirs. We played bridge with Barbara and Leonard, had potluck dinners with Marie and Johnny, and at least once a week went to see Mary and Mama or Doris Washington.

But our relationships were far more than just fun and games. Every time we were in trouble, we knew we could count on at least some or all of these good, kind people to come to our rescue just as we willingly came to theirs. I relied on our new friends and neighbors for emergency telephone calls and transportation. We always helped each other with child care—babysitting, as we called it in those days.

Early in May of 1946 I learned that I was pregnant and that the baby was due around Christmastime. Carlyle immediately applied for a larger apartment, and we were assigned to a two-bedroom unit in block 13. It was the last unit on the far eastern side of the Gardens, not too far from a railroad track. I was pleased enough with the apartment, which had two bedrooms and a bath upstairs and a good sized living room and kitchen on the first floor. I was uneasy, however, about being so close to the railroad track, because on the other side was a mysterious shantytown of White squatters, and I feared they would invade our side of the track. So, despite the reassurance—and sometimes ridicule—of my friends, I kept a wary eye on both the kitchen window and the back door.

Marie and Johnny had an old truck, and together with the Hayneses, the Youngs, and the Harpers, they moved us to block 13. It proved to be a very pleasant summer. Carlyle was still working with the landscapers. I was finding my pregnancy unusually easy. Both Carlyle and I looked forward to September, when Carlyle would begin classes at the University of Chicago. This was the beginning of our climb up the ladder toward the fulfillment of our dreams. We hoped to spend our lives as part of the faculty of a college—he as a professor and I as a faculty wife. Or it might be that we would live in Washington, D.C., with Carlyle serving as a member of the secretary of state's staff or in New York as a representative of the United States to the United Nations. Anything was possible with an education.

In September of 1946 Carlyle began classes at the University of Chicago. It was a very long trip, first by bus, then by train from the Gardens to the university campus. He was gone from seven-thirty in the morning until five or six o'clock in the evening. He took four classes and spent the time between and after classes studying at the library. Professor Gradson, his advisor, was obviously impressed by Carlyle's abilities and not only gave him the ego boost he needed but broadened his knowledge of his chosen field by suggesting books that were not necessarily on the class reading list.

Carlyle worked hard and loved every moment of it. When he came home at night his voice vibrated with enthusiasm as he talked about what he had learned, what his professor had said, what he had said, and all the new and interesting people he had met. Best of all, the veil of pessimism that had clouded his outlook and his ability to make positive plans for the future was lifting. I knew from the beginning that he was an extremely intelligent and gifted man. I was also vaguely aware that the nature of his childhood and the burden of prejudice had hampered him as surely as if he had been handcuffed and chained, but I had no idea that he could change so quickly.

I, of course, was beginning to slow down because of the pregnancy. While Linda was in nursery school I spent a great deal of time reading books that I thought would help me keep abreast of Carlyle—Plato, Veblen, Toynbee, Thoreau.

Meanwhile, I had decided to use the Altgeld Gardens Clinic when it was time to deliver the baby because it made sense to have him at home. Provident, which was the only hospital I would consider because of its staff of Black doctors and nurses, was too far away. I had a dawning awareness of the pervasiveness of racism and knew by then that Blacks frequently received second-class service from White hospital staff. I was not about to subject my family or myself to humiliating treatment at that precious moment when my next child was to be born. I would rather give birth at home.

My doctor assured me I was in fine shape. The baby would probably arrive around Christmastime. And, he added, since I had the "pelvis of a peasant" I should have an easy time—not very flattering, but certainly comforting. I had no morning sickness, and, except for feeling a little tired, I was confident that this pregnancy would cause me no difficulty.

A few days before Christmas a washing machine arrived; it was a present from my parents. Carlyle's mother sent clothes for Linda and a wardrobe for the new baby. Christmas Day passed, and still no baby. It began to snow so thick and fast that you could not see the trees two feet away. It snowed all night and all the next day. Although I had no real pain, I knew the baby had dropped, and I was becoming a little anxious. That anxiety was in no way assuaged when my husband began to cast worried glances in my direction every time I shifted in the chair. The snow changed to sleet by midnight and was forming icicles on the bare tree branches. They were beautiful to behold when the streetlights glistened on them.

My anxiety soon turned to alarm. "You'd better call the doctor," I said in what I thought was a casual manner, but my voice shook. Carlyle called the clinic number and was told that someone would be along as soon as they could.

Gently, Carlyle carried our daughter, Linda, upstairs and put her to bed. Meanwhile, I hauled myself upstairs one step at a time and reached our bed without mishap. Carlyle called the clinic again. The doctor had been informed of my situation and would reach us as soon as he could. The contractions became painful, so I began to walk back and forth, back and forth. Carlyle stood motionless at the door, his face ashen. I tried to smile but nearly lost control, so I began counting between cramps. They were coming faster and faster and harder, too. There flashed through my mind the words from Linda's story *The Little Engine That Could* . . . "I think I can. I think I can. I can! I can! I can!" Carlyle's eyes widened with surprise, and I knew I was smiling.

"We're going to have to do it by ourselves," I said.

He gave me a terrified look but he nodded.

"Get all the clean bath towels. Put two on the bed for me to lie on, and keep the rest for the baby."

His face was gray, and beads of sweat appeared on his forehead.

"Now what?" he asked.

"We just wait," I replied. I lay down on the bed. Within seconds I knew the baby was coming. I had no time to be scared; I just spread my legs and whispered through the pain, "I'll push, and when you see the baby's head, you pull." I didn't even have time to finish the sentence when, with a plop, our new baby arrived. Carlyle wiped the infant off as best he could and then wrapped him up in a clean towel.

"It's a boy," he said triumphantly as though it were all his doing. We didn't know what to do with the cord, and the afterbirth hadn't appeared. I just lay there with the baby in my arms, looking down at him, and he looked back at me as though to say, "Well, now what?" He was an impressive little mite.

The doctor and nurse came within a few minutes and were properly impressed with our amateur performance. The doctor helped with the delivery of the afterbirth while the nurse cleaned and swaddled our new baby boy.

This, then, was how our first son, Carlyle Colin Douglas—whom we came to call simply Colin—made his grand entrance into the world.

When Carlyle's classes began after the holidays, with my parents' financial help, Linda, now two years old, returned to nursery school. I settled down peacefully to take care of my newborn son.

9

Journey with No Return

JOURNEY WITH NO RETURN

Death knows no tomorrow
Every man must learn.
Death knows no tomorrow
No gladness and no sorrow.
Quiet, changeless, stern,
Journey with no return,
Death knows no tomorrow.

—Carlyle Douglas, May 25, 1944

IT MUST HAVE BEEN JUST AFTER New Year's Day in 1947, early in the afternoon, that I opened the front door in response to a rather timid knock. There stood Carlyle's brother, Willie, with a suitcase in his hand. We hadn't seen Willie since we had been chased out of Woodstock three years earlier in 1944. He looked pale and withered, as though he had been ill for a long time.

"Hello," he said, smiling hesitantly as though he were not certain of his welcome.

"Come on in," I said, taking his suitcase. "You look tired," I added, and indeed he did. I thought he might well collapse on the doorstep.

We went to the kitchen and I made him a toasted cheese sandwich along with a cup of instant soup.

"I couldn't stand Detroit," he said, "so I came back here. I got a room on the West Side and a job in the stockyards. It was awful," he said, shuddering.

"Why on earth didn't you come to us sooner?" I asked.

"I didn't know where the place was, and besides, I wasn't sure you'd have room."

He looked so tired, ill, and unhappy that I could do nothing else but make him welcome. I knew something was terribly wrong, that he needed a place to stay and someone to care for him. I wanted to help him, but I couldn't imagine how we could accommodate him in our small two-bedroom apartment, or how Carlyle and I could find time to care for him when we were both working and had two small children for whom we were caring. I was horrified to hear myself say quite blithely that he could stay as long as he liked.

I went upstairs to make a comfortable place for him. I removed Colin's crib from our room and placed it in the front room, next to Linda's bed. Fortunately, our bedroom in back had a very comfortable four-poster. It had been mine on the farm in Chelsea, and my parents had given it and a beautiful maple chest of drawers to us when we moved to Altgeld. The bed had been newly made that morning. I turned back the covers, selected some clean towels and a washcloth from the linen closet, then went down to get Willie. I helped him upstairs, showed him the bathroom, and prescribed a shower and a nap.

Next I went to take care of my son, who, having awakened to find he was in a strange room and that his mother had abandoned him, was yelling in protest. I nursed and rocked him until he finally fell asleep, then put him back in his crib and went to see how Willie was doing. He was sitting up in bed, looking so frail that I was alarmed.

"Lie down," I said, "and rest. The baby will sleep for an hour or so. Carlyle will be home about five. We'll have dinner then. He'll be delighted to see you." I knew I was babbling like a lunatic in an effort to drown my fears about Willie in a sea of words. So I left Willie in our room, closing the door as if to shut out my anxiety, and collapsed on the daybed in the front room, waiting for Carlyle.

At five o'clock I heard Carlyle's feet crunching the snow as he came up the walk. I sat up, combed my fingers through my hair, and hoped I didn't look as bad as I felt.

Carlyle opened the door, put down his books, gave me a kiss, and then stood back, frowning. "What's wrong, Honey? Did you have a bad day?"

"That's the understatement of the year," I said, very near hysterics.

He waited. "It's Willie," I said.

"Willie? What about Willie?"

"He's upstairs in our bed. He's been working in the stockyards, and he's sick."

"For God's sake," Carlyle said staring at me, "what are you talking about?"

He looked and sounded as though he thought I had put Willie to work making bologna at gunpoint.

"You'd better go upstairs and find out," I said. "Something is wrong with him. I think you ought to get hold of your mother."

Without a word he turned and went upstairs. It seemed as if he were gone for hours. In the meantime, Mary, a neighbor, brought Linda home, and I went to the kitchen to find something for my daughter to eat. Linda was sitting on the couch, quietly looking at a picture book when Carlyle finally came downstairs, looking like Zeus about to throw a thunderbolt.

"What the hell is going on here?" he demanded. Then, seeing Linda's frightened face, he picked her up, kissed her, tumbled her hair, and still holding her, sat down.

"He says to call Ruth."

"Ruth?" Now I was lost. Neither Carlyle nor I knew anything about Ruth. Apparently she was Willie's close friend.

"Yes. He gave me her telephone number and said to call and ask her to come."

"What on earth for?" I asked.

Carlyle shrugged his shoulders. "Honey, you know as much as I do."

"What are we going to do?" I wailed.

We finally agreed that I would call Ruth, and Carlyle would call his mother. Meanwhile, Colin awoke and howled from his crib to be fed. Linda clung to her father, asking what was for supper, and Willie called downstairs about whether we had contacted Ruth.

The whole scenario was so utterly absurd that we began to laugh, and once we started, we couldn't stop until Willie's face appeared over the banister as he reproachfully announced that Colin was crying.

I went up to get the baby, coaxed Willie back to bed, then sat down to nurse Colin while Carlyle fed Linda and called his mother. She was still at work. Since he couldn't reach her he tried Ruth. Ten minutes later he came tramping upstairs, wild-eyed.

"She's packing her bag and will be here in a couple of hours."

"Packing her bag!" I repeated. "What for? Where will she stay?"

"How would I know?" he said with a wicked smile. "She's your friend."

I don't know how we ever survived the next few hours. We moved in a daze. I fixed soup for all of us, bathed Linda, and read her a bedtime story. Carlyle attended to Willie's needs and walked the floor with Colin, who, sensing that all was not well with his world, refused to remain in his crib for more than five minutes at a time.

Carlyle looked at his watch every other minute. At eight o'clock he announced with grim satisfaction that, in his opinion, Ruth had taken the wrong bus and was probably by now comfortably established in a motel in Calumet City, a few miles away.

The mysterious Ruth, to Carlyle's surprise and my relief, came a few minutes later. As it happened, her presence proved to be a godsend. As soon as she arrived she took over the care of Willie, who actually seemed to improve from the first moment he saw her, although he continued to complain about a headache and impaired vision. Ruth would stay and care for Willie as long as he needed her. We never knew the exact nature of her relationship with Willie—friend, girlfriend, or lover. All we knew and all that mattered was that she cared for him deeply and provided nursing care for him during this critical period.

Our busy family life became even busier. Carlyle, preparing for his finals, was at the library from morning to night. Mama came over to help with the children. I continued with my job at the doctor's office. Linda continued going to nursery school. Ruth was there to help Willie every day. Everything was moving along smoothly enough when, just three days after Valentine's Day, I received a telegram from my mother.

"Daddy died this morning at 7 A.M. Mother."

I didn't cry—I didn't feel anything at first, except disbelief and emptiness. Carlyle put me on the train for Ann Arbor the next morning. I assumed they informed my mother of the time I would reach Ann Arbor. Ruth bought a breast pump for me to make me more comfortable. I don't remember the train trip at all.

One of my mother's friends met me when I arrived in Ann Arbor and drove me to the farm. Nothing seemed real. My world had collapsed. My mother hugged and kissed me and thanked me for coming. I was so absorbed in my own pain that I was not fully aware of hers. She had been married forty-four years, and in the space of a few days she was alone. I know now how she must have felt—the aching emptiness, the reaching out in the middle of the night, seeking to touch the warm, reassuring presence that was no longer there.

I stayed only a short time. I don't suppose I was really of any comfort to her, but she smiled when she kissed me good-bye and said she would come to see us in a month or so.

I came home to find that Ruth and Mama had held my family together and that everything was under control. However, Carlyle had still been unable to reach his mother, and Willie's illness was becoming more serious. It was obvious to all of us that Willie was becoming weaker each day and that he was almost blind. He could still distinguish light from dark, but shapes were growing dimmer. His speech was very slow, and he did not always seem to be in control of his thoughts.

Thoroughly alarmed, Carlyle made an appointment for him at the veteran's hospital. He and Ruth rented a car and checked Willie in to the hospital. After several days of tests, the doctors told Carlyle that at some time during Willie's tour of duty he must have received a severe blow to his head. The blow resulted in a tumor that was now as large as a grapefruit. Among other things, this was pressing on his optic nerve. It was almost inoperable, but if Carlyle agreed, they would try to remove some of it, at least to relieve the pressure. After one last desperate attempt to reach his mother, Carlyle consented to the operation. It was a success; they were able to remove most of the tumor in his brain. Tragically, however, he lost his eyesight during the operation, leaving Willie permanently blind.

Carlyle's mother finally arrived. She and Ruth took Willie back to Detroit, where he remained until his death about two years later. Ruth simply disappeared, and we never saw or heard from her again.

10

No Negroes Allowed

PRELUDE

Please let me say it while there is still the time
These hours and days so wonderfully fresh
Are but the prelude to a time when I,
With less abandon, much ado with naught,
Shall slip into the pattern culture sets
And lasting truths which now I know, forget.

—*Carlyle Douglas, undated*

DESPITE THE DISRUPTION DURING THE last month before final examinations, Carlyle passed all of his subjects with a B-plus average. His advisor, Professor Gradson, was very pleased and fulsome in his praise. Carlyle began to show signs of self-confidence. At the same time, he was experiencing the sense of social isolation that stems from the race and class divisions in our society. In those days the University of Chicago, like most universities at the time, was almost completely White. There were few, if any, Black members of the faculty.

Always reserved and reluctant to make advances, Carlyle found himself isolated in a sea of carefree upper middle-class White men and women. His fellow graduate students accepted without question the necessity of higher education and entered the academic world with utmost confidence. Free for the most part from the stresses of poverty, they could concentrate on their academic pursuits.

In contrast, Carlyle was bedeviled by the need to provide food, clothing, and shelter for his young family. With only a meager stipend, we constantly teetered on the edge of poverty. The clothes Carlyle wore to campus were always clean, for cleanliness was a fetish with him. Even so, they barely passed the line between shabby and casual. It was hard for him to relate to the other graduate students and hard for them to relate to him. Yet he endured and persisted, intent upon achieving the goal he had set for himself in the long ago days when he worked on the railroad—a college degree.

His second semester was not quite as stressful as the first. My mother gave us my father's car, a 1929 Dodge that seemed to be in perfect condition down to the last tasseled shade and glass flower vase attached to the dashboard. It had belonged to a farmer who drove it only on Sundays and kept it safely locked in his garage the rest of the time. My father had always called it Old Betsy, and we followed suit. Mother also sent us all of father's clothes, which had been especially tailored for him, and fortunately they fit Carlyle perfectly. Carlyle was pleased to have both a car and clothes. Now that he was able to dress well, I knew he would feel more comfortable and confident on campus.

The summer of 1948 mirrored the previous summer. Again Carlyle did maintenance work, and again I was pregnant. Money was very short now, and although Carlyle's stipend would resume in the fall when he returned to college, we really did not see how we were going to make it. My mother paid the fees for Linda's nursery school training. Even so, we struggled to keep ourselves solvent. However, we were reasonably content. We still enjoyed the companionship of our many friends, Carlyle was doing well in school, and my pregnancy was an easy one.

As before, I delivered our baby through the clinic. This time, however, the weather cooperated, and our second son was born without incident. He arrived peacefully enough, unwrinkled and placid, with beautiful brown eyes and a wisp of brown hair. He was a very gentle baby with a charming gurgle and a delightful laugh. We named him David Almerin Douglas after my father.

In the early stages of my pregnancy our friends lectured us on birth control and the necessity of limiting the size of our family for economic reasons. After David's birth the lectures gave way to humor. They simply referred to our home as the rabbit hutch and let it go at that.

Because of the increasing size of our family, shortly after David's birth, we moved to block 9, one of the largest and prettiest courts in Altgeld. There were twelve apartments built around the courtyard. On our end— the open end—was the parking lot, and a little beyond that, the playground. The trees that had been planted along the streets were now tall enough to offer shade. Directly across from us lived the candy lady, and next to her lived the Mathis family. Mr. Mathis was a mechanic, and his wife was a skilled seamstress. They had three girls and a boy with whom our children grew up. Again, the ties were so strong that when we both left Altgeld we still managed to see each other in Detroit or Chicago occasionally.

Right next to us lived Mr. and Mrs. Neighbors. They were an older couple who stayed pretty much to themselves, yet when the grapevine let them know that we were without food, they came to our door bringing chicken dinner and all the trimmings.

Old Betsy eventually wore out, but my mother and Carlyle's gave us enough money to buy a newer car for which Old Betsy served as a down payment. As a result, we were able to drive around the nearby countryside, and this proved to be both a curse and a blessing. The first time we ventured into unknown territory we crossed the Calumet River, which ran between us and a small country town that looked interesting. We had gone no more than a block down the main street of small shops when someone called out "nigger." Fortunately, we were only ten minutes away from the bridge across the Calumet, and we made it back to home territory without incident.

Later on we ventured into another town on our side of the river that was inhabited entirely by Black families living in nice brick stone trimmed homes with well-kept lawns. We felt as out of place there as we had across the river. We felt shut out.

The car enabled us to take advantage of the chicken farm along the highway where we could buy eggs and dressed chickens for far less than in the supermarket. We had planned to go to Rosedale, a quiet Chicago neighborhood, but the first time we went into town we had an unpleasant experience.

Carlyle stopped at a small grocery store to buy us some pop. When he emerged a few minutes later his face was shut tight. He got into the car, distributed the bottles, and, without a word, started the engine.

"What's wrong?" I asked.

"He called me 'Boy,'" Carlyle said flatly.

So much for Rosedale. All it took was one bad experience for us to feel that we weren't welcome. We didn't want to take the risk of exposing our family to more unpleasant and potentially dangerous situations.

The car also enabled us to visit Carlyle's relatives who lived on the South Side of Chicago. There was Uncle Joe, who owned a construction company. His Indian ancestry was clearly visible in his tall, lean body and his finely chiseled features. He and his wife had no children of their own, so they frequently invited us for Sunday picnics. Then there was Cousin Mabel, a nurse, and another cousin, Althea, a schoolteacher, with whom we had very close relationships. It was good for us to have these contacts with his relatives. It gave us the sense of stability and connectedness that we needed.

Unfortunately, to get to their homes we had to go through Rosedale, and no matter how many times we went through that neighborhood we were always uneasy. You might say we held our breath from the time we reached the Welcome to Rosedale sign until we reached Welcome to Chicago on the other side. Welcome to Rosedale did not mean welcome to us.

Only once after that did we venture into totally unfamiliar territory, and that was my fault. I knew that in a suburb west of Rosedale there was a house built by one of my idols, Frank Lloyd Wright. I had read his biography and studied his architecture in college. One Saturday I coaxed Carlyle into taking me to see it. He seemed very dubious and none too happy, but his mother was visiting us at the time and thought it would be a nice outing. We should have remembered the Detroit fiasco.

On a bright Saturday morning we packed everybody into the car and sallied forth. Early that afternoon we came to the wide, welcoming gates of the suburb for which we were looking and whose name I have long since forgotten. The broad, winding streets between shady trees were empty. We drove slowly down one street after another, passing many beautiful homes until at last we found the Wright house. It was unmistakable—clear, sharp lines so simple in design that it looked as though it had not been built but had grown there. We saw no one around and concluded that no one was in residence. After a bit we returned to the main road and slowly drove out between the gates. It was then that we saw the sign posted on the gate: "NO NEGROES ALLOWED AFTER DARK." Neither Mom nor Carlyle nor I made any comment, but I felt cold and frightened. I put out my hand, and Carlyle silently reached for it and held it. "Nothing has changed," I thought, too sick at heart to verbalize it, "and maybe it never ever will."

Sometimes we went farther afield on our family outings: down to the lakefront, to Grant and Jackson Parks, to the museums, and to the aquarium. We did not find it uncomfortable primarily because we were so busy corralling three little ones that we didn't have time to pay attention to the adults around us. The watching eyes were still there. We just paid no attention.

Once we went to watch a Fourth of July parade on the riverfront and found it amusing rather than threatening that those beside us on the curb and passing by were so interested in us that they missed the parade. The same thing occurred when we went driving. Drivers in the cars that passed us were so busy staring at us that they nearly went over the curb. To tell you the truth, we would have been delighted to see them land in the ditch.

120

11

Wind-Twisted Fir

Wind-Twisted Fir

Wind-twisted fir on stretch of golden sand
In stout defiance of the wintry blast
Insisted whirring etched embolden cast
Against the drifting mist of shrouded land.

—Carlyle Douglas, undated

TOWARD THE END OF THE SUMMER of 1949 Carlyle took the entire family to see the University of Chicago. It was an extraordinarily beautiful campus. The buildings were of stone and brick, much like the architecture of the Middle Ages. He showed us the student dormitories, which were not very attractive, and then pointed out the unsightly rows of wooden houses that had been thrown together to accommodate GIs and their families. I understood then why he had never suggested that we take advantage of GI family housing.

That fall Carlyle began his final year at the university. Professor Gradson, his advisor, suggested that he take a course in teaching history at the junior college level as a backup so that he could teach while working on his master's thesis. Gradson also let him know that he needed another advisor for his thesis work. His new advisor would be Dr. Morgenthau, known throughout the academic world as a brilliant teacher of political science and as a perfectionist.

I'll never know what transpired between Carlyle and his new advisor. I can only imagine what happened inside of Carlyle when his fragile sense of self-worth met with Morgenthau's perfectionism. It must have been like an egg being thrown against the Rock of Gibraltar.

When Carlyle came home from the meeting he went into shock. Night after night I talked to him, trying to bolster his sense of self-confidence. I pointed out what a fine record he had so far—what a brilliant student he was, the ease with which he had passed the Signal Corps examinations, and how he stood far and away ahead of so many other GIs who had taken the same test to qualify for the master of arts program.

Nothing I said made any difference. He fended me off by saying that I was blind because I loved him, that I overestimated his abilities, that it was all wishful thinking on my part. I felt sorry for him, but at the same time I wanted to shake him until his teeth rattled. I knew, as did he, that our whole future rested on that master's degree, that we were not able to survive without it. Gradually, I lost hope—it seemed to me that my words were having little effect. Carlyle seemed hopeless and dispirited.

I can see him as vividly now as I did then, sitting in the living room behind the window, his shoulders drooping, his face drawn. I thought of what he had told me years ago—how his mother had sent him by train to his father's home in New Orleans when he was only six. He had been placed in the care of a Traveler's Aid lady. When they reached the New Orleans station she had taken the small, frightened child into the White section of the train. The outraged stationmaster had said, "Get that nigger out of here! He don't belong." It seemed to me that once again Carlyle was struggling with feelings that he didn't belong.

I knew of that wound and of many others that he would not speak of that had left their mark. They had twisted his life out of shape, like a wind-twisted fir, hampering if not destroying his ability to make full use of the gifts with which heredity had endowed him.

All of my pain and anger, which had lain dormant during our years in Altgeld Gardens, came rushing to the surface, but I dared not let Carlyle see it. I did not want to compound his pain by letting him see mine. Subdued and speechless, I struggled to regain my composure. He must have sensed my deep concern. He turned toward me with a bittersweet smile and somehow summoned the strength to comfort me as I hoped he would.

"We'll make it, Darling—I promise you."

I felt as if I were once again in the gazebo covered with snow and remembered how Carlyle had comforted me with similar words so many years ago.

All that semester he worked on the outline for his thesis. He knew and I knew there would be no second chance. As usual, we were living on a shoestring and a frayed one at that. And I was pregnant again.

I felt like a foolish, selfish idiot, so I kept quiet about my pregnancy as long as I could. Surprisingly enough, all of the friends I thought would castigate me and forever dismiss me as a hopeless idiot did nothing of the sort. They came around and supported my pregnancy as best as they could. Mother wrote me a loving letter saying wouldn't it be nice to have one baby born in a hospital and offering to float the expense. I was now forty years old, and she must have been concerned about my safety and the baby's safety during childbirth.

The baby was not due until October. I had settled down to the task of keeping three children happy while the fourth bounced around in my womb.

Carlyle continued to struggle with the outline for his thesis throughout the summer. In September 1950, with fear and trepidation, he turned in his outline to Morgenthau. For weeks he heard nothing, and September stretched into October. Almost before we knew it our fourth child was due.

At four o'clock in the morning of October 7, without prior notice, the pains began. Carlyle called the doctor, who was none too pleased to be awakened at such an early hour. He said he would meet us at the hospital in about five hours. Carlyle and I knew better.

Carlyle then called Mary Ann, our babysitter, who lived just across the court. Next he called Theresa, who came within a half-hour. I dressed in a hurry. Since my bag was already packed, all I had to do was give final instructions to Mary Ann. I waited at the foot of the stairs for Theresa, who came within minutes and took us to the hospital. They would not let Carlyle come in with me, so I went in by myself. The pains were not too strong, but they were coming very fast. They put me on a gurney and wheeled me into the waiting room, where a half-dozen other women in all stages of labor were waiting.

I knew my baby was on the way. I tried to call the nurse, but my voice was too weak. I sat upright, spread my legs, and leaned over to grab my new baby daughter before she hit the floor. I yelled for the nurse, and she reappeared indignantly, wanting to know why I couldn't have waited for help. Meanwhile all around me, like a great chorus, the other women in labor were groaning and wondering why their babies didn't come as easily as mine.

They took the baby from me, cleaned me up, and wheeled me to a room with three other new mothers. In the distance I could hear babies crying in the nursery, and this upset me, so I couldn't sleep. I turned and tossed all night. In the morning when they brought me the tiny infant with a wizened, pale white face and blue eyes, I knew something was wrong. I sat up in bed and demanded to see whoever was in charge. When they came running, I told them this was not my baby. After seeing the tag on the baby's wrist, they agreed that a mistake had been made.

Nothing could stop me then. I asked the nurse to call my husband at once and get the doctor. They both appeared at about the same time. The doctor, having examined me, agreed that I could go home if I wanted to, as long as I got plenty of bed rest. He also released the baby to me. When the nurse brought her in, I rose up in bed, full of suspicion. As soon at they put her in my arms, however, I knew she was mine. Her eyes were a soft brown; her hair was an unbelievable mass of soft, golden-red rainbow curls. Her skin was smooth and creamy like her sister's, and she looked at me with a Douglas twinkle. When we got her safely inside our home, I took her upstairs, snuggled her under the covers of my own bed, and slept peacefully, knowing my baby was lying right next to me and that Mary Ann and Carlyle would manage all the rest of the household.

After seeing our new baby, whom we named Brigid Eileen Douglas, Linda and Colin took her arrival with aplomb. My little one, David, who was only a year-and-a-half old, came to the edge of the bed and looked at me anxiously, his face furrowed and sad. I held out my arms, and he scrambled up onto the bed, beside the new baby. I hugged and kissed him, and he frowned as though the world were coming to an end. He stayed for almost an hour, then suddenly smiled up at me, jumped off the bed, and went to look for Mary Ann and breakfast.

About three days after I came home, Carlyle received a telegram from his mother. Willie had died, and she wanted Carlyle there for the funeral.

Mary Ann agreed to stay with me, and Theresa said she would be on call if needed. Carlyle was gone for five days. An hour or so before he came home, I received a telephone call from Gradson. When I told him Carlyle was not back yet he said he really wanted to talk to me anyway. Obviously, something was wrong. Without preamble he told me that Morgenthau had inspected Carlyle's outline, and Carlyle would have to do it over again.

"Can you get him to do it?" Gradson asked, knowing as well as I what Carlyle's reaction would be.

"I don't know," I said, trying to keep my voice from shaking. "What did he say was wrong with it?"

"Nothing major really, but Morgenthau is a perfectionist, you know."

We talked a little longer, but I really had nothing to say. I knew what Carlyle's reaction was going to be.

Carlyle came home the next day, tired, depressed, and angry. Mom had attempted to have Willie buried in the Woodlawn Cemetery, one of the most beautiful in Detroit, but they had turned her down because they did not accept Blacks. She had to take him far out to a new cemetery in the country—Lincoln Memorial, which had just recently opened to accommodate the Black families in the area.

"Isn't it a nice place?" I asked.

"As a matter of fact, it's beautiful—quiet and open to the sky. They don't allow stand-up stones, only flat stones in the ground, so it doesn't look like a cemetery at all."

He was sitting on the edge of the bed, admiring his new daughter as he talked. Suddenly, he came to a halt and looked at me.

"Something's wrong. What is it?"

"You must be hungry. Why don't you get something to eat? Mary Ann will fix it." I attempted in vain to distract him.

"What's wrong?" He persisted.

"Gradson called," I said reluctantly.

"It's Morgenthau, isn't it?"

I nodded.

He stood up, his face turned away from me, and left the room without a word.

I heard him downstairs talking to the children and Mary Ann. He didn't sound any different. I listened to the dinner dishes clattering, and soon Mary Ann came up with my supper.

"Where is he?" I asked. Mary Ann looked surprised at my tone of voice, but smilingly replied that he was reading to the children. Later I heard Mary Ann leave, and Carlyle came upstairs with the children. He put them to bed, I heard him go downstairs, and then there was silence. I didn't know what to do so I just lay quietly and waited. After what seemed an eternity, I heard him turn out the lights downstairs and climb the stairs. He came into the bedroom quietly and, without turning on the lights, undressed and got into bed.

"Are you all right?" I asked.

"Sure," he said quietly and turned away.

I lay awake for a long time, not knowing what to do. I knew he wasn't asleep, but he wasn't approachable either. When I awoke, the bed was empty.

I was terrified. The thought flashed through my head, born more out of fear than reality, that Carlyle had left permanently. I heard Mary Ann downstairs, talking to the children with the rattle of the dishes in the background, but no Carlyle. Eventually, Mary Ann brought my breakfast. "Mr. Douglas said to tell you he would be back after a while."

That, without doubt, was the worst day I ever had. I went through the mechanics of being a good mother and sighed with relief when Mary Ann took the children to the playground. The hours dragged by; somewhere my husband was fighting his battle alone, and I could do nothing to help him.

Late in the afternoon, Gradson called me to say that Carlyle had come to see Morgenthau. I was still terribly uneasy, but I also thought there might be hope.

It must have been about eight o'clock when I heard Carlyle's voice in the kitchen. I didn't care what decision he had reached; I was just glad to have him home. After a while he came upstairs, kissed me, and said that when the children were asleep he would come back to talk. He seemed calm enough, but I couldn't be sure.

I heard Mary Ann say good night. The children were splashing in the tub, and then Carlyle read to them. Then there was silence. For a second I was afraid he had gone, but then the stairs creaked and he stood in the doorway. He wasn't smiling, but he wasn't grim either.

"Sorry about today," he said, coming to sit on the side of the bed, "but I had to figure this out alone."

I didn't say anything. I just waited. When he finally spoke I could tell that his words had been carefully chosen.

"As you know, my four years will be up at the end of the next semester, and the GI allotment will stop then. Even that isn't sufficient for our needs. It isn't your fault," he said hastily, watching my face. "I'm as much to blame as you. The truth of the matter is that if Morgenthau had accepted my outline I would have been able to hang in there until June. But that's water under the bridge. He and I are what's at odds. I can't do what he wants, and he doesn't want what I can do. So there we are."

"Can't you come to an agreement?"

"No," he said, and I knew from his tone of voice that I had better back off.

"I'm going to finish this semester. That will round out my four years, and then in July I'll look for a decent job. Four years of college ought to count for something."

That was the end of the discussion. I knew as well as he that without a diploma, four years of college meant very little and that our bright, beautiful future had gone down the drain.

From that day on we never spoke of it again. I could not, and he would not. So that was the end of his master's degree and all the dreams that went with it.

Professor Gradson tried to help in another way. He talked with another professor of education who had had Carlyle for a class that semester and was very impressed with him. He suggested that Carlyle come to talk about a class he was giving for qualified students to teach at the junior college level. He encouraged Carlyle to enroll, and Carlyle agreed, and so for the moment at least, we were saved. As an added incentive, the professor of education suggested that Carlyle could tutor students in freshman social sciences. The rest of the semester moved smoothly enough, but our bright hopes for the future became dimmer and dimmer.

12

Dark Clouds

Heart's Desire

The dark clouds, like ebon shrouds,
Hang heavy in sullen gloom;
The lightning's flash, the thunder's crash,
Foretell impending doom.

The dying day fast gives way
To black robed night
While 'cross the sky alarmed birds ply
In homeward flight.
My thoughts to you fly homeward too
Through wind and storm and rain;
My heart's afire with one desire:
To be with you again.

—*Carlyle Douglas, March 26, 1944*

IT HAD BEEN A MISERABLE TWO YEARS since Carlyle's last semester in college. Our social life had ground to a halt. Ted and Helen Young had left the Gardens to live in a house on the West Side that they had inherited from her mother. Louis Harper had been caught in the net of McCarthy's Communist paranoia, and Emile had gone to Florida, where he hoped to find work in a private school. Theresa and Maurice Haynes had moved to Benton Harbor, Michigan, and only a few of our friends in block 13 were left.

Worse than that, after two years of hunting, Carlyle had been unable to land a well-paying job. When Carlyle stopped going to school, he applied for jobs ranging from clerical to minor executive positions in the business world. He was told outright that, although his education and personality were well suited to such work, his color made him unacceptable. Eventually, he took a part-time clerical job with a research organization, but the pay was inadequate. This was followed by substitute teaching, but he only got two calls a week. Then, through the state civil service, he received an appointment as a social worker, but he was unable to support six people on his two-hundred-dollar-a-month salary. So once again, after four years of college, he was back to working as a janitor. We both wondered if his long struggle for education had been a waste of time, effort, and hope.

Shortly after leaving the university, Carlyle took a federal civil service examination on the junior professional level. He received a notice that he had passed the exam and that his name had been placed on the register, but nothing further. He had long since given up all hope of such a job when early in June of 1952 the heavens suddenly opened and sent a shaft of brilliant, exhilarating hope into the Douglas household. It came in the form of a letter from the Joliet Arsenal advising Carlyle that he was being considered for a position as a salary and wage analyst and asking him to come in for a personal interview.

The letter from Joliet lightened our hearts, but I don't think either of us dared to believe that it might be the opportunity we had hoped for over all these long, dreary months.

On the morning of the appointment, Carlyle came downstairs dressed in a gray suit of my father's. It fit him perfectly. He wore a blue tie and had a white handkerchief tucked neatly into his breast pocket. He looked like the president of a bank—erect, dignified, handsome.

My heart skipped a beat, and, despite my agnostic beliefs, I prayed to God that he would get the job, not because of the money, not because of our family's needs, but because he could not stand much more defeat.

The whole family rode along with Carlyle when he went for the interview. I took coloring books and some of the children's favorite stories to entertain them, and we drove off to Joliet. It was much farther than I had expected, and I wondered if Carlyle could possibly drive that distance back and forth every day.

When we reached the fenced-in gardens of the arsenal and saw the armed guard on duty at the gate and the imposing walls, I began to have qualms. How would a Black applicant for such an important job be received in this all-White place?

Carlyle parked outside the gate and showed his letter to the guard; he was admitted and disappeared into what appeared to be the administration building. It seemed to me that he was gone for hours. The children were getting restless, and I was a nervous wreck.

When I saw him coming I knew with absolute certainty that he had been hired for the job. His walk was springy, his head was held high, and he was smiling.

"I got it," he said, opening the door. "I got it without any problem at all. I like the man in charge—he's very nice. He said my credentials were the best he's seen." We rode home on cloud nine. Finally, finally we were going to have enough money and a safe future. All the way home we talked about how we would pay back his mother and mine, start a bank account so that someday we could buy a house, and begin to save for the children's education.

It was true that it was a long way for him to drive, and we decided that eventually we might have to move closer to Joliet, but as long as he had a car it would not be too onerous.

The first two weeks after Carlyle got his job at Joliet passed quickly enough. He was tired when he reached home, but I always had supper ready, and the children were on their way to bed. We spent our evenings sharing the day's events with each other or quietly reading.

It was just about the end of the first two weeks, and I had as usual fed the children and sent them up to bathe and get ready for bed. Carlyle was just a bit late, but not late enough to cause concern. I put his dinner in the oven to keep it warm and sat down to relax a moment before going upstairs to tuck in the little ones, David and Brigid.

When I looked at the clock again, it was a quarter after eight. I began to worry. We had no telephone at this point, and I had no way of finding out whether anything was wrong. At eight forty-five it was getting dark. The children seemed to have settled down, so I ran across the court to get Mary Ann. She came back with me to watch over the children while I went to Barbara's house, where there was a phone. I talked to her for a few minutes, but really there wasn't much either she or I could do since we didn't know where to call. I went home and walked the floor from window to window while Mary Ann sat, patiently waiting. I was over-whelmed with fears. By this time I knew that there must have been an accident.

My heart rose into my throat when I went to the window overlooking the court and saw Barbara coming toward me. I held the door open to let her in.

"The hospital in Joliet called," she said with deep concern in her eyes. "Carlyle was hurt in a car accident. He's at the Sisters of Mercy Hospital." She paused for a moment while I processed the information. "Marie and Johnny have a car," she continued. "I'll call them and see if they can take you."

I dressed so fast that I could hardly fasten the buttons on my shoes. Mary Ann said she would stay with the children, and within a few minutes Marie and Johnny came to take me to the hospital. I settled in the backseat, feeling numb during the long drive to the hospital.

At the hospital, I told the nun at the desk who I was. She looked at me curiously, then proceeded down a narrow corridor. "He's way at the back," she said. All three of us hurried down the hallway she had indicated. It was dimly lighted and seemed to be going nowhere. Finally, we saw a door to what appeared to be the boiler room. Johnny swore under his breath. There were a few cots in the rear, all occupied by Black men. Apparently, this was the "colored ward." In the far corner nearest the locker, I saw Carlyle. He was stretched out in his underwear, his underpants soiled with urine, his head on a thin pad, his feet sticking out over the end. Was this the "mercy" of "Sisters of Mercy Hospital"? I couldn't believe it.

I went over to him and touched his face with my hand. He opened his eyes and tried to smile. He whispered. I saw that his neck had been wrapped in bandages. I pulled the crumpled sheet over him and looked around for a nurse. None was in sight. I went out in the hall and saw a sister was passing by.

I stopped her and asked about my husband. Again, her response was a curious stare. "Nothing serious," she said. "He'll be all right in a day or two." She started to move on.

"Wait a minute," I said. "Who is his doctor?"

She gave me a name and added, "But he won't be in until tomorrow."

I was so angry I could scarcely resist the impulse to shake her; fortunately for her she was a good bit bigger than I.

After assuring myself that Carlyle was all right, I returned to the desk and asked for the doctor's telephone number. I called him, explained who I was, and asked about my husband's condition.

"First of all," the doctor said, "what kind of insurance does your husband have?"

I was sick with outrage. He obviously cared more about the insurance money than he did about my husband.

"Blue Cross," I said.

He then told me my husband could go home in the morning. I couldn't very well leave him there in that horrible place. He would be better off at home. With Maurice and Johnny's help we got him up into a wheelchair, and I signed him out over the nun's protest. We made him as comfortable as we could in the backseat with his head leaning against my shoulder.

Fortunately, I had done him no harm. Our doctor came within an hour after I got Carlyle home, and by midnight he was resting comfortably in bed with a visiting nurse there to help.

The next day Marie and Johnny took me to see what could be done about the car. My stomach turned over when I saw it. It was crushed like an accordion. A truck had hit it on one side and a car on the other. Apparently, Carlyle had skidded on wet pavement. The mechanic who showed the car to me said Carlyle was lucky to be alive. The car, of course, was a total wreck.

I called Joliet the next morning to talk to the administrator, Colonel Edwards, who had hired Carlyle. I explained what had happened and that he required two weeks' care. I liked Colonel Edwards instinctively. He spoke about how well Carlyle was adjusting to his work and how much he liked him. He seemed sincerely convincing.

Carlyle recuperated after two weeks, and with each day became better and more difficult to live with. He was morose about the car and bemoaned the question of how he could ever get to Joliet without one. After moaning about it for nearly a week, making life difficult for the rest of us, he woke up one morning with a pleasant smile and smugly announced that he had solved the problem. One of his coworkers lived in St. Charles, which was about halfway to Joliet on the commuter train line if one took a rather circuitous, indirect route. He could take the bus to the Calumet River Bridge, about a mile down the road, and catch the commuter train there. He could then ride to St. Charles, meet his coworker there, and accompany him to the arsenal. He would use the reverse process to come home. It sounded insane, but I didn't attempt to discourage him, since I saw no other alternative.

Those next two years from 1952 until 1954 were uneventful but exhausting. On weekdays Carlyle left the house at seven in the morning and didn't get home until seven in the evening. He liked the work, however, and his relationship with the colonel was a very pleasant one. He was, of course, fully aware that as the only Black employee at a professional level he was under surveillance from everyone in the office, but as long as Colonel Edwards was there he was secure enough.

While Carlyle was at work I was beginning to put into action the plan we had devised to secure our family against the world. I took the children to the library every week to choose books they might like. I read to them day in and day out, whenever they called for a story. In the evening, Carlyle put aside his work to take over until it was time to prepare them for bed. We started the bedtime routine at seven o'clock on the dot. He and I supervised baths, and bedtime was never later than seven thirty. Throughout the years our children all, at one time or another, complained bitterly that they had to go to bed earlier than anyone else on the block. As adults they humorously claimed it was a form of child abuse, but we are certain that we could not have survived otherwise. During the daylight hours we were totally devoted to our children. We needed the evenings to recover our sanity.

By this time we had acquired a fish tank of guppies, two parakeets (a gift from Helen Young), and a cat named Baldy that came from nowhere and set up house in our downstairs closet. She never was able to fulfill her fondest desire—a meal of fish or birds—but she got revenge by bringing mice into the house and turning them loose.

We bought rolls of wrapping paper and finger paints and spent part of our time with the children painting pictures of every sort. David was especially proud of the painting that we taped to the kitchen wall. He called it "the road with the hole in the middle" because he had worn a hole in the paper while finger painting by rubbing his finger round and round in the same spot.

At my request my mother sent me the collection of art albums I had put together for a course in world art. We bought a folding screen to put between the living room and kitchen, and I arranged copies of famous paintings or pictures of sculptures on both sides of the screen and then called them to the attention of the children, sharing information about the art and the artists whenever I could. We made a point of telling stories about Harriet Tubman, George Washington Carver, Crispus Attucks, and all of the famous Blacks we knew about.

To round off our program we relaxed with hilarious games of hide-the-thimble and Monopoly. Later on as the children grew older we turned to mah-jongg, go-fish, hearts, chess, and checkers. Even when our children were in their teens we sometimes broke down and played such silly childhood games as I spy and pig, as well as more adult games such as Scrabble.

In the evenings we sometimes listened to music, either our own records or music we heard on our radio. Carlyle enjoyed classical and jazz music immensely and took great pride in the high-fidelity system he had assembled. We talked about the children and about the future or his work. Sometimes we played chess. Because Carlyle had to get up so early, we rarely stayed up later than ten. We seemed to have found a pleasant, comfortable routine. On weekends we visited with friends either in their homes or ours, or played games with the children, or just did nothing.

It was on one such weekend that early on a Saturday evening I began to feel ill. I went upstairs to lie down for a few minutes and suddenly realized that I was bleeding. I assumed it was regular menstruation, though it wasn't my time of month, but then sometimes I wasn't that regular. I still was uneasy. I was afraid to get up, so I called Carlyle. He came running up the stairs, frightened by my tone of voice. I told him I thought I was hemorrhaging. He called Mary Ann and then Barbara Jones. I was very fortunate that Carlyle was home. By this time the towels I had put under me and the sheets as well were soaked with blood. When Barbara came, she took one look and said, "Get her to the hospital."

Carlyle expressed fears that our insurance would not cover me. Barbara was already on the telephone calling Provident Hospital, where she worked, on the promise that she would be responsible for the bill. They said they would see me.

We persuaded our nearest neighbor with a car to take me to the hospital. Carlyle bundled me in a blanket and sheets and carried me downstairs. I remember seeing the frightened faces of my children looking up at me and being lifted into the front seat of the car. But I remember nothing else until I half opened my eyes, squinting at the bright white lights overhead and saw a group of strange people with masks and hospital gowns surrounding me.

It was very odd. One minute I was lying on my back, looking up at the doctors and nurses surrounding me, and the next minute it seemed as if I were floating over everyone and looking down at them and my body. A nurse with a white cap was bending over me. I distinctly remember hearing her say, "She's gone." And I thought, "Where?"

The next thing I remember was my husband's face. The bright lights were gone, and there was only one little light somewhere above me. I was lying in a hospital bed with all kinds of machines and instruments around me. Several tubes were attached to my arms.

I tried to smile at Carlyle and say something, but the words wouldn't come. There were tears in his eyes, and I was sorry I couldn't reassure him that I was all right. I didn't hurt, but I felt awkward and uncomfortable. I did not want to be there.

The hours and the days passed, punctuated by hospital personnel poking needles in my arms and legs. I know now, of course, that they were trying to save me, a long slow process. The days and nights flowed by, and after a while I centered my whole being on the tall, erect man who periodically came down the hall and entered my room. He always came in quietly, folded his coat over the back of the chair, kissed me, and sat down with my hand in his. Sometimes we talked, sometimes not, and it was only later, when I was truly convalescent, that I understood what these regular trips to visit me had really cost him.

After work he had to take the commuter train all the way to St. Charles and down to the campus—at least an hour-and-a-half's journey—then walk across the campus to the hospital, spend an hour with me, and ride another hour-and-a-half to get home, just in time to get a little supper, kiss our children, and go to bed. He went through all of this only to face the same tiring journey to work the next morning.

He never once said anything to me about it. He just came. One time I remember he brought me a get-well card from the people at his office. They included a hundred-dollar bill. We were both deeply touched, and I felt gratified that at least something must be going right.

I don't know exactly how long I was in the hospital, but it was long enough for me to become impatient and restless, repeatedly threatening to walk out. The doctor told me that the reason I had hemorrhaged was that I had had a miscarriage. I was quite surprised because I had not known I was pregnant. Since my blood type was AB negative and the baby I was carrying was AB positive, there had been complications. To have any more children might cost me my life, so they were going to tie my tubes if I consented. Since I had four children already, I really didn't mind.

The day finally came for me to go home. It was a Saturday. I was still a little weak, so I rode down in a wheelchair, then walked to the car that Carlyle had borrowed to take me home. When I arrived at home I found my mother there waiting for me. Mom had come to help me out. She told me that every day, little David, not quite four, had stood at the front window looking wistfully out and saying, "I wish my mommy would come." That night, when I tucked him into bed I gave him a special hug and kiss. I promised never to leave him again, and I didn't. Mom stayed a few more days until I was well enough to take care of the children by myself.

Needless to say, between Carlyle's accident and my hospitalization our debts had grown to such an extent that we didn't see how we could ever recover financially.

Carlyle continued to work in Joliet, and I stayed home, helping with homework, settling sibling quarrels, playing games, and keeping a watchful eye on the refrigerator.

One afternoon, as I sat in the kitchen trying to pull myself together to start dinner, I listened to the chatter of noisy little voices humming overhead. I called to them and counted their heads as they appeared in the stairwell. I was shocked at the realization that there were eleven kids in my house. Four of my own, four of the Mathises' children from across the way, two from the house two doors down, and one unfamiliar kid who seemed not at all concerned that he was in strange territory.

No wonder women were off to work in record numbers the first chance they got! I thought about it for a minute. We needed the money. I needed the rest. Working outside of the home had to be easier than this. Why not look for a job?

Considerably more cheerful than I had been before, I announced closing time in Douglas playland and shooed them all out to the playground, guarding the refrigerator as they passed.

For about a week I didn't say anything to Carlyle about wanting to work. I mulled it over, turning the idea this way and that way. The more I thought about it the more I believed the positives outweighed the negatives.

My first consideration was that we needed the money. As I reflected, another more important reason grew in importance: I wanted to work. Three of the children were in school most of the day. David was in school for half a day with nursery school in the afternoon. Brigid could possibly stay with Mary Ann's mother, and Mary Ann could manage all of them after school until I got home if I could pay her enough. For what kind of work was I qualified? Teacher? The less I had to do with children at present, the happier I would be. Salesperson? It was doubtful that I could do well at that sort of thing. I had worked for American Hospital Supply as an office manager—maybe something along those lines.

I bought the daily paper and pored over the want ads. I didn't see anything in the first few lines I checked, but I was getting desperate, so I continued reading. There was an ad in a box with bold letters: Wanted Man or Woman, well educated, good references, to organize travel arrangements for Traveler's Aid. Salary Negotiable.

That evening, after Carlyle had finished his dinner and gone up to say good night to the children, I decided to tell him what I wanted to do. He listened attentively, and when I finished he asked if I had anything special in mind. I showed him the ad in the paper, watching him closely to see what his reaction would be. I saw the corners of his mouth twitch, and I burst out, "You don't think I could do that, do you?"

"Do what?" he mumbled. "I don't think you have any idea what the job entails!"

"There you go!" I said half-amused, half-irritated. "Any normal person would say, 'involves.'" I hated his unusually precise selection of words.

He fumed. "All right then, 'involves'!" I looked at him blankly and launched into a tirade, but I haven't the faintest recollection of what I then said.

"Don't misunderstand me," he said. "I'm not putting you down. I know very well you can do any damn thing you set out to do. But this could be dangerous."

He then explained to me that in all probability the person in charge would distribute tickets to those who would sell them. I might have to keep track of the number of tickets sold, collect the money, and keep all the records.

Ridiculous, I thought. How would he know? In retrospect I can see that his elaborate reasoning was simply his way of trying to maintain the traditional male role of my protector.

"Well," I said, although I was already beginning to waver, "it wouldn't do any harm to go find out." He offered no further objection.

So that is what I did.

I hadn't been to the Loop in downtown Chicago in ten years. In fact, I had not even gone to Rosedale unless I was in a car. I was a little uneasy, but when I boarded the bus at the Altgeld station and saw that all the passengers on the nearly full bus were Blacks, I breathed easier.

By this time I had developed a kind of paranoia about White people. My experiences with Carlyle led me to believe that most of them were prejudiced. I assumed, based on these experiences, that most White people would be horrified if they were to know about my interracial marriage and family. It was safer to assume that White strangers were prejudiced than to trust them and be hurt. Perhaps it was paranoia, but under the circumstances it seemed quite natural. Along with the fear and mistrust was a silent, seething rage for all the injustices that had been inflicted on my family and me, as well as on Blacks throughout history. Many of these injustices continue today.

It took over an hour to reach the Loop even though the bus made very few stops along the way. Once I was downtown I had no difficulty finding the office building on State Street where Traveler's Aid had their headquarters. I was somewhat apprehensive as I walked along the street, looking for the right address. Carlyle was not with me, and there was no visible evidence that I was married to a Black man. Nobody paid any attention to me. My friends in the Gardens had warned me not to reveal that I was interracially married. The chances were that if I said nothing, it would not occur to anyone to ask. This proved to be the case. Interracial marriage was beyond the realm of imagination for most people.

I felt like a traitor, guilty and uncomfortable, but at the time I knew my friends were right in cautioning me to say nothing about my private life. It could easily cost me the job.

As I had expected, everyone in the office was White except a cleaning lady whom I saw in the hall. The woman who interviewed me was very cordial and seemed impressed with the fact that I had a college degree and had worked for American Hospital Supply.

Much to my surprise and delight, she hired me on the spot with the understanding that this was really a temporary summer job. She also indicated that there might be an opening for a desk job as a client interviewer in the fall. The salary was modest, but it was enough to help pay off some of our debts. So I accepted the position, which was to begin immediately. I could hardly wait to share the good news with Carlyle.

The bus was almost full when it finally reached my return stop, and to my dismay, the only empty seats were next to White people. If the day had not been so long, I might well have stood up; as it was, I carefully sat down next to a middle-aged White woman, remaining close to the edge of the seat so that I would not touch her.

As I expected, the woman got off in Rosedale, and I heaved a sigh of relief. This scenario was repeated dozens of times in the years I worked for Traveler's Aid as I traveled on the bus daily. When I boarded the bus, I automatically searched for empty seats next to Black passengers. If there were none, I reluctantly sat next to a White passenger. Thinking back, I see now that my behavior was similar to that of Blacks who sat next to Blacks when possible and parallel to the behavior of Whites who sat mainly next to other Whites. It's clear to me now that inwardly I had developed the feelings of a Black person, although outwardly my appearance was White.

As time passed, my feelings toward Whites got worse rather than better, largely because of the brutal murder of Emmett Till. Now, if you are White, the name may mean nothing to you, but for me and most Black Americans who lived during those times, it is seared into our hearts forever.

I will never forget that heartrending day. It had been an exhausting day, partly because of the heat and partly because of my work. Having finished my work at the office a little early, I had signed out and gone to the bus terminal to wait for the Altgeld bus. While waiting, I picked up a newspaper from the local newsstand. I was drawn to an article on the front page: "Chicago Boy Lynched in the South," read the headline. My hands shook so badly that the paper rattled and the print blurred. Emmett Till, a fourteen-year-old Black boy, had gone to the South to visit relatives. Evidently, he had entered a small country store in the town where his relatives lived. There were conflicting stories about what happened in the store. Apparently, however, the White woman who waited on him claimed he had made some "fresh" remarks that she found insulting. Word passed around. That night, Emmett was kidnapped and taken into the woods, where he was beaten senseless, lifeless, and shapeless by townspeople. His mother could barely recognize her son's battered, misshapen face. The responsible parties were brought to trial but were found not guilty by an all-White jury. A fourteen-year-old boy.

Even now, so many years later, I cannot write about it without tears of rage, frustration, and sorrow. I did not cry then. I was too horrified and enraged to feel anything but hate. All the way home on the bus I huddled in the back seat. I presume other Black passengers on that trip to Altgeld were feeling much as I did, but I was not aware of it. For the first time in my life I experienced a hatred so passionate, so deep that the only way I could handle it was to concentrate on that White shopkeeper whom I was sure had either misinterpreted or just plain lied about that boy. I blamed her as much as I blamed the men who had done the actual beating. As far as I was concerned, it was the woman who had brought this horror about. My hatred zeroed in on her. I found a little comfort in imagining that she herself might be lynched, but that did not seem punishment enough. So I imagined how she would feel if her babies were killed in front of her very eyes.

By the time the bus reached the Gardens, I was barely able to rise from my seat and walk down the aisle to get off at my stop. I sat down on a bench in the late afternoon sunshine trying to pull myself together so that I could face my family. I was so saturated by the depth of my rage and hatred, by all the horrible visions I had of Emmett's horrible end. They were so sharp and keen that I wasn't sure I could make it home.

Fortunately, Mama came out of the drugstore and saw me sitting helplessly on the bench. It seemed that Mama was always there when I needed her. She had helped me to feel welcome when I first came to the Gardens. She had helped to ease my fears when Carlyle was returning from military service. And she was here now. She came across the square to sit down beside me. She put her arms around me as though I were a child and said soothingly, "It's all right, Baby. It's all right. You can't keep it shut inside or you'll blow up. Just let go, otherwise you can't keep going."

It was Mama who pulled me through. How many times in her lifetime had she been confronted with violence and death born from racism? I wondered. I was ashamed for having been so weak, as I realized she had been there many times before and knew all about unbearable pain, anger, and revenge. God knows what would have happened had she not been there to empathize, to comfort, and to help me see the futility of revenge. She helped me to believe that someday if we worked hard enough we could change the inequities that were destroying us all, both Black and White.

I have never confided in anyone except Mama about how I felt that day. The agony in my heart is as fresh today as it was then. Even now, after some forty years, I cannot talk about it without shedding tears. Although my hatred for Emmett Till's murderers has subsided, it still smolders within me like a long dormant volcano, ready to erupt at some slight shifting of the earth.

Beyond the pain and the anger that Emmett Till's killing evoked is the fear it introduced. From that day forward, I was haunted by the knowledge that my sons could someday share his fate. All it would take would be for them, by some small twist of fate, to be in the wrong place, to say the wrong words, or to make some imperceptible gesture, to trigger an outpouring of violence driven by racism.

13

Exodus

To Barbara

May passing time rest lightly on your brow,
And let there be no cares to cause distress;
May all your years be spent in happiness,
Replete with all the bliss the fates allow.
May God, in studied justice, well endow
Your mind with peace, your heart with measureless
Content; and all through life may you possess
The stateliness and poise that are yours now.
The time we've spent together has been sweet,
Containing more of gladness than of tears;
And life for me was never more complete
Than it has been through these delightful years;
May this, our love, inspire you to defeat
All future doubts, my Heart, and future fears.

—*Carlyle Douglas, October 13, 1944*

AT THE END OF SUMMER IN 1956 the manager of Traveler's Aid offered me an office position taking care of the accounts that involved American Indians. I talked to Carlyle about it. It meant an increase in salary and long hours. We could pay off the remaining bills and break even by the end of the year, but we were already spending too little time with our children, and that concerned us both. There was also another catch. With two salaries we would be over the income ceiling allowed for residents of Altgeld, which would mean that we would have to move. I could not imagine living anywhere else. I didn't know how I could live in another integrated neighborhood, nor did I want to live anywhere else.

We discussed the pros and cons for a week, trying to decide what was best for us as a family. It seemed to be a catch-22 situation. If I didn't take the job, we would still have to struggle financially. If I did take the job, we would have to move into an unknown and probably worse living situation.

Then two things happened. Colonel Edwards announced that he was leaving the Joliet Arsenal because they were going to reduce operations and downsize its staff. He offered Carlyle a permanent placement at the arsenal to which he would be moving, which was somewhere in Arkansas. Colonel Edwards had no idea that I was White nor, therefore, what such a move would mean for our family. We knew it would have been foolhardy for us to venture that far south, so Carlyle had to refuse the offer.

The second thing that happened at about this time was that Carlyle's mother came to see us and suggested that we come to Detroit and live with her. She would buy a suitable house in a good neighborhood, and we could live there, paying only a nominal amount for rent until we could find jobs.

She, herself, intended to continue working. Since at that time she was head matron at a correctional facility for girls some distance away, she would be in Detroit only a few days a month. The one flaw would be that her younger brother, Carlyle's Uncle Bob, a half-reformed alcoholic, would also have a room in the house.

We couldn't make up our minds, so Carlyle's mother reminded us that my mother lived alone on the farm and that in time she would be too old to stay there alone. She suggested that it would be nice for her to live with us and be located in an area that was convenient for her friends to visit. That seemed to tip the scales in favor of Detroit, but in my mind there was still a doubt. As far back as I could remember, people in Ann Arbor had made fun of Detroit and looked down their noses because it was a factory town. Nonetheless, there was a house with five bedrooms, three baths, a big finished attic, and a nice quiet street near an elementary school, a hospital, and shopping area. What more could we have asked? With luck we could manage to be there before the end of the first two weeks of school.

Carlyle and I both resigned from our positions, and we informed the Altgeld Gardens management that we would leave within a month.

At that point none of us knew exactly how we felt. The children were already mourning the loss of their friends, but at the same time they were excited about this new adventure. Carlyle and I were still changing our thinking daily. We questioned whether we had made the right decision. Yet all the while we were carried along by the momentum generated by his mom, by the children, and by our own secret hopes.

Mr. Mathis offered to help transport our belongings with his car if we could rent a trailer. Fortunately, we had little furniture of any value to move. We gave the piano—and the guppies as well—to the Mathis family. Our friend Barbara Jones said she would take the parakeets and reluctantly agreed to also keep our cat, Baldy. Carlyle, Colin, and David would ride with Mr. Mathis, and Linda, Brigid, and I would go by bus.

Just as the car was about to leave and we were preparing to catch the bus downtown, Baldy crossed the parking lot, mewing plaintively. I was inclined to ignore her pleas because I felt there was something unnatural about a cat that brought mice into the house and turned them loose. The mouse population in our house had increased because of the cat, rather than the other way around. However, the boys insisted that she come along, so Carlyle, ignoring my protests, took her into the car.

The girls and I boarded a train for Detroit. When we arrived in Detroit we took a cab to the address Carlyle's mother had given us. Arriving in front of an old house on a rather shabby side street, I was a little uneasy. Carlyle's mother was at work, and a short little man with a bald head let us in. This, of course, was Uncle Bob. He appeared to be as dubious about seeing us as we were about seeing him. When I introduced myself, the crack in the door widened enough to let us through. "Nobody here but me," he said. "You Carlyle's wife?" as though he were hoping against hope that I would leave.

I admitted that I was and waited.

"Well," he volunteered after what seemed to me a long time, "guess you better come in. Lucille said to tell you she'd be along."

He motioned toward the door opening off the vestibule, and we ventured into a neatly furnished room with all the amenities one expected to find in a living room. I sat in a chair near the window, too tired to care much what happened next. What happened was that Brigid suddenly announced in no uncertain terms that she was hungry, thirsty, and needed to go to the bathroom. It seemed prudent to take care of these concerns in reverse order: bathroom first, then food and drink. So, after requesting directions from a thoroughly disapproving Uncle Bob, I sent the girls upstairs to the bathroom. Their mission accomplished without incident, Brigid then sat down on the bottom step and let it be known that she had not eaten for a very long time.

Wearily, I pulled myself out of the chair and made my way to the kitchen. I had no idea how Emily Post would have handled this delicate situation, but I was beyond caring. I smiled brightly at Uncle Bob, who was hovering in the background like the proverbial thundercloud, and opened the refrigerator door. To me it seemed expedient to find nourishment for my youngest before she took matters into her own hands, especially since her cheeks were turning pink and her eyebrows were converging, a sure sign of trouble.

I found some milk and cheese and bread, made each of the girls a sandwich, and gave them glasses of milk. There were several cans of beer at the back of the shelf, but since I didn't touch them Uncle Bob became more congenial.

Not long after, the car and trailer pulled into the driveway, and Mr. Mathis, Carlyle, and the boys came in.

* * * *

Barbara's Story

These are the last words Barbara wrote in her effort to tell the story of her marriage. She wrote the better part of the previous chapters in a vortex of creativity from the time Carlyle died in February 1995 until her death in August of that year. Unfortunately, there is no way that anyone else can attempt to tell the rest of the story that she began. Her powers of perception, her passion for her family, her ability to turn a phrase are her own.

On her journey to the next world she carried many secrets. Details about her life in China, the joys and anguish she felt for her children and grandchildren as they experienced triumphs and tragedies in their lives, the depth of her love for her husband, and the ordeals they faced as an interracial couple—we will never know any of these in the way that she wanted us to know. We will never know how she would have finished the story.

The pages that follow do not attempt to complete Barbara's story but to tell the story of one of her children. However, that story sheds a little light on Barbara's unfinished story and gives another perspective of life in an interracial household. It is hoped that the reader will consider the stories complementary and will appreciate the perspective of the child of an integrated household within a segregated society.

Part 2

David's Story
Between Two Worlds

1

The Gardens

MY EARLIEST MEMORIES ARE A COMPLEX collage of colorful characters, wild adventures, childhood friendships, thoughtless vandalism, and numerous encounters with family, friends, and community members around America's curious notion of race.

Life began for me on the South Side of Chicago, but I did not live in the characteristically urban South Side that we know today. Rather, my family and I lived in a housing project located so far from downtown Chicago that it bore a distinctly rural charm. Situated between 132nd Street and the Calumet River, it stood on the city's southernmost boundary.

The housing project, Altgeld Gardens, sprawled over a score or more of rectangular city blocks, filling each with two-story brick row houses. As if cut from the same mold, each block was identical to the others in its arrangement of houses, parking areas, and the centrally located communal incinerator. The only differences were those introduced by the residents themselves: carefully tended flower gardens or grass worn bare by the traffic of children, flowered curtains or bedsheets in the windows, lawns littered with child-battered toys or bloodstains from newly butchered chickens. Although we were all poor, we were rich in the diversity of lifestyles within the project.

Family life for us was full of love and a wonderful variety of simple but meaningful activities. One of my fondest memories is of simply sleeping with my mother and father. I remember as a toddler lying in bed between my mother and father, feeling warm and safe and happy. I hated it when I awoke to find myself in my father's arms, being carried back to my crib. I remember that if I cried long enough and loud enough, my mother would be moved to take me back into my parents' bed.

On one occasion—I couldn't have been more than two—my parents had set me in my crib after having started the night in their bed. Feeling disconsolate and unable to sleep, I lay staring into the darkness. Whether real or imagined, fantasy or reality, I'll never know, but what happened next was all very real to me. Out of the darkness that surrounded me I saw three figures floating toward me in unison. As they drew closer to me their features emerged in detail. All three were men. The first had white skin and a five-o'clock shadow. He wore baggy, pleated slacks, a plaid shirt, a wrinkled sports jacket, and a matching hat. The second was an Indian with a painted face, a loincloth, and a headband that sprouted a single feather. The third was a thin but muscular, bare-chested Black man with unkempt hair and torn pants. As these three strangers floated through my bedroom door toward my crib, fear engulfed my entire being. I wailed with all of the strength my little lungs could muster. I screamed as if my very life depended on it. My parents both came rushing into my room, asking me frantically what was the matter. The figures vanished as my parents entered the room. I told my parents about the strange men. They assured me it was only a nightmare. My father swept me into his protecting arms and took me back to the warmth and safety of their bed.

Another nighttime activity that brought us together as a family was reading. Bedtime stories were a family routine for as long as I can remember. We'd crowd into my parents' bed while my mother or father read from one of the countless library books that were always in plentiful supply. *The Five Chinese Brothers* was one of my favorites. I enjoyed the way each of the brothers used his special gift to avoid being killed. I soaked up the lesson of sharing embodied in the story *Stone Soup*. My father seemed to prefer to read Grimm's fairy tales. I was touched by Hans Christian Anderson's story of "The Steadfast Tin Soldier." Mother read anything we wanted her to read to us. She loved reading and made sure that we loved it too.

During evenings and weekends we spent countless hours playing simple family games. When we were younger we played hide-the-thimble and I spy. When we were older my father bought a deck of cards and *The New Complete Hoyle*, a guidebook of card games and how to play them. We never tired of playing card games: go fish, I doubt it, old maid, hearts, spades. There seemed to be no end to the games that were described in the book and no end to the hours of games we played as a family.

When we were not much older, my parents introduced us to poker. The evening started with a plentiful supply of soda pop, potato chips, a deck of cards, and a candy tin full of hundreds of pennies. My parents divided the pennies between us all. Then it was dealer's choice: five-card stud, five-card draw, seven-card stud, seven-card draw: deuces wild, or deuces and eights wild—the combinations were without limit. Although we gambled in earnest, at the end of the evening all the money went back into the pot. It was all for fun, but great lessons were learned. I learned to count those pennies—first by twos, then by fives and tens. Beyond the lessons in math, I learned sportsmanship and that playing the game is more important than winning or losing.

Saturday mornings were among my favorite times. My parents slept in. As we children awoke one by one, we all piled into their bed and snuggled. We laughed and joked, wrestled, and had pillow fights. On more than one occasion we were so exuberant in our wrestling that the bed went crashing to the floor because the stress and strain of our out-of-control play broke the bed slats.

My parents took great care to make certain that although we lived in poverty we had a rich family life. I never knew the taste of steak until much later in life. I was very familiar with red beans and rice, occasionally flavored with ham hocks. There were times when we went hungry. I remember one particular Thanksgiving on which we would have had our usual fare of creamed chipped beef on toast had my family not won a turkey from the local grocery store raffle. Unfortunately, we were not so lucky that Christmas and had to subsist on apples and nuts for Christmas dinner. On one occasion when my father was jobless and the cupboard was bare, he humbled himself and went begging for food to spare us the experience of going to bed with empty stomachs. He came home with the most wonderful Chicago-style hotdogs I have ever tasted.

None of us ever had a birthday party, but every birthday was celebrated with a homebaked, frosting-less, often lopsided yellow cake. How we looked forward to those celebrations! On summer evenings when it was too hot to stay inside, we sat out on the stoop or went for walks and greeted our neighbors, who also came outside to escape the heat and enjoy the evening breeze. At that time the thought never entered my mind that we were the only mixed family in the project or that my mother was the only White. Everyone on the block seemed to be friendly with everyone else. There seemed to be no thought of color among the project residents.

South of the "Gardens," as we affectionately called our housing project, an inviting field beckoned me and my siblings with urchin treasures: old tires, discarded clothing, variously colored and shaped bottles and cans, pieces of red brick and concrete, and remnants of broken toys scattered amongst a glittering array of abandoned household junk. There were broken chairs, lamps, electronic gadgets, and anything else members of our impoverished community no longer found useful. Small clay hills pockmarked the landscape, interspersed with pools of stagnant water. To the adult mind it was obviously a kind of dump. To my eight-year-old mind, it was a vast and delightful playground.

My brother, Colin, and I spent hours chasing each other over the hills. We threw dirt "bombs" at each other, pretending that we were at war, dodging in and out of the landforms. When we tired of war games we threw rocks at bottles or at the water bugs that skittered along the surface of the stagnant pools. If we felt less energetic we simply searched through the rubbish, looking for treasures.

Occasionally, our search was rewarded with a great find: an old tire. Like children the world over we were absorbed with this modern form of one of the world's oldest machines. There was no limit to the number of ways our creative little minds could discover adventure in a dirty, worn-out, discarded tire. Usually, we simply rolled it down the street, finding challenge in guiding it straight along the sidewalk. When we played more creatively, we put rocks or cans on the inside, taking simple pleasure in watching the objects bounce around inside the rim as the tire spun along until the last object fell out. Other games required two people. One might roll the tire toward the other. The waiting child watched carefully as the tire approached, then, at the right moment, placed both hands on top of the rolling rubber tread and vaulted over it while letting it pass between his legs.

Occasionally, when our parents were not home, we brought the tire inside our simple two-story row house. With great effort we pushed and pulled the tire to the top of the straight flight of cement stairs that led from the first floor to the second floor. Then one of us ran downstairs to serve as lookout and door-holder. When both pedestrians and automobiles were safe from the impending projectile and we were safe from the spying eyes of other adults, the lookout gave the signal that the coast was clear.

"All clear?" my brother shouted from the top of the stairs.

"All clear!" I responded with excitement.

Then with a great heave my brother, stationed at the top of the stairs, propelled the tire downward. We watched gleefully as it bounced down the stairs, out the front door, and across the lawn. Sometimes the momentum carried it all the way into the street. We took great pride in getting the tire to go straight out the door and across the street.

When we really wanted excitement one of us curled up inside the tire before the other one rolled it down the stairs. This thrilling game required three people: usually my brother, Colin, my sister Brigid, and myself. The cannoneer at the top of the stairs propelled the tire with a heaving push so that, aided by gravity, it sped down the stairs, bouncing past the excited door-holder and into the street below with the young passenger curled tightly inside.

It never occurred to us that the thrill seeker riding inside the tire might bash his face on the concrete stairs, or crush his skull on the cement floor below, or break his neck if the tire went askew and crashed into the doorway or a tree. We knew enough to make sure no cars were coming so that we didn't cause or fall victim to an automobile accident. But our biggest concern was having fun and not getting caught by our parents, who would have been absolutely mortified had they known what was going on.

Rolling down the staircase in a tire was only one of the dangerous ways we created excitement for ourselves. Occasionally, my brother and I walked all the way across the hill-studded, debris-littered clay "battlefield" that was south of the projects to the Calumet River. There we climbed down the weed-bristled banks to the muddy shore below and, if our nerve was up, stripped naked and went skinny-dipping.

The river was far enough away from the projects that there was little danger of anyone's actually seeing us. Isolated fishermen occasionally visited the banks, but those occasions were rare enough that we didn't worry. The greatest danger of being seen in the buff came from speedboats and the recreational water skiers who frequently followed in tow. When we heard the loud buzz of an outboard motor we hastily plunged our private parts into the murky depths of the river.

In retrospect, I can hardly believe that we possessed the audacity and stupidity to risk the shame of exposure and the panic of drowning for the questionable pleasure of swimming in those cold, dirty, dangerous waters. The mind of a child is, however, a strange and wondrous creation. It comprehends all of the exciting possibilities and none of the dangers. I never worried about the broken glass that studded the bottom of the river, despite the fact that we frequently broke bottles during our target practice with rocks in the very same spots where we usually swam. Nor did I worry about the foul sewage-smelling waters that poured into the river through the storm drains. And like most children and adults in the pre-Rachel Carson era of the 1950s, I was totally oblivious to the dangers of chemical pollution from the factories that lined the river. So we waded and swam in the muddy shallows of the Calumet, totally unconcerned about the very real dangers of our nude adventures, as much thrilled as worried about the prospect of being discovered by the river's recreational users.

When we weren't skinny-dipping or treasure hunting, we were busy interacting with our friends and neighbors. We knew all of our neighbors in the Gardens. Whether we liked them or not, we dealt with them on a daily basis because all of them were only a wall or a courtyard away.

Immediately across from us lived the candy lady. I think candy ladies exist in all housing projects everywhere in this country. They are a manifestation of the entrepreneurial spirit expressed at the poverty level. They serve the omnipresent need that kids in our society seem to have for sweets. This candy lady, like all candy ladies, operated a kitchen closet candy store. All year round, project kids lined up at her back door with their pennies and nickels tightly grasped in their dirty palms, seeking a fix—a few moments of pure, unadulterated pleasure from the kid-pleasing conglomerations of chemicals designed for that purpose. Lemon drops, orange slices, Milk Duds, candy-coated peanuts, M&Ms, Snickers, Three Musketeers . . . the list was endless, the sight was dazzling, and thoughts of a seemingly infinite array of candy were mind-boggling to the sugar-starved brain of a malnourished kid. It was always hard to decide which of the sucrose delights to squander my few pennies on. In the summer the choice was made easier by the addition of homemade snow cones to the menu. The snow cones were made by shaving a huge block of ice with a carpenter's plane. The shavings were then put into a paper cone with a thick, sugary fruit-flavored syrup squirted on top. The candy lady was the first person I'd see whenever I found or earned a few extra pennies.

Next door to the candy lady lived my best friend, Turner Mathis. We used to call him Turney. Turney was slightly darker and slightly shorter than I. He was also a year older than I and a year younger than my brother, which put him right in the middle of a perpetual struggle for his companionship and attention. My brother usually won. Being older, Colin was able to invoke the argument "You're too little." For example, I was "too little" to play baseball with them because I had trouble hitting the ball. Deep in my heart I knew that I would learn to hit the ball if only I had enough practice, but I was too silent, too passive, and too verbally inept to articulate my needs. I could never hold up to Colin in an argument. If he didn't want me around, the only time I "won" was when Mom intervened and made him take me along. But that became a hollow victory because even though she could force my presence on him, she couldn't force him to have fun with me. He let me know with his scowls and gruff manner that I remained an unwanted tagalong. Nevertheless, there were times when Colin, Turney, and I spontaneously played together and roamed around the projects in search of adventures.

Our adventures, though sometimes dangerous, resulted in little harm. We wandered the projects, went for walks in the woods, wrestled, or played hide-and-seek. On trash day we sometimes looked for treasures in our neighbors' trash piles. "Treasures" meant the broken remnants of toys and household furnishings that wound up in other peoples' trash. We never thought of our activity as garbage picking. To us, it was treasure hunting.

Next door to Turney lived the flower lady. I never knew her real name. She was known as the flower lady because her backyard was filled with the most lavish array of flowers on our block—maybe in the entire project. She had more flowers than I could name. Her yard was all flowers—no vegetables, and not one blade of grass except to serve as a pathway between the numerous flowerbeds. She seemed to have as many kinds of flowers as the candy lady had candy—only I didn't know flowers as well as I knew candy. I recognized tulips, pansies, and roses of course, and even gladiolas, but there were many more that I could not begin to name. Tall ones, short ones, red ones, blue ones, yellow ones, multicolored ones. Flowers near the window. Flowers along the sidewalk. Flowers next to the steps. Flowers against the fence, leaning over the fence, poking through the fence. She had the only fenced-in yard on the block.

Although we never knew her name and we never knew what kind of person she really was, we all had the notion that she was mean. There were only two times that we ever saw her: when she was tending her garden—watering, pruning, planting, weeding—or when one of our balls went into her yard.

When one of our balls, through no fault or misconduct of our own, happened by some unfortunate combination of the laws of nature to pass within the boundaries of her wondrous garden, we panicked, frozen with fright. Typically, after overcoming our initial shock, we argued with each other over whose responsibility it was to get the ball.

"Who's going to get it?" one of us would ask, eyes bulging with apprehension. Then the argument began.

"You get it. I got it last time!"

"You knocked it in there. You should get it out."

"It wouldn't have gone in there if you had caught it like you were supposed to. You get it."

When we finally settled the argument by the prevailing kid-logic, the unlucky party usually stood stock still, staring at the object of his quest as it lay couched in the bed of impending doom. He remained so for some moments until he figured out a plan of rescue. There were two basic strategies: stealth or speed. The first involved sneaking through the garden as carefully and quietly as you could, like a cat burglar; the second, making a mad dash followed by a quick grab and a hasty retreat. It really didn't matter which approach we used. The flower lady almost always caught the person who invaded her property. It was as if alarms went off the minute a ball entered her yard. She would wait, out of sight, hidden behind a curtain or poised behind a door, for her prey to penetrate her territory and come within reach. Then, just before the unfortunate soul grabbed the ball—that brief period when it was too late to turn back and before the culprit could steal the prize and run—she would attack.

We were always afraid that she had a gun and might shoot us while we rescued our ball, but we never saw one. In our saner moments we were afraid she might hurt us with a stick, a hoe, a rake, or a shovel. We knew she had those and could wield them with deadly precision, for we'd actually seen her using those lethal instruments, albeit against nature.

Despite our fears, none of us suffered more than a tongue-lashing and a bruised ego for invading her garden.

"What are you doing in my yard?" she would scream in outrage as if she didn't know.

The culprit froze under her hateful glare like a frightened deer caught in the beam of an oncoming car.

"Nuh . . . Nuh . . . Nothing," the trapped child often said, giving the automatic reply that kids and criminals use when they're caught in the act. "Just getting my ball."

"You know better than to play ball around here. You're killing my flowers!"

We didn't know better, and we weren't killing her flowers, but no one dared say it.

"I spend hours working, trying to make my yard look pretty," she would complain as if we didn't know this, "and you trample all over my beautiful flowers! Take your ball and play somewhere else!" she screamed at the top of her lungs, with fire in her eyes.

"Yes Ma'am," the trapped boy would say, escaping the hateful glare as quickly as possible by retreating hastily from her yard.

Another of our neighbors who had real character was someone we called "Jughead." We called him this because of his curiously misshapen head. Not that it was shaped exactly like a jug, but it was obvious that the combination of a narrow birth canal and a doctor's cruel forceps had left their permanent mark. His head was kind of triangular in shape, almost like a wedge of cheese that had the sharp point sliced off. He had a narrow face, behind which his head broadened until you got to the back, where it curved to resemble the rounded part of the wedge of cheese. His ears stuck out like the handles of a teacup. He was as skinny as a rail, with long arms, long legs, big hands, and big feet. He always wore "floods"—pants that were too short and ended high on the ankle. We called them floods because they were so short they wouldn't get wet if there were ever a flood. Seeing five inches of ankle between his cuffs and his shoes exaggerated the size of his already huge feet.

Jughead had two scrawny little bowlegged twin sisters who were just as skinny as he was. Their mother, in contrast, was tremendously over-weight. She probably weighed at least three times as much as Jughead and the twins put together. She looked as if she weighed at least three hundred pounds. We used to joke that the reason she was so fat and they were so skinny was that she ate all their food. And even when they did get food she made them burn it off by running around doing errands for her while she sat on the porch fanning herself.

Jughead and his family raised chickens. Chickens! Right there in the project and right in their own backyard. It must have been illegal—against the law and against project rules—but they did it anyway. They were the kind of people who didn't seem to care what anybody else thought. They made their own rules, and they lived by them. I don't remember much about the chickens except the day they were slaughtered.

I came home that day to find blood on the lawn—lots of thick, co-agulated blood exuding a sickly sweet smell. The sight and smell turned my stomach. Before I could ask, my brother, Colin, exploded with the excitement of telling me the tale.

"You should have seen it!" he exclaimed, "—how they killed the chickens!" He paused, waiting for my response. When I looked at him in wide-eyed amazement, he continued, the words gushing forth like water from a fireman's hose.

"They were running around with no heads! Jughead would take a chicken, grab it by the head, and swing it around until the neck snapped. Then his ma would take the butcher knife and cut the head clean off. And then the chicken would run all around the yard with blood squirting out of its neck until it died. You shoulda been here! You wouldn't believe it."

I didn't believe it until my mom confirmed the story.

"It was awful," she said, half laughing and half crying. "Mrs. Stewart barking orders at her kids, and all those chickens squawking and raising a ruckus until they were caught! And then the chickens running around the yard—our yard—getting blood all over everything. Why couldn't they stay in their own yard?" she said plaintively, knowing full well that headless chickens have absolutely no respect for property lines.

We may not have liked Mrs. Stewart and her underfed kids, but the family had a certain amount of character, and they were familiar. And we may not have liked the flower lady, but at least she was a known, predictable quantity. We knew when she would appear, what she was likely to say, and what she cared about.

Together, this odd assortment of characters gave us a feeling of community. Our neighborhood was quite social in many ways. When we took family walks on hot summer evenings, we'd exchange greetings and pleasantries with the residents sitting on their front stoops as we passed by. People looked up from their gardens, barbecue grills, or porches and said hello, or made pleasant conversation. We didn't always know their names, but we smiled, made friendly gestures, and shared the news of the day. In the year before we left, the people on our block met together and formed a block club that sponsored parties and dances.

The children had their own informal club. We used to gather on weekends and summer afternoons and evenings in the large, grassy courtyard.

This courtyard was bounded on three sides by long rows of connected housing units. On the fourth side were a parking area and the street. Most of the time when we gathered we played the normal, innocent yet exciting games of childhood. We might play hide-and-seek. Sometimes, if our numbers were great enough, we divided into teams and played red rover until we dropped from exhaustion.

Sometimes our games were not so innocent. One of our not-so-innocent pastimes was rock throwing. We threw mainly at empty bottles in one of the fields near the Gardens. When we tired of stationary objects we turned to water bugs that skated across the surface of the stagnant ponds. Cars driving down the street provided even more challenging excitement, at least until my brother finally hit one. The car he unfortunately hit screeched to a stop, and my brother ran like hell to escape the clutches of the angry off-duty police officer who emerged. While my brother temporarily escaped because he was smart enough to run in a direction away from home, I ran straight home, and the policeman followed me. Needless to say, my mother was mortified to learn that we had a habit of throwing rocks at cars. Yet she didn't spank us. She helped us to visualize the consequences that the people in the cars might experience—damaged paint, expensive dents, broken windows, a panicked driver, a serious automobile accident. Somehow we felt guiltier and more shameful without a spanking. She was good with words; we never threw rocks at cars again.

I am horrified now as I remember some of our escapades. My brother and I, despite my parents' best efforts, seem to have lacked any sense of social responsibility or conscience. One evening neighbors on the other side of the block threw a party. They danced beneath colored lights strung from the trees and played some of the popular music of the era. Under the cover of darkness my brother and I decided it would be fun to throw stones into the crowd. We thought our bombardment was ineffective and unnoticed. It was so dark we couldn't even see where the rocks landed. They had no noticeable effect as far as we could tell—until suddenly out of the shadows several human figures came charging around the corner.

Apparently our missiles had attracted enough attention to bring a scouting party to investigate their source. The scouting party left the group unnoticed by us and sneaked around behind the buildings to our hiding place on the next corner. We tried to run, but the older children easily captured us. They led us against our will to our parents, who properly chastised us for our delinquent action. That was one of my most blatant acts of disregard for social mores. I felt thoroughly ashamed of myself and never again did anything else that showed such a wanton lack of concern for other human beings.

That is, except for the block fights. Each individual block in the projects had a number. We lived on block 9. Across the street sprawled block 13, where we had lived before moving to block 9. As children of the projects, we possessed a strong sense of territoriality. If you lived on block 9 you were regarded as an enemy alien by block 13 children. I always felt a certain degree of apprehension when I traveled through other blocks. I knew it was enemy territory, and I believed the rumors about children being beaten up by gangs because they were on the wrong block.

Occasionally, these mutual feelings of hostility and mistrust erupted into violent rock wars. Scores of children on one block hurled bricks, rocks, and pieces of pavement at the children of another block. These rock wars excited me. With little regard for the very real danger of getting smashed in the face with a hunk of cement, my friends and I gleefully joined the fray. We had no more concern for our safety than if we were joining a snowball fight. I thoroughly enjoyed heaving stones at the faceless enemy across the street and ducking behind parked cars to dodge incoming missiles. Like many modern wars, there was never a clear winner or loser. Thus my greatest disappointment came not from losing or being injured but from being forced to retire from the battle when it was ended by disapproving parents. The hostility that existed between children on different blocks was only one of the ways that us-and-them thinking affected me.

In later years I learned many forms of us-and-them thinking: rich versus poor, educated versus uneducated, men versus women, Democrats versus Republicans, saints versus sinners, the saved versus the damned. And of course the most troublesome form of us-and-them thinking: Black versus White.

At that time the troubles of our divided world were only beginning to impinge upon my innocent mind. More than anything else, my memories of that period are filled with the warmth of my family's love, the wonderful diversity of characters in the housing project, and the excitement of simple childhood adventures. Despite the trials we experienced, they were happy years for my family.

2

"You White, Ain't You?"

My EARLY RECOLLECTIONS OF RACE are clearly stamped in my memory with the ink of embarrassment. As an eight-year-old, I had just started third grade. During kindergarten, first grade, and second grade, I had been conscious of color and of race but had only a dawning awareness of the social nuances of a racially divided society. My classmates and teachers were all various shades of brown, but I don't remember categorizing them as "Black" or "Negro" back then. The way that I looked at people changed, however, in the third grade.

On a bright, clear, crisp autumn morning, just before school, the children were beginning to line up outside of our two-story school building. We thrilled in anticipation of rushing in at the sound of the bell. We all wanted to be first—first to take his coat off and get into his seat. It wasn't that we were eager to learn; no, school was drudgery. Rather, we wanted the honor of being first. Not necessarily first in math, first in reading, or first in life. Just to be first—ahead of everyone else. First in line, first in the building, and first in your seat. These little firsts were enough. We didn't know about the big firsts that are associated with power, status, money, and great achievements. Back then, being the first to get to your classroom seat was enough.

I stood in line behind a boy named Melvin as he turned and smiled up at me. Melvin was shorter than I, younger than I, and darker than I. In contrast to my café au lait skin color, his skin tones were rich chocolate, the color of a Hershey's bar. His hair was cropped short, typical of the hairstyle that Blacks wore in 1957. My looks, however, were distinctly atypical. If one were to try to identify my race by hair color and texture alone, he would probably say I was Caucasian. My facial features and skin color revealed the rest of my family background. My lips, while definitely not as broad or as thick as my African ancestors', might be described as somewhat full were they on the background of a White face. I thought my nose was a dead giveaway of the secrets of my heritage. While it was not as broad and flat as the stereotypical Black nose, neither was it as long and pointed as Caucasian noses generally are. It was more or less medium length and somewhat bulbous—neither a Negro nose nor a Caucasian nose, but something in between. Melvin, on the other hand, like most other children in the project, was clearly Negro. From the tight curls of his well-groomed but coarse hair, past the tip of his wide, flat nose, through the breadth of his broad lips, there was no mistaking his racial identity.

We were both in the third grade. I don't really know if he was younger in years, but he seemed boyish to me, somewhat impish. As we stood in line, waiting for the bell that would signal the start of our morning race to be first, thoughts of racial heritage were far from my mind. I was simply enjoying the beauty of the clear blue sky and the warmth of the Indian summer sun. Melvin, however, must have been contemplating my unique appearance.

Standing in line in front of me, he turned around with his back to the building to face me. He looked me over rather thoughtfully, his eyes sparkling, and then without warning asked me a question in a somewhat quizzical and accusing tone.

"You White, ain't you?"

Shocked by the question, I hid my surprise behind an impassive mask. By that time I had learned from my father's example how to hide my feelings. Why did he ask me that question? Where did he get the idea that I was "White"? Although there was only a little accusation in his tone, I felt that there was something wrong. His question unleashed deep feelings of anxiety buried within my psyche. I suddenly felt different from him and the other children. I squirmed with discomfort. After an awkward silence I spoke.

"I'm a mulatto," I said in controlled, measured tones that belied my true state of anxiety.

He looked at me with blank, uncomprehending eyes.

I covered my embarrassment with a carefully worded explanation of my racial background. I had developed a tendency early in life to hide my feelings behind intellectual showmanship. I drew upon the reservoir of racial knowledge my parents had given me in some previous and heretofore forgotten discussion.

"My mother is White," I continued, "and my father is Black. So I'm half White and half Black. That's what a mulatto is—someone who's half-and-half."

I didn't know then that "mulatto" also meant "little mule" in Spanish or that the term stemmed from the idea that mixing Blacks and Whites was like breeding horses with donkeys to produce mules. All I knew was that mulatto was the term my parents taught me to apply to mixed children like myself.

The look on Melvin's face changed from incomprehension to disbelief. He didn't say a word. He probably thought I was inventing my Black racial heritage to cover up the fact that I was really White. It was as if it were normal to be Black and White people were anomalies one saw occasionally in buses or stores. I guess Melvin, having been raised in a housing project that was 99 percent Black, thought that the rest of the world was that way too. And of course a "mulatto" was almost beyond the realm of imagination because Blacks and Whites didn't even mix socially, let alone marry and have children. So, in his mind, I had to be lying about this half-and-half stuff to cover up the fact that I was White.

That ended the conversation for that day and forever as far as Melvin was concerned. Our lives were quickly taken over by the demands of school and by the exciting release and relief of playground activities. Melvin and I never talked of race again. But it remained a subject that continually perplexed me from my early years in Chicago through my college years in Ann Arbor and into my adult years in the small town of Benton Harbor, Michigan.

My thoughts concerning Melvin and his conclusions about race were not my only observations on the subject. I knew by then that the predominantly Black Altgeld Gardens community was sandwiched between two all-White communities—Rosedale to the north, and Riverdale to the south.

Living in the Gardens was more like living in a small town than living in a big city, even though technically we were within the city limits of Chicago. The population of our small enclave consisted of no more than a few thousand residents. In many respects it was a self-contained community. We had our own schools, a drugstore, grocery store, dime store, library, and, loosely speaking, our own parks. We had an identity as a community. People were relaxed and friendly toward each other.

We were self-contained socially but not economically. The Gardens offered a few jobs to people—store clerks, stock boys, maintenance people, and so forth—but the majority of residents who worked had to leave our rural island for jobs in the more urban parts of the city. We were also forced to go downtown for any major shopping and for any cultural events other than block parties.

In those years our family did not own a car. We could not afford to replace the car that had been destroyed in my father's horrible accident. When the consumer necessity of acquiring goods not available at the local five-and-dime struck, or when our parents wanted to expose us children to cultural experiences not available in our ghetto, the family would make trips to downtown Chicago by bus. Most of the trips were for shopping. However, there were enough cultural trips that my dearest and fondest memories of downtown Chicago are centered around the library, the Art Institute, and the museums, rather than department stores.

Yet even clearer than the memories of downtown Chicago are the images and feelings evoked by memories of the bus ride to and from the city's business district.

We lived in a time and a place in which Blacks could sit wherever they wanted on the bus. It was not a question of being discriminated against or being forced to sit at the back of the bus. What I remember most is the attention my family commanded.

The bus rides always started at the bus stop near the well-littered parking lot of our small project shopping center. As all bus rides seem to, ours usually started with a long wait. The stop was at the end of the line. It was the turnaround point at the southern end of the route from downtown Chicago to our remote stop at the southern end of the city.

As soon as the bus arrived at our stop, all of the remaining passengers got off. My family and the other project residents boarded an empty bus. We enjoyed the opportunity to sit anywhere we wanted. Wherever we sat, we usually all sat together and waited until it was time for the bus driver to start heading back downtown. Other people sat where they chose: friends with friends, family with family, loners alone.

When the bus started on its long, winding journey, my mother was the only White person on the bus. But there was nothing unusual about that from my point of view; she was the only White person in the projects—at least she was the only White person I ever saw. As the bus wound its way past the fields and factories along the banks of the Calumet and into residential areas of the city, more and more people boarded. At first the people who entered the bus were all Black. Then mixed groups of riders got on the bus. These groups were partly White and partly

Black. Then we came to stops where all the people who entered the bus were White.

One curious pattern I noticed when people selected seats on the bus was this: As new people visually scanned the aisle of the bus looking for the best place to sit, Black people sat with Black people and White people sat with White people. Although no one ever told me, I knew intuitively that there was a reason for this. Black people and White people were uncomfortable with each other. People feel comfortable with familiar surroundings and familiar people; like naturally gravitates toward like. But I knew there was more to it than that. Don't ask me how I knew. I don't know how I knew. Maybe by intuition or a subtle form of emotional osmosis, or perhaps by body language. By whatever means, I knew somehow that Whites did not like Blacks and therefore sat with other Whites, and that Blacks often held a host of emotions toward Whites, including fear, mistrust, anger. I was beginning to develop those feelings as well. Blacks therefore sat with other Blacks. I think I also knew that beneath the mild exterior of many of the calm White faces was a boiling cauldron of hatred for Blacks. Only later did I learn that many Blacks held a similarly seething hatred for Whites. And still later I learned of the tragic hatred that many Blacks hold toward themselves. The rule that Blacks sat with Blacks and Whites sat with Whites had only two exceptions. The first exception occurred when a Black person or a White person got on the bus and all of the seats next to people of his color were taken. Then he or she would sit next to a passenger of a different color. The other exception was my family. We created an integrated seating pattern wherever we went.

The people in the Gardens must have become used to our racially mixed family. I don't remember encountering any stares when we were in the project or at the beginning of the bus ride. It was only as the bus left our little sheltered community that we began to attract attention. Invariably, when people outside of the projects got on the bus, their eyes were irresistibly drawn to us. While they took pains to appear as if they were looking for a seat, it was obvious that they had to tear their eyes away from us in order to actually find one and sit down.

We must have been quite startling: my blue-eyed, fair-skinned, beautiful mom, with her coffee ground–brown, well-groomed, kinky-haired husband, and their four café au lait, brown-eyed children.

The stares we attracted diminished as the bus filled and it became harder to tell who was attached to whom. But the brief respite from the unwelcome stares was only temporary, for when we arrived at our destination and my parents herded us off the bus, all eyes were once again riveted to us.

It was literally impossible for us to have normal shopping or cultural excursions in Chicago. Wherever we went, we attracted attention. Heads turned in astonishment and disbelief as we left the bus and walked down the street. People seemed to abandon the restraints of courtesy that normally prevent unabashed staring in public. Whatever street we turned down, whatever building we entered, the prying eyes of an unaccepting public invaded our lives.

However discomfiting the stares were, they were not enough to prevent my persistent and courageous parents from exercising their duty to expose us to the inexpensive cultural experiences that Chicago offered. I have vivid memories of touring the Art Institute, the Museum of Science and Industry, the Field Museum, and the Shedd Aquarium. I enjoyed our family field trips and looked forward to them despite the fact that our mixed racial menagerie often attracted more attention than the formal museum exhibits.

When we returned to the privacy and safety of our cement-floored project apartment, we made light of the attention we attracted. We laughed about the people who nearly fell out of their bus seats, twisted their necks, or stumbled over themselves in their effort to get a better view. We mirthfully joked with one another about how people must have thought of us, referring to ourselves as a "traveling circus," "sideshow," "zoo," or "freaks." Even so, we always took the attitude that other people's outrageous reactions to us were their problem, not ours. My parents made us believe that there was nothing wrong with us. The society that surrounded us was racist, and the shame of racism belonged to society, not to us. Mom and Dad explained that in this country Blacks and Whites rarely mixed socially and that interracial marriages were almost unheard of. That's why people stared. The explanations helped us understand the reason for the stares. They also taught us to use humor to turn the pain and embarrassment of ostracism into a joyful, even self-affirming, experience.

Although I knew interracial marriage was extremely rare, I didn't realize in my Chicago years that it was taboo. I didn't know anything about the mythological attraction between Black men and White women. I didn't know that White women were supposed to be untouchable when it came to Black men. I didn't know that many White people were enraged at the very thought of mixed marriages and interracial relationships. I didn't know that some Whites lived in fear that their progeny might date and marry outside of their race. I didn't know that my parents' marriage had been illegal in twenty-seven states at the time of their wedding. I didn't know that my parents had been chased out of Woodstock when their neighbors had discovered that the GI married to my mother was Black. I didn't know about the thousands of Black boys and men who had been beaten, lynched, and burned because they dared to look at a White woman in the wrong way, or because of some imagined offense to the pristine purity of White women.

My parents were aware of these harsh facts, but they shielded us from them by bolstering our pride, lifting our spirits, and making light of those whose staring eyes silently chipped away at our fragile sense of self-worth.

Nevertheless, I think that the thousands of staring eyes must have taken their toll over time. As tiny bits of seemingly harmless dust borne by gentle winds can eventually wear away the surface of the hardest rock, so the silently expressed opinions of the thousands of glaring, staring eyes can eventually alter the character of even the strongest person.

Throughout these years I developed a growing awareness of the extent to which American society is racially divided. In most cities where there is a substantial ethnic minority, the minorities are confined to certain areas. They are usually separated from the majority population by some clearly visible geographic characteristic—a railroad track, a street, or, as in the case of Altgeld Gardens, a river—the Calumet River.

Across the murky expanse of the Calumet River lay the gleaming white city of Riverdale. I can't tell you much about it. I only visited it once, and I was too scared to accurately perceive, understand, or remember anything but my own fear-tinged personal impressions. Riverdale was not actually white. It was, however, "white" in the sense that it was relatively clean, compared to the dirty projects in which I lived. It was also "white" in the sense that many of the houses were painted white in contrast to the dingy brown brick of the projects. But—most important—it was "White" in the sense that all of the residents were White. There were no Mexican-Americans, no American Indians, and absolutely no Blacks. None. Zip. Zilch. Nada. Not one. Just bone-white Caucasians.

I don't know how, or where, or when I learned it. I don't know who taught me this, nor whether they were friends, family, or total strangers. All I know for certain is that sometime before I was eight years old, sometime in those few short but crucial years in my development, under circumstances I can only vaguely remember, these impressions were thoroughly ingrained in me: that the residents of Riverdale were White and that many held a deep, abiding hatred for Blacks.

I have mental images that, to me, prove the hatred I saw being expressed toward Blacks—images that are now permanently etched on the once blank slate of my mind. I don't know where these images came from, nor do I know whether they are actual memories of my experiences, images formed from stories others told me, or merely creations conjured by the mind of a frightened child. But they are real to me regardless of their origin, for if they are not actually based on concrete facts, they are most certainly rooted in the spiritually sick reality of a racist society.

The images are simple. They involve two children walking over the bridge that led from a road near the projects and across the river to Riverdale. One of the children is me, the other is my brother, Colin. He is about nine years old, and I am about seven. We are nervous and excited about the adventure of exploring this new territory. It is our first time venturing into this unknown White land. We don't get more than a hundred yards into this strange new land before fear overcomes us and we decide to head back.

We turn around and head toward home. A car drives past us as we head toward the bridge and the comfort and safety of familiar territory on the other side. It is an old car from the late 1940s. On the passenger side of the car a young White male with a tormented look of hatred on his face shouts something. I hear the word "nigger" ringing in my ears. As the car speeds past, I panic for an instant, worried that it will stop, that the passengers will get out and we will be harmed. But the car speeds past, and we are safe.

We are halfway across the bridge now—halfway home, halfway to safety. Behind us, near where bridge meets land, is a small group of boys. They are our age or perhaps a little older. I don't know where they came from. They are throwing rocks at us. This time I don't hear the words—

I feel them. I feel the cold hatred. Whether the words are actually uttered or not, I don't know, but I feel them in the very core of my being. They are more powerful, painful, and damaging than the rocks that are thrown. They say, "Get out of here, Nigger! Go back where you belong!" None of the rocks hit us, for we are too far away—just the words. We are scared, and we run, afraid for our lives. Back in the safety of the Gardens we say nothing to each other. We are too shocked to know how to process the incident. We also say nothing to our parents because we know that we have gone into forbidden territory and don't want to be punished for it.

These images are simple. They don't depict the dehumanization and cruelty of four hundred years of slavery. They don't show the atrocities, the burnings, the rapes, the mutilations and lynchings that America ignores as if they were all in the past. But they are important. They were permanently embedded in the mind of an eight-year-old mulatto in the city of Chicago during the 1950s. They proved to him beyond a shadow of a doubt that Riverdale was a dangerous place for Blacks.

My early experiences created fears and anxieties that lasted well into my adult life. As a child in Chicago I had the persistent feeling that our housing project was safer than the surrounding communities because the Black people who lived there accepted me and the White people who lived elsewhere didn't. Later, when we moved to Detroit, I had similar feelings. Detroit was safe, I felt, because it was inhabited by Black people. The all-White suburbs were filled with White people who had moved there primarily to get away from Blacks. Even though I was different from other Blacks because my mom was White, I was Black and felt most comfortable in a community of Blacks.

3

A Different World

THE MOVE TO DETROIT MARKED a major change in the outward circumstances of our family. It came suddenly. I had no idea where we were going, and I didn't know the purpose of the move. All I remember is that one day we piled all of our worldly possessions into a U-Haul trailer and left town.

Turney's father pulled the U-Haul because we were too poor to afford our own car and professional movers were totally out of the question. My brother and I went with my father by car while my sisters went with my mom by train.

We arrived in Detroit in the middle of the night. I don't remember much about that night except staggering up the stairs of an old two-story house and stumbling into bed. In the morning I awakened to a whole new world.

Instead of living in a project on the outer edge of Chicago, we were now living in a house in the center of Detroit. No longer in the middle of the winding labyrinth of project streets, we were in the midst of a vast grid of square city blocks. We had traded the slow trickle of two-lane residential traffic for the fast streams of rush-hour commerce along Woodward Avenue and John R. Street. The familiar faces of old friends and neighbors were replaced by the unfamiliar faces of our new neighbors.

We were in a drab, low-income Black neighborhood with houses so close together you could barely walk between them. The postage-stamp backyards made us miss the large, open courts provided by our old projects. Instead of being built from actual bricks, the wood frame houses were covered with brick-patterned tar paper. We really had no place to play but the sidewalks and streets. This was classic inner city. And to top it all off, we had to deal with grouchy, beer-drinking Uncle Bob, my grandmother's brother who came with the house.

These were all major changes, but the biggest change loomed ahead of us. We stayed in our new home on Harmon Street in Detroit for only three months and didn't even bother to enroll in school. There was hardly enough time to explore the neighborhood or make new friends before, to my relief, we moved again.

The plan had always been that we would stay with my grandmother in a new home she had just purchased on Virginia Park Street. The house on Harmon, her old home, was simply our temporary residence while we waited for the new house to become available. I did not know about the plan so I was totally surprised when, after only three months on Harmon, we moved to another part of Detroit. My surprise grew when I later discovered that Grandmother would not only be sharing her new home with us but with Uncle Bob as well. He followed right along with us from Harmon Street. Although we paid my grandmother rent for the privilege of staying there, and we had to share the house with both her and Uncle Bob, from my perspective, the new home belonged to our family since we occupied most of the space and hardly ever saw Uncle Bob or Grandmother. Uncle Bob secluded himself in his room with his beer and his crippled cat, making daily excursions to the kitchen for food and drink. Grandmother had a live-in job at the Michigan State Training School for Girls, a correctional facility in Adrian, ninety miles away. She only came home a few days each month.

The home that she purchased for us made our previous Chicago home seem like a hovel. In the projects, we had lived in a small three-bedroom home with concrete floors, a living room, a kitchen, a single bathroom, and no basement. Our new home had that much space on the first floor alone. It was a real mansion. Downstairs there was a living room, a dining room, a kitchen, a den, and two bathrooms. Upstairs there were five bedrooms and two bathrooms. On the third floor there were two additional fully finished rooms. Altogether, there were eleven rooms, not counting the basement, which offered a partially finished recreation room. It was more than I'd ever imagined.

We nearly went wild with excitement as my parents, my siblings, and I ran from room to room discovering the opulent treasures of our new palace: crystal chandeliers, two fireplaces, stained glass windows, hardwood floors, a staircase with a landing and window seat, a back staircase, a second-floor balcony, walk-in closets, French doors here, sliding doors there, wooden paneling, bay windows, a laundry room, a wine cellar, a recreation room, three back doors, a fenced-in backyard, and a two-car garage. It was more than my limited experience had allowed me to imagine. I had had no idea that such houses existed.

The biggest change, however, was not in the size of the house that we lived in. It was in the color of the neighbors and in the character of our relationship with them. We were the only Black family on the street. Everyone else around us was White. And there was always a distance between us.

We didn't experience any open hostility from our neighbors. Like many middle-class Americans, they were much too reserved for such open displays of emotion. Instead, we experienced isolation. No one welcomed us when we moved in. No one brought us cakes, or bread, or any other welcoming gifts. No one befriended us. We were the only people of color on our street.

In Detroit, there were no trash piles and no Turner Mathis with whom to share the joy of exploring. We didn't have the hordes of friends or even the wide open spaces we needed to play our large group games. There were no flower ladies in our neighborhood and no one with whom to share the blame for an out-of-control ball. There were no block parties and no bowlegged twins, no headless chickens and no block fights. To make matters worse, there were no candy ladies in our new Detroit neighborhood. In the Gardens, we may not have liked all of our neighbors, but at least we knew them.

Our new Detroit neighbors were completely unknown to us. People kept to themselves. They stayed in their homes and didn't even interact with each other as far as I could tell. Our neighbors seemed to be mostly older people whose children, if they had any, were grown and gone. We never went to their homes, and they never came to ours. They were White faces who appeared at certain times: They took care of their lawns, they walked to and from their cars, they got mail from their mailboxes. If they ever spoke, whatever they said was so insignificant it didn't register. They were the embodiment of politeness but without personality. We never knew who they were or what their families were like. They never shared their hopes and dreams with us, and we, in return, never shared ours with them.

I really missed the family-like intimacy of our old neighborhood, but moving to Detroit had its positive side. We moved away from an area that became part of the ubiquitous culture of poverty that envelopes housing projects today. By moving into a middle-class neighborhood and lifestyle, we also escaped some of our tendencies toward juvenile delinquency and gang behaviors.

The days when the excitement of playing or fighting with large groups of children were forever ended when we moved to Detroit. When we first moved into our new mansion, there were three children on our street. My brother and I made friends with the two boys on our block, Milton and Gene. The friendship lasted only a short time, however, because their family soon moved away. That left only one White child in the neighborhood and no Black children outside of our family. Fortunately for me, he became my good friend.

My years of living in the house on Virginia Park were dominated by that single friendship with the only boy who lived on our street, a White boy of Serbian heritage named Joey Caravic. He was one year younger than I and about four inches shorter. He wore a crew cut and came from a conservative, racist family. In retrospect, all that we really had in common was the fact that we were the only two kids our age who lived on the street.

Shortly after we met, Joey informed me that we could only play in his house when his mom's live-in boyfriend, known as "Uncle Frank," was not at home. He told me that Uncle Frank didn't want "niggers" in his house. Uncle Frank's attitude never really bothered me. On the few occasions when I accidentally encountered him while visiting Joey, he was courteous, even friendly. I knew of his attitude toward Blacks only through Joey. I accepted it as a fact of life that there were many Whites who outwardly accepted Blacks but privately used the "N" word or held deeply rooted racist attitudes. Joey said Frank accepted me because I was different from other "niggers." Like many Whites, he accepted me as an individual, thinking that I was somehow different from other Blacks. He didn't realize that his image of other Blacks was a stereotype that few, if any, Blacks really fit. Instead of challenging his stereotype, he chose to view me as an exception to the rule. So I played happily with Joey at his house, giving little thought to Uncle Frank when he was not around.

Unlike some of my more barbaric childhood activities in the Gardens, my childhood pursuits with Joey were slightly more socially acceptable— more middle class. Instead of throwing rocks at people whom we imagined were the enemy, we threw rocks at each other's toy soldiers. Instead of swimming naked in the murky shallows of the Calumet River, we'd go to a public beach on Belle Isle and swim in bathing suits in the polluted effluents of the Detroit River. We no longer heaved missiles at bottles to break them; we shot at them with Daisy BB guns. The search for "good things" was redirected from our neighbors' trash piles to the neighborhood five-and-dime store.

But there were other more important differences. To move from the Gardens to Detroit was to move from a close-knit community to the city. One single, solitary White friend replaced the masses of children with whom I had played and fought in the Gardens. There were other children in the neighborhood, but they lived on other streets—Euclid, Seward, or across the John Lodge Expressway—streets that I traveled on and through, but which were forever filled with strangers. I wasn't lonely, mind you; in fact, I spent very few lonely hours at that time in my life. Between the company I kept with my brother and sisters, Joey Caravic, and, of course, my parents, I was quite busy. Still, it was different having just one real friend on the street with whom to play. It was different living in the city and having no community. This was the beginning of a period of social isolation that would characterize the rest of my formative years.

4

School Years

WHILE JOEY CARAVIC WAS MY ONLY real friend outside of the family during most of the years that we lived in the house on Virginia Park Street, I had many school acquaintances. Our neighborhood school, Fairbanks Elementary, was mostly Black with a handful of Whites in each class. I didn't realize it at the time, but when I first started at Fairbanks in the middle of the third grade in 1957, it was my first interracial school experience.

My school friends at Fairbanks were both Black and White. I usually paired up with only one person at a time. That person became my "best" friend. Sometimes he was Black, and sometimes he was White. It made no difference to me.

With females, however, it did seem to matter. I knew by then that White females were untouchable, not just in the physical sense, but in relationships, too. I was familiar with the fate of Emmett Till, the fourteen-year-old Black youth who had been killed for allegedly flirting with a young White woman. I knew from discussions with my parents that Blacks in the South had to avert their eyes when passing Whites, especially White females, or risk negative and possibly catastrophic consequences. I was aware that Black men were looked upon as being beneath White women. I knew from my parents' experience that interracial relationships were abhorrent to most of White America. Nevertheless, the females I was most attracted to were either light-skinned Blacks or Whites.

At the time, I never stopped to think about my attraction to the White-looking girls. In retrospect, I think many factors were involved. Perhaps the most important reason is the largely self-perpetuating racist indoctrination that American society fosters. Simply put, it is a fact that being White in America carries more status, class, prestige, and opportunity than being Black. Unfortunately, Blacks know all too well that their skin color automatically and permanently consigns them to second-class citizenship in this great land of equality. But there was more to my attraction to White females than the conditioned feeling that Whites are better-off than Blacks. There was also the indoctrination that we are all subjected to through television, magazines, and billboards that Caucasian features are more attractive than Negroid features. Add to this social indoctrination the fact that my mother was White and—if you believe Freud—that every boy has a primal Oedipal attraction for his mom.

Finally, I think that there was more cultural similarity between me and my White classmates than between me and my Black classmates. Culturally, I was middle-class White: Both of my parents were college educated, I spoke Standard English, I had middle-class mannerisms, and my attitude toward school was middle class. It seemed natural for me to be attracted to people who had the same mannerisms, speech patterns, attitudes, and values as I did. None of my Black classmates looked like me or spoke like me. I sometimes wonder how my social development might have differed had I had more exposure to middle-class Black America. Perhaps I would have had a stronger Black identity or would have felt more strongly attracted to my Black female classmates. Unfortunately, there were few middle-class Blacks in my school.

Although I had feelings for girls at this stage of my life in elementary school, whatever attraction I felt never developed beyond a crush. I knew which girls I "liked" and talked about them with my best friend, but I never directly communicated my feelings of puppy love to any of them. At that age boys in my school simply did not do that, because they knew it would result in embarrassment and teasing. My boldest assertion of feelings for the opposite sex came when I was in sixth grade. I signed Barbara Portee's autograph book, "To My Future Wife."

Barbara Portee was beautiful. She was a light-skinned Black with a delicate nose and thin lips. She had long, straight brown hair that hung nearly to her waist. In fact, she was so close in appearance to being White, I wondered if maybe she were. But there was a yellowish tinge to her skin that made me think otherwise. She was shy and never spoke up in class. I have no idea what her personality was like underneath her shyness. Somehow I got her phone number—whether directly from her, through a friend, or from the phone book, I don't remember. I called her up, and when she answered, I didn't know what to say. Between her shyness and mine we were incapable of carrying on a decent phone conversation. Because of our mutual immaturity, the relationship never went any further. All this is to say that I was attracted to her purely because of her appearance. She was the Whitest-looking Black in my sixth-grade class. I never questioned my attraction to White-looking females until years later, when I learned how thoroughly racism pervades our society, and how I had internalized many of the values projected by the dominant White society on Blacks—including standards of beauty.

Despite my feelings of loss for my old community in the Gardens, my elementary years in Detroit were happy. They lasted from the spring of 1957, when I left Chicago in the middle of the third grade, until 1960, when I graduated from Fairbanks Elementary School at the end of the sixth grade. Even though I didn't have the mobs of friends that I had had in Chicago, I did have some friends at school and at least one good friend in my neighborhood. I enjoyed school because I was the kind of student teachers loved. I did my work, I never broke the rules, I always knew the answers to questions, and I was eager to answer. I nearly always got straight A's without effort.

After school I filled my time in a variety of ways. If I wasn't playing with Joey or one of my brothers or sisters, I read or played alone. We often played childhood games in the backyard or took long walks exploring the city. When we wanted to go farther, we went on bike explorations. We often rode or walked the three-mile distance to downtown Detroit or the eight-mile distance to Belle Isle—the island park in the middle of the Detroit River.

Those were years when I felt relatively comfortable with who I was and what I was doing. However, two race-related incidents that occurred during those years stand out in my memory.

Not too long after we moved to the house on Virginia Park Street, my brother and I were exploring the neighborhood. We were walking along Woodward Avenue, one of the main streets of Detroit not too far from our home, when we were stopped by two White police officers in a squad car. They questioned us and in a few minutes allowed us to go on about our business. This was the first of many times that we were stopped and questioned just because we were walking down the street. These queries became so routine that I assumed they happened to everyone—that is, until one day, returning from one of our neighborhood excursions, we mentioned to my mom that we'd been stopped again by the police. She was shocked. When we told her that this was only one of many occasions, she was livid. She revealed that she had never been stopped and questioned by the police in her entire life. It was then that it dawned on me that many police have a racist attitude in their approach to public service. Young Black males are either prime suspects for crime or prime targets for harassment.

The other incident occurred in a Black neighborhood far from home. The neighborhood was poor, like so many in Detroit, the houses were run down, and the streets littered with glass. Many houses were vacant, with boarded-up windows. Joey, Colin, and I were on one of our explorations, cruising down the street on our bicycles. We could see a group of about ten Black children on the streets ahead. As we approached the young ruffians, they picked up stones and other pieces of street debris. I knew what was coming—perhaps because I remembered encountering territorial ruffians in Altgeld Gardens. My brother and Joey had no trouble reading the hostile looks and body language. We increased our speed in a frantic effort to avoid the impending hail. Fortunately, the volley was not released until we were well past the juvenile mob. None of the hastily aimed projectiles found their mark. Nevertheless, I was quite frightened by the experience.

I rode away from my attackers with a new lesson engraved on my heart and mind. The experience was reminiscent of more than the block fights in the Gardens. It also reminded me of the incursion my brother and I had made into Riverdale, only this time my attackers were Black.

I began to realize that Whites are not the only people to fear and that police are not the only ones who harbor prejudice. Poor Blacks in any neighborhood you're not familiar with can be every bit as threatening. My young mind did not yet make the connection that only a few years earlier my friends and I had also treated others—people outside our block—in the same hostile way. I did not realize then that buried within the hearts of all of us are the deadly seeds of prejudice against strangers, that the potential for bigotry is universal. Nor did I realize the varieties of prejudice that exist in our society: prejudice of class, prejudice of language, prejudice of culture, and—most insidious of all—prejudice against one's own race—internalized racism.

5

Family Life

FOR MY PARENTS, THE YEARS FROM 1957 to 1963 in Detroit were filled with the hope of continued progress toward making their dreams become reality. Both were overjoyed at the physical beauty of our new home and neighborhood, and both were determined to become teachers as a stepping stone to greater things. My mother had ambitions of changing the world through her writing. My father still had aspirations of earning his master's degree and perhaps joining the State Department as a diplomat. Those were the days when they both still believed in America and cherished the values that they thought America represented. They were encouraged by the Civil Rights movement and the hope that equal educational opportunities would be available for their children and other children of color. They believed in the democratic process and became active in the Democratic Party at the precinct level, believing that their actions would make a difference. They hoped that the progress toward equality seen in the educational arena would extend to the housing and job markets. They were thrilled at the prospect of seeing their children go to integrated schools. Finally, they hoped to establish the same kind of network of friends that had supported and sustained them back in the Gardens.

The house itself was truly a blessing for the family. Although it was old, it was in good condition and had no major problems. There were five bedrooms. Colin and I shared one, our two sisters Linda and Brigid had one, our parents had another, and grandmother and Uncle Bob each had their own. Grandmother worked as a matron at the Michigan State Training School for Girls, a young women's correctional facility in Adrian, Michigan, so we only saw her occasionally on weekends. She kept pretty much to herself, retreating to her bedroom when she came home for visits. Likewise, Uncle Bob kept to himself, staying in his bedroom except when he came out to eat. Neither of them seemed to enjoy using the dining room, living room, or den, so our immediate family had exclusive use of most of the house.

My parents immediately set about making our house on Virginia Park Street into a home. My mother had a flair for interior design. Using furniture donated by her mother and other items that she carefully selected at secondhand furniture stores, she created a beautiful home that was comfortable to live in. Every piece of furniture was thoughtfully placed. Each picture and mirror hung in just the right spot. Small ornamental statues were perfectly poised for effect as if they were in a museum. It was a joy just to sit in the living room and take in the physical beauty of our new surroundings.

My father warmed to the task of maintaining and improving the lawn and gardens. In addition to mowing and weeding, he planted a bed of peonies of which he was particularly proud. At my mom's request he made a beautiful goldfish pond in the back yard, sinking a washtub in the ground, filling it with water, and painstakingly landscaping the area around it. The washtub was meticulously painted so that unless you were really observant, you would not guess that it was a washtub. My parents delighted in ordering dwarf fruit trees from a nursery and planting them in the garden. My father even went so far as to make a compost pile, which he regularly turned and sifted so that we could fertilize our lawn and gardens naturally.

My parents both worked as substitute teachers while my father went to school at Wayne State University. He was in the peculiar position of having four years of successful college experience but no degree. The master's program in which he had earned all of his previous college credits had not required a bachelor's degree, nor did it offer one as a stepping stone toward the final master's degree. Because he had not completed his master's dissertation, he had nothing concrete to show for his four years of study. Fortunately for the family, the Wayne State University School of Education accepted many of his credits, and he was able to work toward a bachelor of arts degree in education. By substitute teaching in the day and taking courses at night, in a short time he earned a bachelor's degree with a teaching certificate.

It was even easier for my mom to become a teacher. With a bachelor's degree in English and experience in substitute teaching, she had no trouble getting her application for a teaching certificate approved.

During the months before they both had full-time work as teachers, my father's mother helped to supplement their meager wages. My parents made modest rental payments to my grandmother, but if they were ever short of money she was there to pick up the slack. By 1960, they were both employed as full-time teachers—she as a high school English teacher, he as a junior high civics teacher.

These were very happy times for our family. For the first time in more than seventeen years of family life since their union in 1943, my parents felt financially secure. As a double-income family, we were able to live comfortably and even buy a car for the first time since my father had totaled the old Hudson back in 1952.

Furthermore, although both parents were working, we managed to spend a lot of time on recreational activities together as a family. Evenings were spent playing the card or board games that we had learned in the Gardens. In addition my father taught us chess, and in desperation for partners, taught us to play bridge as well.

Weekends were frequently spent doing family activities. They would start raucously on Saturday mornings when Colin, Linda, Brigid, and I stormed into our parents' bedroom and piled onto their bed before they were up. We bounced on the bed, tickled and wrestled each other, and made it impossible for my parents to sleep. Their only choice was to laugh and join the fracas. As in the Gardens, we were so energetic in our early morning frolics that on a couple of occasions we broke the wooden slats that supported the mattress and box springs. We had a delightful time. When my grandmother was home, of course, we refrained from such rambunctious morning activities. We knew she needed to rest and dared not incur her wrath with our noisy activities.

Sometimes on weekends we went for family outings, which consisted of piling into the family car and driving around town. My father always drove because my mother didn't have a driver's license. She had not been afraid to travel halfway around the world by herself as a recently graduated student, nor had she been afraid to break all of the social conventions about interracial marriage, but she was afraid to learn to drive a car.

Our favorite place to go was Belle Isle, Detroit's five-square-mile island park. We'd drive around the island and occasionally stop to watch the river traffic. My mother loved to watch large freight ships go by. She'd get a dreamy look on her face as if she were imagining all of the exotic, faraway places that ships sometimes go. She loved to travel and made no secret of the fact that she dreamed of returning to China. When her heart was troubled by family problems or by world events, she would take great solace in riding to Belle Isle to watch the boats go by.

Sometimes instead of going to Belle Isle we would just drive. Some days we'd drive to the country, looking at farms and farm animals. My mother missed country life and always had hopes of someday moving away from the city. She loved wide open spaces and flowers and green plants. My father held similar feelings, although he never spoke of them until years later, when he and my mother bought acres of land in Canada.

My mother was much more vocal about everything than my father was. He would save his words as if they were money in the bank and only allowed them to come out of his mouth in a very guarded fashion, making sure that each word was precisely chosen for the exact meaning he intended to convey. But when the words came out, they were pure gold. He had a rich sense of humor and a prodigious vocabulary, which came from studying the dictionary in his youth. His speech was filled with double entendres and puns, yet when he spoke seriously, you always knew exactly what he meant.

My father often told the story of his attempt to teach my brother the correct word for "pee." At the age of three, Colin was urinating into the toilet. My father, standing nearby, heard Colin refer to his "pee." My father, correcting him by using the proper word, quickly said, "urine." My brother responded proudly, "Mine!"

My father was very concerned with the proper use of language. If you were ever sloppy in your use of language, he questioned you until you realized how stupid you sounded and, shamefaced, corrected yourself. But those occasions were few. One of the things that I remember most about my father, even during those happy years, is his brooding silence, interspersed with occasional sparks of levity kindled by our family activities. In retrospect it is clear to me that the challenge of daily living was overwhelming for my father and that his only source of happiness was my mother and the family he and she had created.

Sometimes we simply drove around the city, through various neighborhoods, looking at houses. We loved to drive through Palmer Woods, which had houses bigger and newer than ours, and Grosse Pointe, the home of those who, from our perspective, were filthy rich. We spoke with envy of the people who lived in homes where the lawns were manicured by gardeners and the servants lived in the carriage houses. We openly dreamed of living like that ourselves someday, not realizing that in many respects the family life we shared was worth far more than anything money could buy.

Although we enjoyed our family outings immensely, there was one very noticeable irregularity. In Detroit, no matter where we went and no matter where we stopped, my father never got out of the car with us. If we stopped at Belle Isle, both parents stayed in the car—she to watch the boats, he to remain in the car without explanation. When we stopped at stores for shopping, my mother took all of us children with her while he waited in the car. We managed to have lots of fun as a family, but after leaving Chicago we never again went to movies, amusement parks, or museums together. Although my father never explained, I knew the reason: He was no longer willing to be a public spectacle. He was unwilling to passively entertain all of the staring strangers we encountered everywhere we went. Though we always had a good time when we were together as a family, our excursions were limited to local car rides—that is, until we met Margaret Zook and her family.

Margaret Zook was a short, blond math teacher who exuded energy from every pore of her pudgy body. She taught in the school where my father landed his first full-time teaching position. An experienced teacher, she was assigned to be his mentor.

Margaret's father had been an active Civil Rights worker—a freedom rider who had put his life on the line by riding buses down South to help desegregate bus stations and lunch counters. On one of his freedom rides he had been beaten senseless by an angry mob of White separatists. The beating paralyzed him and left him confined to a wheelchair for the remainder of his life. Having been raised to act on her belief that people of all races deserve equal treatment, Margaret went out of her way to extend friendship to people of color. She had divorced an abusive first husband several years before meeting our family, and she had two boys and three girls of her own. When she met my father she was dating a Black man, so when she found out that my father's wife was White, she wanted to meet the whole family. Thus began a friendship between our two families that lasted for the rest of my parents' lives.

Margaret's five children were just the right ages to mix socially with our family. Her oldest daughter, Debby, was one year younger than my brother and one year older than I. Billy, a rebellious youth who challenged his mother at every turn, was my age. Emma was a year younger than I and exactly the same age as my younger sister, Brigid. Johnny was a year younger than Emma, and Dorothy, the "baby," was one year younger than Johnny. When our families visited, we were like one big family. We laughed, talked, and played games together. Colin and Debby immediately became romantically involved. Emma and Dorothy competed for Brigid's attention, while Brigid and I competed for Emma's attention. My older sister, Linda, had a wide array of friendships but found no particular social match in the Zook family. Johnny and Billy pretty much kept to themselves, except when they were busy annoying their sisters.

We had many wonderful times with Margaret and her family, but the greatest adventures that we all shared and enjoyed were our family camping experiences. Margaret introduced us all to camping. My parents were financially stable for the first time after nearly two decades of marriage. Driven by her wanderlust, my mom noticed an advertisement in a local magazine offering land for sale in Ontario. It was a hundred acres of woodlands on Manitoulin Island at fourteen dollars an acre. My parents couldn't resist. They were both employed and had recently inherited a small sum of money from my mother's mother. Ignoring all the rules of real estate investment, they purchased the land, sight unseen. When they shared news of this with Margaret, she suggested that we all take a camping trip to see what the land was like.

All of us found the idea exciting. Margaret had camping equipment and camping know-how. Because all of us would have two weeks off from school for spring break, we decided we would go then.

This trip was, for us, the mother of all adventures. It was filled with the excitement of new places, new people, and new experiences. We piled into my parents' newly acquired 1957 Dodge DeSoto and Margaret's Volkswagen van and struck out for Canada. On the first night, we stayed with Margaret's Uncle Oscar in Sault Sainte Marie. On the second night, we stayed in one of the Canadian national parks. At that time of year there were hardly any campers, so we had the campgrounds almost to ourselves. Since it was below freezing at night, we spent lots of time huddled around the campfire or quivering from the chill in the two tents that slept the twelve of us. It was so cold that we slept with our clothes on. We enjoyed sharing the responsibilities of pitching the tents, gathering firewood, tending the fire, cooking, and cleaning—laughing and talking all the while about the experiences of the day.

When we talked and shared experiences, we often laughed at the reactions of others to our strange party of twelve—one Black man traveling with two White women, five White children, and four mongrel-looking half-breeds. People didn't know what to make of us, and we laughed at their consternation.

We spent the third night on Manitoulin Island after finding a small public campground on the banks of Lake Wolsey a few miles from our property. We decided to use the campground as a home base until we had explored the property enough to discover whether it was suitable for camping. It was so cold that night that the water on Lake Wolsey froze near the shore. In the morning we had to break the ice to get water for cooking and cleaning, but for us that was all part of the adventure.

When we finally reached our property on the morning of the fourth day, we were overjoyed. It was beautiful. It was a half-mile back from the main road, but there was a two-rut dirt track that led back to the edge of the property, which consisted of one hundred acres of untouched pines and hardwoods. A stream meandered along the property's edge. Beavers had dammed the stream that ambled along the two ruts that passed as a road, making a large pond. Several beaver mounds studded the pond, giving hints of the life beneath the surface. Wildlife abounded above and below the surface. When we looked carefully we could see a variety of fish in the stream and pond. Animal tracks along the edge of the stream revealed the presence of raccoons, squirrels, frogs, and more birds than we could ever recognize.

The next week was filled with hauling supplies back to our campsite, exploring the property, and enjoying the rigors of wilderness camping. We carried water, food, and camping gear half a mile back into the woods. We hiked along trails and through the woods to explore as much of the property as we could. My father used a compass and a measured length of cord to crudely survey the property. In some places the underbrush was so dense that we could not penetrate it. For me, the dense underbrush made our explorations even more exciting. We had heard that there were bears and deer on the property. In my mind, the impenetrable thicket only made the prospect of large wild animals more real.

We found an abandoned hunting cabin on the property and pitched our tents near it. Although we had seen no evidence of bears, we scared each other by conjuring up images of a bear raiding our campsite at night, searching for food, and carrying one of us off into the night, screaming.

That night we all slept in the cabin, except for Colin, who scoffed and said there were no bears around. I have always suspected that he said this to impress Debby, but I never voiced my suspicion because I could never prove it. In the end, Colin came off as the only member of our party with courage and common sense. The only animals that visited us were the cows that wandered from a neighboring farm into the clearing where the cabin was situated on our property. After that first night on the property, we all slept in the tents.

After a week of camping on the island, we began the trip home. We enjoyed this trip as much as we had enjoyed the trip up. On each of the three nights of that journey, we stopped at a different Canadian provincial park. When we returned home from our two-week adventure, we were exhausted but happy. We had started the trip as new friends and returned feeling like family.

Traveling in Canada was different from traveling in Michigan. We attracted attention wherever we went, of course, whether in the United States or Canada. How could we not? Yet there was a difference in the way that people from the two countries interacted with us. In the United States, people stared coldly and turned away disdainfully if you stared back. In Canada, they sometimes stared, but they were generally warm and friendly and often smiled and started a conversation with members of our party. We all agreed that we felt more accepted in Canada than in the United States. I believe it is no coincidence that my father described these camping trips in Canada as the happiest times in his life. They gave him a feeling of family that he had not experienced when he was growing up. More important, our family found acceptance in Canada that we didn't find in the United States. In the United States we were outcasts. In Canada we were just people.

6

Alone

MY LIFE BEGAN TO CHANGE AGAIN when I entered junior high school. The neighborhood school to which I would normally have gone, Hutchens Junior High, was reputed to be one of the worst in Detroit. My older brother, Colin, had gone there and had come home with stories of foul-mouthed, violent children who disrupted class, fought constantly, and carried knives. My brother felt compelled to carry a knife for self-protection. My parents would not have approved, but I don't think they knew about it.

The horror stories my brother brought home were enough to convince my parents that the school was too rough for me. They arranged for me to go to the junior high where my father taught, Durfee Junior High School.

Durfee was about three miles from our house. I rode the bus every day to get there and back. While there is no doubt in my mind that it was a better school than Hutchens, going there meant that I was more isolated than ever from my schoolmates. No one else from my neighborhood went to Durfee. During my two-year stint there, none of my friendships at school grew into after-school relationships.

My loneliness was compounded by the fact that my brother and I were growing apart. Colin had entered high school when I entered junior high. We no longer played the childhood games that we had once enjoyed.

The most significant interaction I remember occurring between the two of us at this time was a negative one. Colin, on the one hand, had just entered Cass Technical High School's exclusive science and arts program. Only the top 2 percent of all students in Detroit were invited to enroll in the program. Most of his classmates were middle-class Whites. I, on the other hand, was attending a school that was almost entirely Black. There could not have been more than a dozen Whites in the entire school, and none were in any of my classes. In an effort to gain my peers' acceptance, I was beginning to abandon the Standard English I had been raised with in favor of the Black English my peers were using.

I don't remember the exact words that my brother used. More vivid in my mind is the feeling that they gave me. He was sharply critical of my "improper English." I remember feeling ashamed and defenseless, as if there were nothing I could say to justify using Black English. The fact that I just wanted to fit in with my classmates didn't seem to be a sufficient reason to give up "proper" English. I didn't know at that time that Black English had its roots in African dialects. I didn't realize that the dialect I was adopting was part of African American culture, nor did I realize that by giving it up I would be creating a barrier between myself and most of the African Americans with whom I interacted.

My brother didn't know it, but his critical words marked a turning point not only in my use of the language but also in my social development. From that day onward I spoke only the Standard, precise English of my parents and never the emotionally rich dialect of my peers.

My brother's influence on my use of the language was ironic. After one year of attending Cass Tech, he entered an all-Black high school. Years later I discovered that when he was among friends who spoke Black English, he temporarily abandoned his cherished Standard English for the vernacular of his Black peers. He became, in effect, bilingual, switching back and forth from Black English to Standard English according to the peer group he was in. Yet I totally abandoned Black English in favor of Standard English.

Driven by the need for friends, in eighth grade I began using other tactics besides speaking Black English to gain the acceptance of my peers. I began to fool around in class. I'd spend my time talking with friends instead of paying attention to my teacher. After school I worked my paper route and then read or watched TV instead of doing my homework. For the first time in my life I was afraid to have the teacher call on me in class, because I didn't know the answer. Needless to say, my grades plummeted. I went from being an all-A student to being an all-F student.

The sacrifices I had made in language and grades were all for naught. The physical separation from my schoolmates was only one of the insurmountable barriers I encountered. There were cultural barriers, too. My Black classmates, like many Americans, were prejudiced. They frequently made disapproving remarks about Whites. When they did, I had nothing to say. I knew they were wrong. I knew their remarks were as prejudiced as those of any KKK member, but I believed there was nothing I could say or do that would change their minds. When my friends made racist remarks, I was silent, afraid that if I spoke my true feelings I would lose their friendship.

My first year of high school was even worse than my experiences in junior high. Despite my abysmal academic performance in eighth grade, my test scores were high enough to earn an invitation to attend Detroit's exclusive Cass Technical High School. I was flattered and thrilled.

However, warm feelings of pride and excitement changed to cold fear when I entered Cass. The school was enormous. It filled an entire city block and was eight stories high. The student body must have been the size of a small college, and it seemed to be all White, or at least 90 percent White. My classmates, the freshmen in the science and arts curriculum, consisted of at least one hundred students. There were only one or two other Blacks in my entire cluster of classes.

Skin color wasn't the only difference between me and my classmates: I wasn't the smartest kid in the class anymore; in fact I felt stupid compared to some of my classmates. I was always afraid of what they'd think of me. When I raised my hand to answer a question, I could feel my heart pounding in my chest. I was so nervous I actually broke out in sweat. Nobody ever criticized me, but I was always afraid they would.

During my one-year stay at Cass, I developed no friendships. Not a single one. To what extent was my social isolation due to race? I don't really know, but I'm pretty sure of several things. I'm sure that my feelings toward my classmates were shaped in part by my general experience with White strangers. I had come to expect cool nonacceptance. Because that's what I expected, I was hesitant to take the first step in developing friendships. I had the same feelings of awkward speechlessness I'd known with Barbara Portee, my first crush. Today I know that these feelings were due to the racist social conditioning that many other Black Americans experience as well. Blacks are often aware that they are regarded by many Whites as inferior or worthless, while Whites seem to have unconscious feelings of superiority.

I'm also certain that my classmates regarded me as different simply because of my race. It is almost unheard of for Whites in this country to initiate friendships with Blacks. Blacks are usually treated either neutrally, negatively, or with a sense of cool reserve. I didn't think my White classmates had anything against me. They probably didn't know what to make of me and didn't know how to treat the withdrawn young Black in their midst. They did the easiest thing they could: They ignored me.

Sometimes I wonder if I had been friendlier, or less reserved, or more outgoing—would things have been different for me? My own warmth might have been enough to break through the barrier of color conditioning. After all, I was just like many other Blacks who are accepted into White social circles as long as they show themselves to be White culturally and don't threaten any of the racist views of their White friends. And of course as long as they don't bring up the subject of interracial dating or marriage.*

Michelle, one of my Black classmates at Cass, was like that. She was so light-skinned that she could probably pass for White in some circles. Her hair was silky and curly, not kinky. She was a real social butterfly, always talking about high school trivia with other classmates. She was definitely accepted by our classmates to a greater degree than I was. I attribute the difference in our school social lives, at least in part, to our differing personalities. She was outgoing while I was introverted. She was confident while I was shy and reserved. She was in. I was out.

In fact, I was not only out socially, but within a year I was out academically as well. If I floated on my intelligence throughout my elementary and middle school years, I sank on lack of self-discipline and loneliness in high school. My grades were not high enough to keep me in the exclusive school, and I was asked to leave Cass at the end of the school year.

Once again, my neighborhood school—this time Northern High—was reputed to be one of the worst in the district. Again, my parents pulled the necessary strings to transfer me to a school they thought would be more appropriate. Instead of my father's school, this time it was the school where my mother taught, Northeastern High.

My three years at Northeastern High were better than the previous three years at Durfee and Cass Tech had been, even though I didn't have any more friends at Northeastern than I had at Durfee Junior High or

---

* A national survey by the *Washington Post,* the Henry J. Kaiser Family Foundation, and Harvard University found 86 percent of Black respondents said their families would respond in kind. Still, the Current Population Survey estimates that there are more than 450,000 Black-White marriages today, compared with 51,000 in 1960 (Lane Hartill, "A brief history of interracial marriage," 25 July 2001, <http://www.csmonitor.com/cgi-bin/wit_article.pl?script/2001/07/25/p15sl.txt>, [9 September 2002]).

Cass Tech. The racial composition of Northeastern was about the same as Durfee, almost 100 percent Black. There were still a few Polish Americans who had not managed to move to Hamtramck, the nearby Polish enclave to which Detroit's Polish population fled as Blacks moved into the area. Most of the Black students there were worlds apart from me. While I had been raised on van Gogh and Tchaikovsky, they'd been raised on *Jet* and B. B. King. They used the subjunctive form of the verb *to be,* as in "Sometimes he be jammin'," and added *s*'s in places where they didn't belong, as in "womens." I was psychologically locked into Standard English. I had a well-developed vocabulary from reading Poe, Steinbeck, Hemingway, and Hersey, and I used it to impress my teachers. My Black classmates had a freedom of speech from a rich oral heritage filled with creative metaphors and wordplay. Teachers appreciated my European-dominated cultural heritage more than they appreciated or understood the heritage of my classmates. That gave me status at my new school. Furthermore, I changed my attitude toward school.

That was the main difference. At Cass and Durfee I had no friends and was a nobody. At Northeastern High I still lacked friends, but at least I was somebody. I had learned my lessons from Durfee and Cass. I studied and I did my homework. My teachers loved me. Once again I knew all the answers. My fellow students may not have accepted me as a friend, but they respected me as a student. I played on the chess team. I was president of the student council. Like my brother, I had flunked out of Cass but graduated from Northeastern at the top of my class.

While my social life during my teen years was almost nonexistent, I was not totally isolated, thanks to Joey Caravic and the Zook family. Our two families—the Zooks and the Douglases—were very close in general, but my brother Colin had developed an attraction for the older Zook daughter, Debby. As I saw their relationship move from friendship to romance, I began to feel twinges of jealousy. I was powerless, however, to alter the course of their relationship.

As my brother's romance with Debby grew, I turned my attention to her younger sister, Emma. She was one year younger than I—Brigid's age, in fact. As I in my awkward, boyish ways began to show interest in her, she responded in her shy, feminine fashion. We never kissed—we were both too young and too timid—but we enjoyed the gentle sweetness of holding hands for hours. I enjoyed the warmth of our blossoming friendship until disaster struck.

The catastrophe took the form of a pair of conspiratorial mothers—Emma's and mine. The only story that I was given was that Emma was my younger sister Brigid's only friend. My relationship with Emma amounted to taking away Brigid's only friend. The time Emma spent with me meant less time for Emma and Brigid. Emma and I both thought our parents' interference was misguided and just plain rotten, but there was nothing we could do but comply.

For the next year there were no real friends in my life. About that time, my closest friend, Joey Caravic, moved to Bloomfield Township, one of Detroit's all-White suburbs. Now I not only had no friends at school, but none at home, either. I found ways to pass my time—walking our dog, reading, playing the piano, or mowing the lawn—but there was an emptiness within me that could only be filled by companionship with another human being.

One year later, when I was fifteen, something magical happened. Colin broke up with Debby. I never knew precisely why. He never divulged such secrets to his kid brother. But I surmised that it probably had something to do with his new girlfriend at high school. Debby was staying at our house temporarily. She was having difficulty getting along with her mother. Margaret, despite her egalitarian spirit, could be a very demanding parent at times, and Debby had the tendency to dig in her heels when she believed in what she was fighting for.

While things cooled down between Debby and her mom, she was staying in the bedroom next to my parents'. We spent hours together talking about books, school, or anything else. As our friendship grew into romance, we became more interested in each other than in what we were talking about.

We never kissed or became physically involved, but I remember how sweet it was just to hold Debby's hand and spend time with her. I stayed in her room late into the evening, just to be with her—that is, until my parents intervened. This time, however, when the hatchet fell, it didn't sever the entire relationship; it only curtailed it. I was not to stay in Debby's room so late into the night. Although our relationship was innocent, my parents wisely saw the potential problems of having two teenagers visiting each other in a bedroom so late at night, and they stepped in.

My relationship with Debby did two important things for me. First, it removed the terrible loneliness from which I suffered. Debby was my principal friend and companion from the time I was fifteen until the time I reached twenty-one. Without her, I think my teen years would have been unbearable.

The second thing my relationship with Debby did was to teach me how vulnerable I was to the disapproval of the public. Debby and I went places together—the movies, window-shopping, or an occasional school basketball game. When we went out in public together we attracted the same kind of attention my family attracted. We were an interracial couple—a novelty, a curiosity, and a natural attention-grabber in a racially divided society. My reaction to the stares of Detroiters was much different from the way I had reacted years earlier, when the stares had been directed at my family and me. Back then, I felt amusement mixed with mild anxiety about the fact that many of the stares were hostile, but I definitely felt it was "their" problem.

With Debby it was different. The anxiety was no longer mild—it was intense. While I continued to believe that the people who stared had a problem, deep inside I felt guilty. I felt I was doing something wrong by dating someone who was White. I felt somehow that I was betraying Black people—that I was letting them down by dating someone who was not Black. I had these feelings only when I encountered Blacks— never when I encountered Whites. The feelings were so deep that when we walked down the street, I had trouble looking Blacks in the eye. I felt their accusing stares as I averted my eyes. No one ever said anything to me. No one had to. I knew my relationship violated a very strong taboo and consequently attracted scorn—but why should I feel so deeply that I was betraying Blacks? Where did these feelings come from?

Clearly, I wasn't born with them, nor did they come from my family. They didn't come from White America, either. I was used to White racism and was callous to it. Not that I didn't feel the pain of rejection, but the pain was deadened by my intellectual understanding—the belief that I was okay and what I was doing was okay. The feelings of guilt came from Black America. They came from the burgeoning Black separatist movement that said "Black is beautiful." They came from the well-dressed followers of Elijah Muhammad, who called White people "blue-eyed devils." The feelings came from realizing there were people who thought my dating a White girl was a rejection of my Blackness. They came from knowing there were Black people who thought that Blacks belonged with Blacks and Whites belonged with Whites. Although I knew that all of these people who believed in separatism were wrong whether they were Black or White, I believed that there was nothing I could do to change them. I felt that they would never understand. I wanted the acceptance of the Black community and knew I couldn't get it with a White girl-friend.

The shame that I felt came from my identification in part with the Blacks who were fighting to elevate the status of African Americans. They were the very same people who spoke out against interracial dating. My shame was compounded by the fact that I was ashamed of being ashamed. I felt even then that I should stand up proudly for my belief in racial equality. Although I did stand up for it in private conversations and by the act of free association with Whites, I did so in what felt like a weak and cowardly way. I averted my eyes whenever I encountered the hostile, staring eyes of Blacks instead of standing proud. While I desperately wanted the approval of the Black eyes that condemned me, I also wanted to stand up for my beliefs as those on the front lines of the Civil Rights movement had done.

The Civil Rights movement had influenced me profoundly. I remember sitting in front of our black-and-white television screen during the fifties and sixties, watching the news of the freedom riders and Civil Rights protesters. I viewed those horrible scenes with a tempest of mixed emotions. There was the shock of seeing innocent people—both Black and White—being mauled by vicious attack dogs at the command of local law enforcement officers. There was anger at officers who ordered the dogs to rend human flesh and at other policemen who bludgeoned their victims into submission. There was gut-wrenching sorrow at the thought of the agonizing pain and suffering that the freedom riders were going through. Most of all there was the feeling of admiration for the people who were willing to leave their comfortable homes in the North to risk their lives for the freedom of others.

From the beginning of the Civil Rights movement, I knew there was something special about the nonviolent protesters. Many left the safety and security of their homes to fight for justice and equality. Black and White, together they risked life and limb by violating the time-honored Southern seating arrangement that placed Blacks at the back of the bus and Whites at the front. These noble souls were willing to sacrifice themselves for the sake of integrating previously all-White restrooms and restaurants. They were true heroes. I felt hurt, angered, and inspired to see their majestic self-immolation.

I followed the news of the marches and protests of Martin Luther King, Jr., with swelling pride, as if his victories were mine. Like every other Black in America, I felt that when he triumphed, I triumphed. On that awful day when bullets ripped through his body and his heart was forever stilled, something of the dream that he had worked so hard to realize continued to live in me.

There were other Black leaders whose influences on me were not as positive but were nevertheless significant. These were the leaders on the radical fringe of the Civil Rights movement—leaders who claimed that Whites were devils, leaders who wanted to overthrow the United States government and replace it with a socialist republic, leaders who led the clarion call "Power to the people," leaders who wanted to form a separate Black country within the United States because they saw no hope of eliminating White racism.

As crazy as these folks seemed to me, in a way I identified with them and wanted to help them. Although they had insane, impractical goals, they all seemed to understand how deeply rooted and wantonly destructive racism in America was. All of these people wanted to save Black Americans from their assigned place as second-class citizens. Because I sympathized with their view of Black oppression and their desire to free Blacks from their remaining shackles, I was attracted to them even though their goals were too drastic for me to accept.

The people I had the most trouble dealing with were those Blacks who, while condemning White racism, were themselves steeped in prejudice. They were the people who called Whites "crackers" or "honkies." They were the ones who, in spite of the magnificent achievements of the Civil Rights movement gained through Black and White cooperation, rejected working with Whites to achieve even greater gains. It seemed that in retribution for four hundred years of slavery, they were prepared to dish out four hundred years of revenge.

What made these people so difficult for me to deal with was that I empathized with their feelings. I understood their rage at the four hundred years of slavery, dehumanization, economic deprivation, and political oppression. I shared their desire to improve the welfare of Blacks around the world. At the same time, I thought that their means were excessive. It was a troubling feeling of inner turmoil, understanding the cause of the rage but not wanting to condone it. So whenever I went walking with Debby and encountered disapproving Black eyes, I felt like a traitor. I felt that their anger was in some measure justified and that I was completely defenseless.

I was in the middle of adolescence, trying to find my place in a society that had no place for me. As a biracial adolescent struggling for identity, I did not yet have the self-assurance to disregard the nonverbal rejection we received from all sides.

Debby Zook was my only real friend during high school and my first year in college. Even though I was always uncomfortable with her in public, she was my only companion during those lonely years, and I will treasure that companionship for eternity.

7

Trouble in Paradise

THE YEARS THAT I DESCRIBED as lonely for me were filled with turmoil for the rest of my family. In 1962 when I was thirteen years old my maternal grandmother, having no one to care for her in the area of her Chelsea farm, had moved into our house on Virginia Park Street. She had lived with us for only a few months before she succumbed to kidney failure, leaving my mother a small sum of money, about twenty thousand dollars.

My parents had both been working for a few years, lifting us from the realm of poverty into the lower fringes of the middle class. Yet that was not enough. My parents wanted a home of their own. Although my paternal grandmother was gone so much that she was more like a visitor than a resident, my parents always felt that it was her home. They wanted the independence that only comes with establishing and maintaining one's own home.

They quickly searched for and found a house even larger and more elegant than the one in which we were living. It was in a neighborhood that was changing from White to Black, and they got it for a fraction of its real value. It was perfect for our treasure trove of newly acquired antiques. It was the house on Boston Boulevard. The money my grandmother left had given them enough for the down payment of the house with enough left over for investing and indulging in wants that had long been put on hold. After investing some of their newfound wealth in the Canadian land on Manitoulin Island, my parents became engrossed in antique hunting. Every weekend they went to garage sales, estate sales, or antique shops looking for priceless bargains. They searched the want ads looking for the most promising sales and relentlessly hunted for rare furniture and household items. They returned from each expedition with rich assortments of beautiful old relics—couches, statues, coffee tables, rosewood end tables, antique stools—the list seemed endless. Their treasures amply filled all of the nooks and crannies of our huge house in an artistic and decorative fashion, transforming its interior into a beautiful museum.

Yet all was not well in paradise. A few years prior to our move to Boston Boulevard, my older sister, Linda, had started growing away from the family and getting into serious trouble. She had always had difficulty in school and had been classified as a "slow learner." She was given extra help through her school's remedial reading program, but it wasn't sufficient to help her feel successful in school. She dropped out of school in tenth grade and began running the streets. "Running the streets" was the term used by respectable Blacks at the time to refer to people who partied, hung out on the streets, and indulged in alcohol, drugs, or other criminal activities. When Linda started running the streets, I never knew exactly where she went or what she did. I only knew that she disappeared, sometimes for days, and that my parents were worried sick about her. When she returned my father would greet her with cold interrogations amidst my mother's hysterical tears. Linda responded to the arctic questioning with introverted silence. She answered my mother's flood of tears first with anger, then with tears of remorse.

Linda had always been a troubled child, somehow different from the rest of us. While Colin and Brigid and I were all considered bright, she was always considered a "slow learner." We were all at the top of our respective classes in school, but she qualified for and was placed in special reading classes. When it came to religion, Linda was a born-again Christian, having accepted Christ at an early age, while the rest of us were all atheists and agnostics, doubting the very existence of God. Furthermore, we were all culturally middle-class White. She had more "soul" in her than all of us put together, enjoying Aretha Franklin and every Motown record that had ever been produced. The rest of us were so self-conscious and body awkward that when music started to play, we were clueless on the dance floor. Linda, however, danced with a zeal and fervor that belied her utter lack of rhythm. Despite the fact that she was consistently off the beat in dancing and off-key when singing her favorite soul music, she participated in Black culture more than any of the rest of us. She traveled in Black social circles, spoke Black English unabashedly, and enjoyed Black entertainment.

My mother attributed Linda's growth away from the family to two factors. She explained that Linda had been just as bright as the rest of us until she was afflicted with German measles at the age of four. During the course of the disease she ran an exceptionally high fever. After that she was never the same quick-witted child. It was as if the fever had caused permanent brain damage, robbing her of her natural intelligence.

Although my sister's brain damage was never confirmed by a doctor, my mother was thoroughly convinced that her child's keen intellect had been destroyed by the ravages of her childhood disease.

Added to the aftereffects of Linda's illness was my father's apparent rejection of her after she recovered from it. My mother explained to me that my father was so grieved over my sister's tragic life that he was never able to accept his mentally disabled daughter after that. He clearly preferred his other children to her. To make matters worse, we—the "unafflicted," "brighter" children—preferred each other's company to Linda's. We were not intentionally cruel. It was simply that we had more in common with each other and gravitated in our play toward one another. I know now that our rejection wounded Linda deeply.

Rejected by her family, Linda sought solace in her peers, members of the Black community who had also been rejected by society or had family problems. As a teenager, she fell in with a crowd of people who partied on weekends. Alienated from her father, she was attracted to men who accepted her and paid attention to her. I later learned that she became a binge drinker at this time. Shortly after her disappearances began, she came home pregnant with her first child, Elizabeth. That was only the beginning of the troubles that haunted us in the house on Boston Boulevard.

During the first winter we were there, the ancient furnace—a coal burner that had been converted to gas—broke down. My parents had no choice but to replace it with a modern, efficient, and costly gas furnace. Then, during the following spring, one of the four-inch drainpipes that conducted wastewater from our house to the main sewer line burst. Our basement was flooded with four inches of sewage for weeks while my parents tried to figure out where they would get the money to pay for repairs. Unfortunately, they had exhausted their limited financial reserves on antiques, the down payment for the house, our Canadian real estate venture, and the new furnace. When they finally reached the point of desperation, they approached my grandmother to borrow the funds needed for plumbing repairs. It was hard for them to ask her, because they knew that she would regard their financial predicament as a problem caused by their poor judgment.

And the problems continued. About a year after we moved into the house on Boston Boulevard, my father lost his job as a teacher. Then, as now, teachers are very rarely fired and are almost impossible to let go without just cause and due process. Yet my father never appealed his termination. My parents never talked openly about the details of his problems on the job, so I asked my mom privately. She explained that my dad was just not cut out for teaching at the junior high level. He had problems with discipline. His desk at school was piled high with uncorrected papers. Although he might have done well at the high school or college level, where students were more motivated, the challenge of hormone-wild junior high students was just too much for him. He was simply overwhelmed.

Moreover, his heart wasn't really in teaching. He really wanted a position in government, perhaps in the State Department. My mom explained that Black people simply were not hired for the positions in which he was most interested. Yes, there was Ralph Bunche, but he was several shades lighter than my father, his lips were thin, and he didn't have kinky hair.* He also had a Ph.D. in political science from Harvard.

There was a lot of truth to my mother's explanation of my father's predicament. His greatest strengths were his intellect and his vocabulary—tools that are useless with groups of pubescent children whose chief concern was the latest hit song or who had a crush on whom. He lacked the skills necessary to build relationships with youth and to motivate them to learn. Furthermore, he had the same problems with organizing his papers at home as he did at school. His desk at home was piled high with bills, magazines, newspapers, and junk mail. The conclusion that he wasn't cut out to be a junior high teacher made sense. The real tragedy, however, wasn't that he lost his teaching position—it was that he never pursued his dreams. The obstacles he had encountered during the preceding four decades had by then become psychological barriers that were difficult to overcome. By the time he was forty—a time when most men are well established in their careers—he had only just begun his career and had failed at it. Whatever dreams he may have had of becoming a college teacher or a diplomat ended when he lost his first teaching position. His dreams died, then, long before his physical life was over.

My father did not gather the courage to apply for another professional position for two years. For the first few months he drove a cab six, some-

---

* (1904–1971), a U.S. diplomat, key member of the United Nations for more than two decades, and winner of the 1950 Nobel Prize for Peace for successfully negotiating an Arab-Israeli truce in Palestine in 1948.

times seven, days a week in an effort to meet the family's financial needs. Even though he often worked fourteen-hour days, it wasn't enough, so he took a civil service test and was able to get an entry-level position with the Michigan Employment Securities Commission. Unfortunately, he was laid off every few months and had to resume his cab-driving job to try to make ends meet.

Our family's financial situation became precarious. We simply couldn't survive on my father's sporadic income, even though my mother was still bringing home a teaching salary. We sold our car and began to sell off the antiques, but it was not enough. There was never quite enough money to pay the bills. To complicate matters, my father had a dispute with the gas company about a particularly high heating bill. He claimed he had paid it; the gas company claimed he hadn't. Before the dispute could be resolved, the gas company cut off our gas service, and as a result we went without heat for an entire winter.

I'll never forget that winter in Detroit, the winter of 1965. Things weren't too bad during the fall. It was chilly, but we had two working fireplaces, and we relied heavily on electric heaters. When we were cold we simply moved closer to the fire or the electric heater. It was much harder when the temperature dropped below freezing, because then you could never get really warm. Even when you moved closer to the fire or the heater for warmth, your front side roasted while your backside froze. We would sleep with our clothes on for extra warmth, changing to clean clothes in the morning. We still had hot and cold running water because my parents paid the electric bill and kept the water running in the bathrooms to keep the pipes from freezing. This ensured that we would have water to wash our faces and brush our teeth. However, it was extremely uncomfortable to bathe or take a shower in a subfreezing house. Fortunately, I had gym classes at school every day, so I showered at school. The rest of the family made out as best they could, washing their bodies in subzero temperatures with damp washcloths. Doing our laundry at home was out of the question. Although the washer worked, we had no dryer, and the wet clothes turned to ice. We hauled our laundry in plastic garbage bags several blocks to the nearest laundromat.

Going to the bathroom was yet another ordeal because it meant exposing our sensitive organs to frigid temperatures on a regular basis. In addition sometimes the toilets froze. The first time this happened we made the mistake of pouring boiling hot water into the bowl in an attempt to thaw the ice. It cracked the ceramic, rendering the toilet non-functional—perhaps symbolic of my family at that point. Fortunately, we had four other working toilets in the house.

The most depressing moment came when one of the bathrooms flooded. It happened in the middle of winter during a particularly cold spell. We had stopped using one of the back bathrooms because it was located off of a back bedroom that no one was using at the time. When I went downstairs one morning I was dismayed to see icicles hanging from the beautiful cherry beams of the living room ceiling. The icicles were dripping as they melted onto the flawless hardwood floor below. I rushed upstairs to see what was happening in the bathroom above.

The door stuck as I pushed to open it. I rammed my shoulder against it several times before it sprang open. When I finally forced my way in I was horrified to see a bathtub full of ice and at least an inch of frozen water covering the bathroom floor. We had left the water running slowly so the pipes would not freeze, but the water had frozen in the tub's drainpipe. Since no one used that bathroom, the ice had gradually built up until it filled the tub. The still-trickling water had eventually begun to drip onto the bathroom floor, where it gradually formed a thick layer of ice and began seeping and freezing through the floor to the living-room ceiling below.

I informed my parents, and we did our best to remedy our hopeless situation. We turned off the water in that bathroom, realizing that the pipes might freeze on that side of the house but wanting to avoid the immediate and continuing damage that would result if we allowed more water to freeze on the bathroom floor and drip down into the living room. We chipped as much ice as we could off of the bathroom floor. However, we could think of nothing to do with a tub full of ice except wait for spring. We cleaned up the ice in the living room, moving the few precious remnants of furniture out of harm's way, and hoped for the best.

For the rest of that winter every thaw brought more drips from the bathroom and more damage to the living room ceiling and floor. The frozen bathroom pipes had sprung leaks, and it took a while before we figured out how to shut off the water for that side of the house. Meanwhile, the ceiling was ruined, the hardwood floors were stained and warped, and we had watermarks on the cherry beams. Worst of all, there was no prospect of getting enough money to make the necessary repairs to the plumbing or to the living room. I saw no hope of improving our financial situation. I envisioned our once-beautiful home gradually crumbling around us.

As the problems with our house mounted, so did the problems with our family. In 1964, Linda, now in her twenties, had given birth to her first child, Elizabeth, out of wedlock. Linda had dropped out of high school in 1961. She had not held a job and relied on my parents for support. After Elizabeth was born, she continued to live with our family, relying on their generosity to supplement her meager welfare benefits. Against their will, our parents gave her the luxury of vanishing whenever she wanted to get away from the responsibilities of motherhood. Linda knew that they would take care of Elizabeth in her absence. My parents were torn between the desire to help Linda become a responsible parent and the need to provide Elizabeth with a stable environment. Since Linda—still engrossed in her own emotional turmoil—proved to be so unreliable, they were more like parents than grandparents to Elizabeth. Until their dying days, Elizabeth called them "Mom" and "Dad."

Around this time, my older brother, Colin, began his own troubled family life. Toward the end of his senior year, he got his high school sweetheart pregnant. In love and believing it was the best thing to do, they got married. Colin had already been accepted at the University of Michigan, so he went to college in the summer of 1965, leaving his pregnant wife to live with us. He became a weekday scholar and a weekend husband. But he soon discovered that it was impossible to be a good husband, father, and student simultaneously. That winter, after only one semester in college, he dropped out and began working at the post office to support his family.

My younger sister, Brigid, encountered another set of difficulties. Since my parents viewed her local school as inadequate, she went by bus across town to a school with a better reputation. There, she unfortunately had a classroom teacher who, when angry with the class, made racist remarks. Disturbed by the nature of these remarks, Brigid reported them to my parents. Incensed by the teacher's language, my parents immediately made an appointment with the teacher to confront him. Although he made the appropriate apologies to my parents, he was extremely angry with my sister. He singled her out in class and let her know that he was disappointed in her tattling on him. His daily glares and scowls let her know that he would not forgive her. As a result, she was extremely uncomfortable in class and, at the age of sixteen, dropped out of school, unwilling to face him any longer.

To make matters worse, Brigid's only friend, Emma Zook, had discovered boys and was no longer available to her. In the midst of our family difficulties, Brigid, no longer in school, retreated into a world of fantasy and literature. She shut herself in her bedroom, where she furiously read and wrote romance novels. In her own way she was withdrawing from the world just as my father and I had. The only difference was that our withdrawals could not be seen as easily since I was still going to school and because my father was driving a cab. Now neither my parents nor Brigid nor I had any social life, and my father had no professional life.

These were years of struggle and defeat for my family. The decade of the sixties had begun with the promise of hope: hope for renewed family life in our new home, hope for a new career for my father, hope for the success of all the children in school. Yet before the decade was half over, hope had nearly vanished. Both sisters had dropped out of high school. My brother had started his college career and abandoned it to support his new marriage and shaky family life. As an adolescent, I struggled to find friendships and identity in a world that had no place for someone who was neither Black nor White. My father was again relegated to menial jobs. The beautiful dreams we had once entertained were frozen in time as the icicles that hung from our cherry wood beams were frozen in space.

8

Escape

IN THE SPRING OF 1967 I ESCAPED from the crumbling ruins of our family and our once beautiful home by entering the University of Michigan, my mother's alma mater. I had graduated in January from Northeastern High School with a 4.0 grade point average. My parents were proud but apprehensive. I was following in my brother's footsteps. After flunking out of Cass he had also gone to Northeastern and had graduated at the top of his class, two years before me, and had enrolled in the University of Michigan. He had dropped out after an unsuccessful first year to support his new family. My mother wondered if I, too, would fail to fulfill my academic potential because of some unforeseen trouble and drop out of school.

My parents were unable to contribute financially to my college education, but because of their financial difficulties I received enough from scholarships and grants to cover all of my expenses. I left our decaying mansion and our family problems and traded my inner-city Detroit life for the small-town campus life of the university.

My college years brought changes in my social development and in my attitudes about race. For the first time in my life there was an advantage to being Black. The Basic Educational Opportunity Grant I received paid most of my tuition and room and board. The grant was one of the fruits of the Civil Rights movement and the equal opportunity laws passed in the mid-sixties. It was designed to give Blacks of low-income status access to higher education. Without that grant it would have been very difficult for me to attend the University of Michigan.

When I arrived at my new dormitory room in May of 1967 and settled in, I was pleasantly surprised to find that my roommate was Able Feinstein,* one of my former classmates from Cass Tech. Able was one of a half-dozen graduates from Cass who had also enrolled at the University of Michigan. They had graduated in January as I had, also taking advantage of the early graduation to get a head start on their freshman year by

---

*A pseudonym.

enrolling during the summer trimester. As freshmen, we were all housed together in a dormitory known as the East Quad. Oddly enough, most, if not all, of this small group of graduates from Cass Tech were Jewish suburbanites from the Detroit area. Able was a pudgy, balding, intensely nervous person. Before tests he would pace our dorm room, talking rapidly, half to himself and half to me.

Knowing Able and others from Cass made my introduction to university life much easier than it might have been. During my one-year stay at Cass I doubt that I said more than ten words to the group; yet the fact that we recognized one another made it possible for us to form an ephemeral bond. Few of us had previously shared time at Cass, but we were thrown together in a university of some forty thousand students from all around the world. That gave us enough in common so that I avoided repeating my experience at Cass. We knew each other, and we had something in common—not a lot, but enough to break the ice.

The Jewish contingent from Cass Tech formed a kind of clique. Needless to say, the tight little group never accepted me as a member. I couldn't overcome all of the barriers of race, class, and religion that separated us. Nevertheless, I hovered on the fringes of this clique by virtue of our common experience at Cass and the fact that Able was my roommate.

Although Able and I got along relatively well, we never became close friends. We were, in fact, worlds apart. The measure of the galactic distance that separated us became clear when the race riots erupted in Detroit in 1967. Twelfth Street, one of the central streets of the riots, was less than a mile west of our house on Boston Boulevard. The Algiers Motel, the scene of the horrendous massacre described by John Hersey in his book *The Algiers Motel Incident,* was on our old street—Virginia Park. It was less than two blocks from our old home and about twelve blocks from where my parents now lived. My parents were gripped by a mosaic of feelings as they watched the news and saw familiar buildings burning, heard and saw tanks rumbling down their neighborhood streets, and listened to the frightening reports of nearby gunfire.

My parents understood the rage of the rioters. They knew the hopelessness felt by people trapped in the cycle of poverty. They understood the difficulty of acquiring education in substandard schools. They had experienced job discrimination, housing discrimination, and racial harassment. Although they felt the same anger as the rioters, they also knew the futility of allowing that rage to be vented by burning the buildings owned by the absentee landlords. They were afraid that the riots might spread to their area. They cringed at the possibility of stray bullets coming their way. They worried about irresponsible members of the National Guard taking advantage of the shoot-to-kill orders that defined the National Guard's relationship to rioters. Fearing for their lives, they stayed in their home and watched the riots unfold on television.

My first reaction when I heard of the riots was to phone home for reassurance that my parents were safe. Frustrated because the lines were busy and I could not get through, I turned my attention to Able.

I have a very clear image of Able anxiously pacing the floor of our small dorm room as he listened to news of the riots on the radio. He was wearing a white T-shirt, as was his custom in the evening hours. He threw his hands into the air in a mixture of despair and incomprehension as he repeated over and over again, "Why are they doing this? Why are they doing this?"

Part of me understood his question perfectly. On one level, the race riots in Detroit were an act of insanity. Blacks were burning their own neighborhoods. They were looting stores at the risk of being shot. They were throwing bricks and bottles, even shooting at the firemen who risked their lives to put out the fires that threatened the homes of the rioters. They were fighting battalions of National Guardsmen who were there to protect the lives of innocent men, women, and children as well as the property of law-abiding citizens. Why were they having this senseless orgy of violence, especially when they had gained so much through the Civil Rights movement? Blacks now had laws that gave them equal access to jobs, housing, and education. What more did they want?

Yes, I understood Able's question perfectly, but I hated him for not knowing the answer to it. I hated him for not knowing what it was like to go to the worst schools in the city instead of the best. I hated him for not knowing what it was like to go job hunting when you didn't have the right clothes, a car, or money for bus fare. I hated him for not knowing what it was like to have no hope of becoming a doctor, a lawyer, or an engineer because you had gotten poor grades in poor schools from the time you were in kindergarten. I hated him for not knowing what it was like to see fair housing laws passed and still find yourself unable to move to the suburbs because you didn't have the money or because no one would sell you a house. I hated him for having no idea what it was like to feel as if nine-tenths of your fellow citizens looked down on you with contempt.

While Able's biggest concern was that the riots might break into the suburbs where his home and family would be endangered, my greatest concern was that I wanted to be at home with my family so I could be closer to the action. While Able wanted to see the riots contained, part of me wanted to see them spread not only to the suburbs but also to the entire United States. It was entirely irrational, but I saw the riots as a well-deserved rebellion against racism in America. I secretly hoped they would lead to a revolution that would establish a more just society.

When Able paced the floor and asked why I felt this way, I attempted to explain it, but words failed me. It wasn't that I was inarticulate. I was, in fact, quite able to express my feelings and thoughts in both writing and speech. Yet whatever I said, no matter how well I argued my point, Able could not understand. He lacked the experience of being poor, downtrodden, and hopeless, which leads to the deep-seated rage that was being unleashed against American society. He had no "soul"—no basis for compassion with the underclass—and there was nothing I could say in that dorm room to give it to him.

When I finally got through to my parents, I was relieved to find that they were safe. I contacted them frequently throughout the summer for news about them and the riots. My parents were stunned by the devastation the riots brought to Detroit. They were shocked by the murder of three unarmed Black men in the Algiers Motel. They believed that the reason for the executions was the irrational anger that White male National Guardsmen, police, and state troopers felt when they confronted White women who were staying with Black men at the Algiers. The two White women were beaten brutally by the uniformed troops. This incident only confirmed my parents' well-founded belief that racism was deeply entrenched in our society. It took away their hope that real progress was being made in race relations.

In the fall of 1967 when the new semester started, Able and I parted. Though we both moved to the same dormitory, the South Quad, we lived on different floors. Since we were no longer roommates and had little in common, our relationship gravitated toward acquaintanceship rather than friendship. Not having any real friendships among the student body, I left it to the housing authority to assign me a roommate.

If Able Feinstein lacked compassion, my new roommate, Mike Morgan,* appeared void of understanding. While Able could not comprehend Black rage, he was at least generally sympathetic to the Civil Rights movement. Mike was not only against the Civil Rights laws that were

---

*A pseudonym.

designed to bring about equality, but he also had a thinly veiled contempt for Blacks.

I think he must have accepted every negative stereotype of Blacks ever invented. Blacks were poor because they were shiftless and lazy. They didn't do well in school because they lacked intellectual capacity. Their basic moral depravity inclined them toward crime and promiscuity. But, boy oh boy, did they have a lot of natural athletic ability and rhythm. Mike and I had many long and interesting conversations.

During my year with Mike I learned a couple of things about racism. First, I learned that racism has its roots deeply embedded in the emotional side of the human psyche. No matter how persuasively I argued, no matter how well-researched my facts were, no matter how logical my statements were, Mike's feelings about Blacks never changed.

Another thing I learned was that a racist KKK sympathizer and a Black Panther sympathizer could live in close proximity for almost a year without killing each other. Sure, we argued back and forth, and we never agreed on a single point related to race. I was enraged by his thoughts, arguments, and feelings toward Blacks, but I didn't hate him. I'm sure he detested my position as much as I despised his, but he never expressed any personal animosity toward me. Needless to say, the icy, yet peaceful coexistence that characterized our relationship had no chance of ever developing into a friendship.

My social life still consisted of visits with my high school girlfriend, Debby Zook. I needed my relationship with her. She was my only friend and companion. I was nineteen years old, but I was still afraid to reach out to other people—Black or White. With Whites there were still the old feelings of not belonging—of knowing from subtle and not-so-subtle indicators that most of them had no interest in friendship with me. With Blacks on campus, there were new reasons for my reluctance to reach out to them.

The Blacks I met on campus were a new breed—new to me, at least. They were mostly middle or even upper class. They had been the top students in their high schools. They had money and clothes, and some even had cars. Furthermore, they stuck together and walked and talked in groups. Once again I found myself on the outside. I was scared of them, and my fear kept me on the outside.

What was I scared of? I was terrified that the Black students wouldn't accept me. I was different from them. I wore jeans and plain shirts instead of high-fashion clothes. I spoke plain White English without the slightest flavor of Black dialect. I didnʼt particularly like soul music, and I couldnʼt dance a step. But most of all I was afraid that my attitudes toward Whites would not be accepted. We had entered the era of Black pride, and Black pride in many instances meant rejecting Whites and relegating lighter-skinned Blacks to a lower status. Although I didnʼt see it then, I can see now that my feelings about Blacks grew out of the soil of my own insecurity and were watered from the springs of my own prejudice. By the time I was nineteen, I felt there was no group of people with whom I could be comfortable. I was different from Blacks and different from Whites, not only on the outside but on the inside as well.

A friendlier, more outgoing personality might have enabled me to overcome the barriers of race and culture and realize earlier what I now know to be true—that people of all colors are basically people. We all love, hate, fight, and reconcile. We are all almost always fiercely proud of our families and want the lives of our offspring to be better than our own. And we are all unique individuals. I may have known that people were just people, but I didnʼt feel it and shied away from my middle-class Black peers. With a little bit more courage I might have been able to find Black friends on campus.

My sophomore year at the University of Michigan brought about another great change in my life. I had spent the summer of 1968 working as a field monitor for United Community Services. I was hired to visit summer recreation programs to ascertain their degree of compliance with the program proposals for which they were funded. The programs were organized by neighborhood and community organizations. The job was interesting because it gave me an opportunity to see another side of Black urban life. I saw small church groups and block clubs struggling to give Black children organized alternatives to street life. Deeply committed Black community members and leaders who understood the culture of urban poverty to which many Black families are consigned usually organized these groups. They worked long hours with little pay, motivated by the desire to improve the lives of the Black urban poor. I saw these community leaders and the work that they performed to help these children avoid the pitfalls of poverty, and I was proud.

I stayed with my parents while I worked that summer, saving my earnings so that when I returned to school in the fall of 1968 I was able to live in off-campus housing. No more randomly assigned bigoted roommates for me. I went to the university one week early to look for a house or an apartment I could share with someone. I arranged to stay at the YMCA during my search. While at the YMCA, I met a lonely blond graduate student who wore gold-rimmed glasses and a shaggy moustache. His name was Henry Ellsworth, III.*

His character was diametrically opposite to his stiff, formal name. He wore long, shoulder-length hair and faded blue jeans, and his conversation was replete with classic hippie phrases such as "Wow!" "Out of sight!" "Far out!" and "Power to the people!" Henry spoke with a very curious drawl, as if he were high. He was against the Vietnam War, capitalist oppression, and racism. He supported free love, free speech, and the legalization of marijuana. He fit the stereotypical image of a hippie perfectly.

Henry and I took an instant liking to each other. I agreed with his politics, his views on race, and his general attitude toward life. I felt that he completely accepted me as I was. I had found a male friend, a buddy, for the first time since elementary school.

I quickly discovered that Henry, like me, needed a place to stay. We were both temporarily staying at the Y while searching for a more permanent place to stay, so we naturally agreed to search for a place to rent together.

My year with Henry proved to be my complete academic undoing. We found a spacious three-bedroom apartment just north of campus. Our furnishings were spartan. They consisted of two mattresses, a table, and four chairs. We had no living room furniture, nothing on the wall, and no dishes. It was barren, even by university student standards.

If our apartment was barren, our social life was anything but. Henry quickly collected a group of dope-smoking radical hippie friends of both sexes. Oddly enough, many of them were Jewish. Most of our social life consisted of small gatherings in friends' apartments, listening to rock music and smoking dope. Those evenings were interspersed with discussions of radical politics—the Black Panthers, the Rainbow People's Party, Students for a Democratic Society, and how to bring about "the revolution." The revolution was to be the culmination of the sweeping liberal reforms that the activists of the sixties were pressing for. It was to bring about an end to unbridled capitalism, the Vietnam War, the military industrial complex, racism, sexism, and capitalist oppression.

---

*A pseudonym.

Our endless political discussions and doped-filled evenings were interspersed with occasional demonstrations. We marched on the university to get it to admit more Black students. We marched on Washington in protest of the Vietnam War.

While Henry remained my best friend, his numerous other friends were merely acquaintances to me. Though we all shared common values and I felt accepted without reservations based on race, most of these folks had no idea about the world I came from. My past history of racial anguish was something I kept to myself. I could have shared it, had I wanted to, but I didn't because I was not comfortable sharing my deep level of pain.

My social life—filled with coffeehouses, folk music, marijuana, and politics—resembled a meal of bacon without eggs or toast. I enjoyed it to a limited degree, but it failed to eliminate my hunger. I was still famished for a kind of social interaction I had not yet experienced.

Nevertheless, it was enticing enough to lure me away from my studies. Under Henry's tutelage, my grades dropped from an A average to a C average. At the end of my first semester I was heartbroken at the loss of my nearly perfect average. My grades were even worse the second semester, but this time I was a little smarter. Instead of continuing to watch my grade point average plummet, I dropped most of my courses as soon as I saw how poorly I was doing.

I finished off the school year with one or two additional incompletes. I dropped out of school and went back to Detroit, and Henry went back to Berkeley. I only saw him once after that when I visited California briefly.

I moved back to Detroit with its crowded buses and blank, unsmiling faces—back to the boarded-up storefronts, back to a Black city with all-White suburbs, back to Motown, back to childhood memories of loneliness. I rented a small apartment and began my life as an independent adult. I was twenty years old.

My return to Detroit marked the culmination of my arduous struggle to define myself and determine where I fit into society. Part of the reason I had dropped out of school was because the goal I had held as a freshman—to become a university academician—was no longer relevant. I had lost the motivation to study. It was no longer important to me to get good grades or to excel in my studies. In my younger years, much of my self-worth was based on my grades and academic achievement. I had come to realize that my worth as a person was not related to what professors thought about my work. In addition, I knew from my association with my hippie "revolutionary" friends that the revolution would never come. Most Americans believe in America's economic system. If they are not actually content with their station in life, they are comfortable with the hope that they can change it. The small percentage of those who are dissatisfied, who feel oppressed, is not enough to bring about revolutionary change in America.

Having given up on the revolution, I returned to a more limited personal goal—to make enough money so that I wouldn't be trapped for life in a job I didn't like. I wanted enough money so that I wouldn't be limited to living in a single locality or be bound to a particular lifestyle. Naively, I thought that I could make enough money to begin building my fortune by working hard, living frugally, and investing. In my mother's eyes I was following in the footsteps of my brother by giving up my promising college career. Although my parents were deeply disappointed in my decision to drop out, they supported my decision and offered guidance in my search for gainful employment.

I held a series of jobs that I hoped would both support me and enable me to save. During the next year I successively drove a cab, taught school as a substitute, sold encyclopedias, and worked as a summer program monitor. The jobs I was able to find and the money I was able to make quickly convinced me that it would be to my advantage to finish school before entering the job market permanently.

During my first two years in college from 1967 to 1969, there had been several positive developments within my family. My sister Brigid, who had dropped out of high school at age sixteen, had resumed her education. At seventeen, she had gone to night school and was able to earn the equivalent of a high school diploma by taking a state examination. She had then enrolled in Wayne County Community College for a year and afterwards transferred to Wayne State University.

After two years as a cab driver, my father had found a civil service position with the Mayor's Commission on Human Rights. Although it was steady work, it did not provide enough income to repair our now dilapidated mansion, but it was enough to pay the mortgage and the bills.

My brother, Colin, was beginning his climb toward a successful career as a journalist. Having failed at the University of Michigan, and finding his job at the post office infinitely boring, he looked for other career options. Although he never discussed it with anyone, writing had always been one of his ambitions. Confident in his ability to write, he penned a letter to the *Michigan Chronicle,* a small Black-owned weekly newspaper, claiming that he could write better than their current staff. His letter was so well written that they encouraged him to submit freelance articles for publication. Within a matter of months they hired him as a full-time reporter. Within two years he was promoted to an editorial position. Within three years he submitted samples of his writing to Johnson Publications and was hired as a writer and editor for *Ebony,* one of the most respected Black periodicals in the country.

The entire family was proud of Colin's meteoritic rise to success. It was not simply because he had become a successful journalist. Instead of falling into a life of menial work after dropping out of college, he had, through a combination of hard work, talent, and bravado, shaped a career for himself as a professional journalist. We were all proud of the fact that he, a college dropout, held a position in which he supervised writers with masters' degrees in journalism.

In contrast to the otherwise improving conditions of our family, Linda continued to have problems that added to the strained circumstances of our family. She had been dating a man named Leslie, a recently discharged marine who had served in Vietnam. Leslie was one of the few men in her life who was not interested in exploiting her. He was a kind, gentle man and wanted to marry her when he found out she was pregnant with her second child. She refused, however, because he would not accept her first child, Elizabeth. He wanted Linda to put Elizabeth up for adoption. To Linda, who was struggling to be a responsible mother, this was unthinkable, so Chris, her second child, was born out of wedlock in 1967, adding to my parents' concerns.

Despite the problems involved with having Linda and her two children living with her, my mother found time to write. These were my mother's most productive writing years. Liberated from many of her previous financial worries and detached from material ambitions, her spirit was free to express itself in the art of writing. She spent hours every day writing and revising her work. Her writing took the form of a novel about the Detroit riots, *When the Fire Reaches Us,* which was published in 1970 by William Morrow and Company.

Sadly, our family's good fortune did not last long. In 1970 the school system transferred my mother to a new school, Western High School, where she felt very uncomfortable. She missed the close, caring relationships of her previous school and found the students more difficult to deal with. She resigned at the end of the year, preferring to teach a couple of community education classes in which the students were more serious. She was sixty-two and eligible for retirement and social security. Since my father was working full time for the state, he and my mother agreed that they would have enough to live on.

Unfortunately, in 1971, after only two years in his new position, my father was fired. Again, I never heard the full story, but I know that it had something to do with his socializing on the job. For the first time since leaving Altgeld Gardens, he had found in his coworkers—a group of African Americans—colleagues who accepted him socially. I'm not sure how much they knew about his family life, since he never brought his new friends home. Nor do I know much about these new friends, since he never talked much about them. I do know that he participated in a bowling team with his coworkers and that their favorite bowling spot, the Twenty Grand, was also a nightclub.

I can't help but wonder if my father's need for friendship and approval didn't drive him to socialize too much at work. After all, I had gone through that experience in junior high and in college. It had been fifteen years since our family had left the Gardens, and my parents had had no real social life since that time. I'm sure my father felt the same sort of negative peer pressure I felt from disapproving African Americans. My parents repeatedly had the disturbing experience of bringing home coworkers who were so shocked to find themselves in the midst of an interracial family that they never wanted to return. I think about the pressures that drove me to experiment with Black English and that made it more important for me to socialize in eighth grade than to earn good grades. Is it possible that similar pressures kept my father from bringing his coworkers home and tempted him to socialize too much at work?

After losing his job with the Mayor's Commission on Human Rights, my father brooded daily, slept long hours, and drank a lot. He was the only person I have ever heard of who could drink a fifth of Scotch without showing any outward signs of inebriation. Instead of resuming the struggle to achieve his goals, he turned all of his emotions inward. He would talk to no one but my mom about his unemployment. He returned to his job as a cab driver, working long hours for meager wages. When I attempted to encourage him to apply for another job, he replied despondently, "What's the use?"

With the decrease in both of their incomes, my parents soon fell behind on their bills, including the house payment. My grandmother was always ready to help in times of need, but it became more and more difficult for my father to face her. It was hard for him to face the fact that even with a college degree he could not support his family. After struggling for two years he fell so far behind in his mortgage payments that the bank foreclosed on our house. My parents once again went to live with my father's mother.

She had purchased yet another house, smaller than the other had been but large enough to accommodate our changing family. My parents moved into two small rooms on the third floor. This move forced them to sell, give away, or abandon almost every remnant of their previous material possessions, including their furniture, china, and books. They were consigned to a much more basic level of existence.

Linda continued to have difficulties with drinking and men. The whole family hoped that her life would improve when she married Reggie Jones* in 1970. Unfortunately, their marriage was brief and turbulent. Shortly after Linda left him, she discovered she was pregnant again, this time with her third child, Kevin. My parents insisted that she begin making efforts to become a more responsible mother. She got an apartment of her own, not too far from my parents. Supported by welfare, she tried to rely as little as possible on my parents' limited resources.

The decade of the sixties saw the rise and fall of my family's fortunes. My parents had gone from being renters to becoming homeowners back to becoming renters again under my grandmother's roof. I had progressed from making a shaky start in junior high, to becoming an outstanding student in high school and college to being a despondent dropout who had lost motivation. My older sister, Linda, had gone from being a carefree high school dropout to becoming the struggling mother of three young children with little prospect of financial independence. My parents had started the decade full of hopeful career possibilities and ended it disillusioned, without any clear vision of their future careers. The only bright spots for our family as we entered the seventies were Brigid's promising college career, my brother Colin's newfound career as a writer, and my mother's newly published book.

---

*A pseudonym.

9

Resurrection

WHEN I RETURNED TO SCHOOL in 1971 after a two-year hiatus, I was a different person than when I left. Living on my own and supporting myself had given me a great deal of confidence. I had worked successfully at several different jobs. I had earned the respect of my coworkers—Black and White. I had developed friendships with people of all races. More important than that, I had transcended the limitations of the racial identity imposed on me by American culture.

Throughout my childhood and adolescence I had accepted the racist labels that were put on me. The prevailing American attitude was that if you had one Black ancestor somewhere in your heritage, no matter how remote, you were Black. In the case of Native Americans you had to be one-quarter Indian, or in some cases an eighth or sixteenth, to count as an Indian. However, Caucasians have to be 100 percent Caucasian to stake their claim as members of the White race. As I grew up I wondered why the opposite wasn't the case. Why shouldn't one only be counted as Black if he were pure African and considered White if he had only one White ancestor? It seemed to me that if we were to use this definition we wouldn't have a racial problem in America because most African Americans would then be counted as Whites. Why couldn't someone be counted as White if he were one-sixteenth White? It was apparent to me that being White was regarded as better, and somehow purer, than being mixed. If you had any Black or too much Indian ancestry you were irrevocably cast into a lower class. I concluded that the American definition of race simply served the function of maintaining the social hierarchy. It wasn't just about color—it was about status, power, and privilege.

Although my mind rebelled at the complete lack of logic of this racial system—regarding it as vile, unfair, and demeaning—I had accepted it because it was the prevailing view of American society and because everyone else in America seemed to accept it. Blacks seemed to accept this definition of race even though it implies that races are inherently unequal. Blacks continue to accept it today even though it is an ideological remnant of the days when Blacks were thought to be subhuman.

My family accepted the American definition of race for social reasons. We knew it would do a Black man in America no good to suddenly say that he wasn't Black—to say that he was now White on the basis of his limited White ancestry. People would think he was a fool or just plain crazy. Blacks have been powerless to change the definition, because it has been imposed upon them just as slavery was imposed on them by a dominant White society. It would be pointless for them to try to change the way they are labeled if it would make no difference in the way they are treated by White people. Americans still, by and large, have a feeling that Blacks are different from and inferior to Whites, no matter what they call themselves. For many, a nigger by any other name is still a nigger.

Yet by the time I was twenty-one I was willing to take the step of renaming myself despite the prevailing dictates of American culture. I knew then, as I know now, that the way Americans categorize people as "Black" or "White" is one of the greatest evils of American society. To look at people in racial terms—Black, White, Yellow, Red, Negro, Caucasian, Mongol, half-breed—is a serious defect in our culture. Americans think that race is important. They train their children to perceive racial differences, and in doing so they train their children to be racist.

Yes, I had come to believe that in calling myself Black, I was not only acquiescing to American racism but participating in it and perpetuating it. So when I returned to school that fall I returned not as a mulatto, half-breed, or Black but as a human being.

I did not announce my newfound identity from a stage, podium, or soapbox. I didn't proclaim it to the world in any earth-shaking or wave-making manner. I simply carried it with me in the quiet, fanatical certainty that I was right to deny any and all racial labels that might be applied to me or others and that those who applied them were wrong.

During the summer before my return to the university I had a conversation I will never forget. I was working as a field monitor for United Community Services. Part of my job demanded that I contact the organizers of the recreation program and make appointments for on-site inspections. I remember calling a woman who ran a program in northwest Detroit. I was immediately attracted to her voice. She sounded warm, friendly, and open, and she spoke with a slight Southern accent. I was attracted to more than just her voice. She seemed intelligent and showed real concerns for the needs of neighborhood children.

I pictured her as a light-skinned, freckle-faced Black woman in her late twenties or early thirties with fairly Caucasoid features corresponding to her skin color. From her choice of words and the depth of her understanding, I imagined her to be college educated. I liked her enough to engage in a little flirting over the phone.

When I arrived on the scene of her summer program, her appearance shocked me. Here was no fair-skinned, freckled octoroon. The woman I had been speaking to was a deep brown, about the same color as my father, or darker. She had a broad nose, high cheekbones, and thick lips. Although she looked much different from what I'd expected, I found her very attractive and began developing a friendship with her.

I saw her several times during the course of the program after work. I discovered that I wasn't the only one who had preconceived notions about the other's appearance. She had assumed that I was White based on the sound of my voice.

There's something wrong with a society in which racial stereotypes prevail. Both of us had stereotypical views of how Blacks and Whites speak. We automatically thought we knew the color of each other's skin because of the way that we spoke. She had assumed that I was Caucasian because of my impeccable Standard English and my Midwestern accent; I had assumed that she was a light-skinned Black because she sounded educated and spoke Standard English as well. Both assumptions were rooted in racism.

As my friend and I got to know each other I revealed that I had very few friends. When she asked me why, I explained that I felt uncomfortable around most people—Blacks and Whites.

Wanting to know more, she asked me what my ideal social milieu would be. I thought for a moment and then described the kind of people I thought I would be comfortable with. I imagined a group of people sitting in a coffeehouse and talking. They were educated and intellectual, but that wasn't the most important thing. They were also free from prejudice. They were Black, White, and all other colors as well, and they interacted with each other without regard to race.

"It will never happen!" she blurted, looking down with a skeptical expression.

The words sliced the air between us and cut me like a knife.

"It's a dream. It will never come true—not here in America. Not in your lifetime, anyway. I used to believe in that dream too, but not anymore. There's too much prejudice!"

"Too much prejudice!" The words echoed in my head. I could hear in the echo of her voice the disillusionment she must have suffered. I pictured the young, idealistic woman she must have been when she belonged to "Up With People," an interracial youth group dedicated to improving cross-cultural relations. I knew that her youthful idealism must have been smashed when it collided with the rock-hard reality of racism in America.

At the same time, I hoped she wasn't right. I hoped there was a group of people out there somewhere who would react to me as a person—not as a Black. People who would care about what I thought and felt and not about the color of my skin. I hoped, but my hope was not strong. It was a faint, dying, desperate hope.

I wasn't sure when or if I'd find my social group. In the meantime I was prepared to fight my battle with racism individually. My fight was a simple, quiet one. It meant that I would try to include people of all colors in my small circle of friendships. On university registration forms I would write "human" in the race section instead of checking the box that said "Black." I would continue to refrain from using derogatory racial terms. I didn't have enough courage or inner strength at that point to fight racism more actively or openly. I stood on no soapboxes. I challenged no George Wallaces, Black or White. I simply continued going to classes, meeting people, and taking care of my daily needs while trying to avoid participating in America's racism.

As I went about my student life, attending classes and studying at the library, I soon forgot about my conversation concerning my ideal social group. I never expected to find that ideal social group. Yet without looking, at a time when I had given up the search, I found it.

It was October 29, 1971. I was deeply troubled by a variety of social issues. It was clear to me by that time that America was not the land of opportunity for Blacks, Hispanics, or Native Americans. I could see that systematic discrimination in the way schools were funded left minorities at a significant educational disadvantage. It seemed clear that minorities faced active discrimination in the workplace, and there was clear evidence that our legal system was slanted against poor people and minorities. The American political system was embroiled in turmoil over the

Vietnam War. Hundreds of thousands of people protested in the streets against America's military involvement in Vietnam's civil war, and there seemed to be no end in sight. Our society was deeply divided on the issue. Conservative patriots saw the war as a fight against the spreading menace of communism, while radicals believed that the United States government was engaged in the war purely for economic and political reasons. America had a history of supporting repressive dictatorships in foreign countries when it was economically or politically advantageous and in many countries only gave lip service to the notion of working toward democratic reforms. Our American political system seemed totally inadequate to solve the social and economic problems of the world.

Deeply concerned about these problems, I searched for answers. I concluded that the most effective leaders were people who held deeply spiritual values. I began to entertain the proposition that what America needed most was moral reform. We needed leaders who were willing to work for the ideals embodied in the Declaration of Independence: ". . . that all men are created equal, that they are endowed by their Creator with certain unalienable Rights, that among these are Life, Liberty and the pursuit of Happiness. . . ." We needed leaders who would fight for democracy and human rights around the world, not presidents who set up dictatorships using the clandestine power of the CIA to advance capitalism. Where could I find leaders like that in America?

America needed both moral and spiritual reform. Political reform would not be effective without moral reform. Upon reflection, I came to believe that moral reform must spring from spiritual renewal. Yet I was deeply suspicious of organized religion.

I had learned from my parents that mainstream Christian churches were riddled with racism. I later learned that the Catholic Church had a long history of sanctioning slavery stemming from the fourth century, when a pro-slavery statement became part of canon law.* I discovered

---

* B. A. Robinson explains that the Christian Council of Gangra circa 340 A.D. issued a resolution that stated, among other things, "If anyone . . . teaches another man's slave to despise his master and to withdraw from his service, and not serve his master with good will and all respect, let him be anathema." This resolution became part of the Catholic Church's canon law and was quoted as an authoritative source until the mid-eighteenth century (B. A. Robinson, *Christianity and Slavery: The Move from Acceptance towards Abolition,* <http://www.religioustolerance.org/chr_slav1.htm>, [5 July 2000], Ontario Consultants on Religious Tolerance).

that Protestant churches in America had been segregated from the time they were founded and that many had supported slavery. The Bible had been used to justify inequality, segregation, and slavery. During the nineteenth and twentieth centuries most Christian churches were visibly absent from the struggle against Jim Crow laws in the South and from the struggle against rampant racism and discrimination in the North. I came to believe that if there were any truth to Christianity it was to be found in the Bible, not embodied in the church. Indeed the principal problem with American churchgoers seemed to be that they didn't follow the teachings of Christ.

Yet it was undeniable that many people found inspiration in the Bible and that Christ, through his life and teachings, inspired people to noble heights of self-sacrifice. I had learned from my parents that the same could be said of Buddha, Muhammad, Moses, Krishna, and the founders of other great religions. I was stunned by the fact that each of these religious leaders had inspired millions of people over a span of centuries. This seemed to me to be proof that they were somehow different from other people. They had somehow gained access to eternal spiritual truths that inspired mankind across generations. What was that spiritual truth, and how could I gain access to it?

The only answer I could come up with was to study the holy books of these religions and to relentlessly ask questions of those who seemed to know more than I did. I began reading the Old Testament and the New Testament. I read religious tracts. I started reading the Bhagavad-Gita. I talked to anybody and everybody who was interested in religion. At the invitation of friends, I attended charismatic renewal services. I listened to people speaking in tongues and prophesying. I read books by the current gurus, including *Be Here Now*, by Ram Dass, and *Science of Being and Art of Living: Transcendental Meditation*, by Maharishi Mahesh Yogi. I meditated and recited mantras. I took a course on Hinduism.

This intense spiritual search lasted for months, and it gradually led me from agnosticism to theism. I began to accept the proposition that God was the source of all spiritual truth. For the first time in my life I began to pray, though not out loud. I figured that if God existed He was omniscient, and, being omniscient, He could tell what I was thinking. So I prayed silently as often as I could remember to, mindful of the apostle Paul's admonition to pray constantly.

At noon on October 29, 1971, I was praying silently for direction as I

248

was leaving my class on Hinduism in Mason Hall at the University of Michigan. Which way should I go?

I don't know whether it was simply chance or guidance from God, but on that particular day, instead of turning right as I usually did when leaving the room, I turned left. The hallway was strangely empty. Students were either still in class or had gotten out earlier than usual. The end of the hallway opened into a broad lobby commonly known as the Fishbowl because one of its sides was a fifty-foot-long wall of windows.

The Fishbowl was frequently lined with display tables filled with either political or religious information and staffed by ideologues. I often stopped there to talk to members of the various groups about their political or religious opinions. As I glanced around the Fishbowl to survey my options for engaging someone in conversation, I spotted a banner that read "Bahá'í."

I remembered a few previous encounters with this unusual religion. A few years earlier, when I was sixteen and my brother was eighteen, he had dated a member of the Bahá'í Faith. Colin had attended discussions about religion at his girlfriend's home. I vividly recall one discussion he and I had about the Bahá'í Faith at that time.

"So what's this Bahá'í thing about?" I had asked as we stood in one of the attic rooms that served as my bedroom in our house on Boston Boulevard.

"Unity," he replied. "It's all about unity. They believe that there is only one God and that people of all faiths worship the same God. They also believe in the brotherhood of man."

The ideas he shared with me aroused my excitement. They appealed to my personal ideals about our human family. I also liked the idea of a religion that did not claim to be the only road to salvation. These statements piqued my curiosity, and I wanted to know more. I searched in vain for a way to ask if I could go to the meetings with Colin sometime, but I knew he would view this as just another case of his tagalong younger brother impinging on his social life.

"Do you think you'll join?" I asked.

"Nah," he said with some hesitancy. "I'm not sure I accept their concept of God. They believe in God."

I understood. It would be pretty hard for an agnostic to join a religious group. But the seed of a thought began to germinate in my mind, and I felt as if I'd like to find out more about this religion. Perhaps they would have teachings about God that I could accept. This thought had lain dormant within me until I entered the Fishbowl that day at age twenty-two.

As I approached the Bahá'í display table, several florescent posters captured my attention. Bright neon orange, pink, and green, they all bore simple, almost childish, line drawings and had a short caption or quotation: "Ye are the leaves of one tree," "Independent Investigation of Truth," "All of the Prophets of God proclaim the same Faith." I agreed with the sentiments the posters expressed. I walked up to the table and began looking at the literature displayed before me.

A tall, thin student standing behind the table and wearing wire-rimmed glasses, bell-bottom pants, and an eye-catching shirt characteristic of the seventies eyed me as I approached.

"Hi, my name's Carl," he said nervously. "Can I help you with anything?"

"Tell me about the Bahá'í Faith," I gently demanded.

His smile brightened. "Well . . . er . . ." He seemed to be searching for the right words. "Bahá'ís believe there is only one God, that all religions are one, and that mankind is one human family." He gave me essentially the same description my brother had given me eight years earlier.

"What do Bahá'ís do?" I inquired. I believed that the actions of people, particularly religious people, were more important than what they said or taught. After all, I had learned from my parents that hypocrites abound in religious circles.

"They pray, they meditate, they attend firesides, they go to Feasts—"

"What are Feasts?" I asked eagerly, interrupting him before he could complete his sentence. The word "Feasts" caught my attention, conjuring visions of tables overloaded with an array of sumptuous foods, people in togas, and gorgeous women feeding me grapes.

"Feasts are spiritual gatherings where Bahá'ís pray, conduct their community business, socialize, and, of course, eat." I'm sure my face fell in disappointment with his answer.

"I'd like to go to a Feast," I asserted, certain that the best way to find out about the Bahá'í Faith would be to meet members of the Bahá'í community.

"I'm sorry, you can't." His words interrupted my fantasies. "The Feast is for Bahá'ís only." He explained that because Bahá'ís conduct their community business at these meetings, they are not open to the public, only to members of the religion. "But we have other gatherings you could go to," he offered apologetically.

I didn't like being excluded from Feasts and was determined not to let that happen.

"How do you become a Bahá'í?" I asked, thinking that I would join so that I could see what a Feast was like.

"You simply say, 'I'm a Bahá'í.'"

"I'm a Bahá'í," I declared almost before he had finished saying the words himself. He nearly fell over backwards in surprise.

"Well . . . well, it's not quite that simple," he stuttered. "You have to accept Bahá'u'lláh as the prophet of the religion." He went on to explain that Bahá'u'lláh was the founder of the Bahá'í Faith and that his followers accept his teachings as a revelation from God.

"Are these Bahá'u'lláh's teachings?" I asked, pointing to the posters and literature.

"Yes, they are," he answered, still recovering from his surprise.

"If they are, I can accept Bahá'u'lláh as one of God's prophets."

I sincerely felt that the teachings of the Bahá'í Faith expressed spiritual truth, but my chief motive was to get to a Feast to find out what the Bahá'í Faith was really about. I reasoned that Bahá'u'lláh was probably a great teacher of spiritual truth, and if I later encountered information that caused me to change my mind I could always back out.

"It's not quite that simple," he said cautiously, trying not to drive me away yet wanting to be honest and accurate. "There are laws you have to follow, and you also have to accept the Báb as a prophet of God." The process of becoming a Bahá'í was suddenly getting a lot more complex, but I persisted.

"Who's the Báb?" I asked.

"He's the one who foretold the coming of Bahá'u'lláh. He lived a very saintly life and was martyred because of his teachings."

"I can accept him as a prophet," I said. After all, he had foretold the coming of Bahá'u'lláh. Furthermore, he had suffered death because of his teachings. I knew that was the common fate of many deeply religious people.

"What are the laws I would have to follow?"

Carl patiently explained the laws of prayer, fasting, chastity, and avoidance of alcohol and drugs. My search into religion and religious practices had led me to understand the importance of spiritual discipline. I knew that prayer and fasting were an important part of every major religion. I had begun to pray daily for guidance and had recently fasted for three days as part of my spiritual quest. I understood that dedicated followers of every faith practiced a variety of spiritual disciplines including chastity and dietary restrictions. So it was no surprise to me that such spiritual laws were embedded in the Bahá'í Faith. In fact, finding such laws in the Bahá'í Faith helped me to see it as a legitimate religion. I later accepted the Bahá'í laws, understanding that these spiritual laws are the laws of God and form the core of every revealed religion. I came to understand that following the laws of God is the only way to achieve our spiritual purpose of learning to know and love our Creator.

"I don't think a spiritual person like you would have any trouble following any of these laws." He said this with a flattering smoothness, yet he was sincere.

"I'm willing to follow the laws," I said, eager to join and be allowed to go to a Feast. My commitment was still tentative and short-term. I mentally reserved the right to quit if I didn't like it.

Carl explained that to become a Bahá'í I had to sign a card declaring my belief in Bahá'u'lláh and the Báb and stating my commitment to follow Bahá'í teachings. After frantically looking for a card and not finding one, he invited me to meet him later that afternoon to sign an enrollment card. I met him at the appointed time and signed the card, not knowing the profound changes this act would bring to my life.

I had just joined a religious group. I had become a member of the Bahá'í Faith without knowing much about it.

Carl Schwartz invited me to go on a trip to Cass City to share my new faith with others. We left Friday evening after school.

When we arrived at our destination, a meeting hall in Cass City, I felt overwhelmed with the experience. In that small meeting hall, people of all colors associated in love and harmony. Not only were there Blacks and Whites, there were Bahá'ís from Ethiopia and Germany as well. I immediately fell in love with these people. They had dedicated themselves to the conviction that humankind is one family. They believed it, they lived it, and they wanted to share this belief with the world.

For the first time in my life, I found a social setting in which I felt comfortable. I knew that everyone accepted me on the basis of my character, not my skin color. I enjoyed being with people who believed color to be only a superficial difference among people. I relished the social climate in which no one used derogatory racial terms and in which racial and ethnic jokes were unheard. In subtle ways—not just in words, but through gestures, facial expressions, and attitudes—the Bahá'ís conveyed that they truly believed all men and women are brothers and sisters. I soon realized that the Bahá'í Faith wasn't merely a passing curiosity but something I could commit to wholeheartedly.

My membership in the Bahá'í Faith marked a major turning point in my life. Gone were the years of search for people who shared similar attitudes about race. My feelings of guilt over my lack of support for Black separatist groups vanished. I no longer felt the shame that had flooded over me whenever I encountered the accusing stares of Blacks while in the presence of White friends. Instead of feeling isolated and apart from the rest of the world, I felt a strong sense of membership in a group of people who shared my deepest ideals. The voice of the alluring siren of Black separatism was forever stilled by the musical strains of unity. Feelings of guilt and shame were replaced with feelings of pride. I beamed inwardly at being on the cutting edge of a spiritual and social revolution that has the prospect of changing the world.

The experience convinced me that humanity can no longer afford to divide itself along the traditional lines of race, religion, nationality, or politics. Though there are obvious physical differences between people from different parts of the world, these physical differences do not need to be the cause of separation, alienation, fear, or hostility. We can no longer afford to teach our children to identify with only one race, one nation, or one religion. Where people divide themselves into separate groups they are sowing the seeds of misunderstanding, cultivating weeds of fear, and choking out the nurturing plants of love and harmony. The harvest in such a garden is war and bloodshed.

Membership in the Bahá'í community provides more than a supportive non-racist environment. The Bahá'í Faith enables me to consolidate many deeply held, yet previously fragmented, social and philosophical tenets. The members of the Bahá'í Faith stand for, believe in, and live according to tenets of racial unity and hold equally strong convictions about world peace, the equality of women and men, and universal education. They recognize the need for a vast reorganization of society to bring about justice and to pave the way for the end of violence as a means of settling political disputes. They understand that all social changes inevitably must begin with self-directed individual spiritual transformation. They demonstrate their understanding of these principles by integrating them into their daily lives.

These principles had all been part of my personal belief system before I encountered the Bahá'í Faith. When I found the Faith, I found a group of people who believe deeply in the same things that I believe. After years of social and psychological isolation, I had genuinely found a home. I had discovered an extended family that not only accepted me physically but also shared my deepest convictions and beliefs about the world. I discovered in the Bahá'í Faith a worldwide organization with philosophical and theological underpinnings that merged with my own views. I threw myself zealously into Bahá'í community life.

I can say with absolute certainty that becoming a Bahá'í changed my entire life. Beyond my feelings of satisfaction with being part of an accepting community, I began systematically to develop a spiritual life and a spiritually based lifestyle. I incorporated prayer and meditation in my daily routine. I chose a career in education ultimately because it offered the opportunity to help change the world. Whatever reservations I might have had about choosing a wife of a different race vanished before the teachings of the Bahá'í Faith. I now spent much of my spare time working to establish the principles of the Bahá'í Faith in society at large. For the first time in my life I was part of a community in which I felt inner peace and an indescribable spiritual joy.

This joyful, exciting, almost inebriating spiritual experience convinced me that my entire family would want to join me in my newfound religious community. I could hardly wait to go home and tell them about it. At the very next opportunity I explained the teachings of the Bahá'í Faith to my family members. Just as I had expected, they were attracted to its principles. When I introduced my family members to the Bahá'í community, they felt the same sense of kinship that I experienced. But, unfortunately, they could not accept the possibility of its divine origin. In their view the Bahá'í Faith was a beautiful religion, but they didn't believe in God and therefore could not accept its divine origin. Joining the religion was completely out of the question for my father, my mother, my sister Brigid, and my brother, Colin.

However, there was one bright spot in my attempt to share my new beliefs with my family, and that was my sister Linda. She, too, was attracted to the teachings of the Bahá'í Faith and began to attend Bahá'í meetings. Later she declared her belief in Bahá'u'lláh, the founder of the

Faith, and signed an enrollment card. It may seem paradoxical that Linda, who seemed to have less intellectual capacity than my other family members, had little trouble seeing the beauty and truth of the Bahá'í revelation. Yet this same apparent paradox presents itself in some of the remotest regions of the world. The Bahá'í Faith, one of the most sophisticated and intellectually appealing religions of the world, is often embraced by uneducated peasants or aboriginal peoples more rapidly than by highly educated scholars. Some people take years of study to embrace the Faith while others accept it in a matter of minutes. Bahá'u'lláh explains that recognition of a Prophet of God is not dependent on education or learning, it is only dependent upon purity of heart. Brigid, Colin, and my parents were too attached to their atheistic or agnostic views to consider the possibility that Bahá'u'lláh was a Messenger of God. Linda, it seems, had a heart pure enough to see and feel the light of God as it shone through the teachings of Bahá'u'lláh.

10

The Next Generation

THE DECADES OF THE SEVENTIES and eighties were filled with a series of family triumphs and catastrophes as my parents, my siblings, and I struggled to carve our respective niches in society. We all succeeded to varying degrees, yet each of us also met with our share of failure.

Linda's story is the most tragic. She left her husband, Reggie, after a brief and stormy marriage. Although she is still married to him because she can't afford to divorce him, she hasn't seen him since she fled their apartment in 1970.

Linda struggled to raise her three children, but between her abject poverty, her mental disability, and her own drinking problem, the odds were against her. To complicate matters, her second son, Kevin, at age two began to show signs of mental retardation and emotional problems. His language development was delayed, and he threw violent head-banging tantrums. Periodically, when life became unbearable or the lure of the streets wafted over her, Linda got drunk and abandoned her children, sometimes leaving them with my parents and sometimes leaving them by themselves. Eventually, someone reported her to children's protective services, and the children were taken from her.

Away at college during those years, I only heard the general rumblings of the problems my family was experiencing back in Detroit. My physical separation from the family spared me many of the painful details. I continued to enjoy my relationship with the Bahá'í Faith, developing many new friendships among its members in Ann Arbor and Detroit. One of those friendships, with a woman named Alice Johnson,* blossomed into a romance. We were soon married, after having known each other only six months. Unfortunately, it was destined to become a miserable marriage for both of us.

We settled in Ann Arbor, where Alice worked and where I could finish work on my bachelor's degree at the University of Michigan. Before we

---

*A pseudonym.

had been married long enough to gauge the extent of our misjudgment, my mother called us in from Detroit, desperately pleading for us to take Linda's three children. Linda and her three children had moved in with my parents and grandmother. My mother found the ensuing circumstances unbearably chaotic. Alice and I gravely discussed the situation, agreeing that we could only manage two of the children. Our apartment was the upstairs portion of an old farmhouse. It had been converted into a small two-bedroom apartment. With four of us in the apartment it would be very crowded. Five people was absolutely out of the question.

Although we agreed that two of the children should come to live with us, we couldn't agree which two. I favored taking the two most needy children, Elizabeth and Kevin. Elizabeth, now eight, seemed very insecure and had begun to develop the habit of eating her troubles away. Kevin obviously needed extra attention because of his emotional and mental handicaps. Alice was particularly attracted to Christopher, who dealt with his problems by withdrawing from the world. Outwardly, he seemed to be coping with the problems that came his way while inwardly he was building deep resentments toward his family.

One evening while I attended my college classes, Alice went to Detroit without my knowledge and made arrangements to take custody of the two boys. When I came home from class that evening, Christopher and Kevin were already installed in our apartment. Alice had made and executed her plans without me, and there was very little I could do without causing even more disruption to the boys' lives and to our family life. To my dismay, Elizabeth remained with the rest of the family in Detroit. I had hoped to provide a stable home for her, but there was no way that we could raise three children under the circumstances. So I resigned myself to the choices Alice had made.

Our marriage was further jeopardized by the fact that Alice was convinced that I didn't love her—and I didn't—at least not in the way that she wanted me to love her. Her heart yearned for an intensely romantic relationship, while I wanted a working partnership based on common values. We were mismatched from the start.

Shortly after we took the boys, Alice announced that she was pregnant and was planning to separate because I didn't love her. She had arranged, prior to this announcement, to become the guardian of the two boys. I had already consented to the guardianship, ignorant of her plans to separate and believing that our marriage would endure despite our difficulties. I was devastated but felt powerless when she announced her intentions to separate. The last thing I wanted was to be separated from my two nephews and from my child-to-be. Furthermore, I had faith that with enough effort our marriage would work out. But at that point Alice called all of the shots, and there was nothing I could do.

Alice found an apartment in a nearby complex while I moved in with some Bahá'í friends who were about my age. We spent the better part of Alice's pregnancy apart while I tried to effect reconciliation. About a month before the birth of our little girl, Alice succumbed to my persistent attentions and agreed to get back together. Our daughter, born by cesarean section, had sparkly blue eyes and sported a crop of beautiful red hair. We were both surprised at first, but upon reflection, realized there were corresponding genes on both sides of our family. We named our daughter Jen-Ai after one of the characters in an old Ingrid Bergman movie, *The Inn of the Sixth Happiness.* It means "one who loves all of mankind." I thought it was a good name because it symbolized our intent to raise a child who was capable of loving people of all national backgrounds.

Linda continued to struggle with her drinking and social problems. She seemed to attract the wrong sort of man like a magnet. Inevitably, she wound up with men who only wanted to use her. In 1976 she gave birth to her fourth child, a boy whom she named David, after me. She tried to summon the determination to be a better mother for David than she had been for her other three children. She was there for him more than she had been for the others. Within the limits of her welfare check she was attentive to his material needs almost to a fault. He always felt loved by her. As he grew older, she cooked his favorite meals, and when she had money she took him to McDonalds or bought him his favorite junk foods.

When David was three years old, Linda fell victim to a tragic accident. A car struck her while she crossed the street. The accident shattered her pelvis and broke her knee. After hours of reconstructive surgery, the doctors managed to pin her pelvis and piece her legs back together with steel rods running through her hips and knees. She had a long recovery period, spending weeks in the hospital and almost a year in a nursing home.

During that time, protective services consigned David to a foster home. Although all of us had grave misgivings about the foster care system because we had read horror stories in the local newspaper about children who were abused in foster care, there seemed to be no alternative. My parents were still living with my grandmother and taking care of Elizabeth. They were stretched to their emotional limits. Alice and I were continually plagued by marital difficulties. Our marriage, on the rocks from the first year due to very strong personality conflicts and differing expectations in the relationship, was further strained by the challenge of caring for Chris and Kevin. So into the foster home David went.

His foster parents did a good job of taking care of his physical needs, but he hated being with them. In his view they had too many rules, and they were just no substitute for his mom, who catered to his every whim. He was glad when his mom recovered sufficiently to care for him herself.

With my parents' assistance—sometimes in the form of child care, sometimes in the form of transportation, and sometimes in the form of money—Linda managed to provide for David until he was about eight years old. She did so well that Alice and I somewhat reluctantly returned Kevin to her custody. Alice and I had endless disagreements about how to discipline Kevin. She was emotionally volatile and lost her temper when he disobeyed her. I could not tolerate such emotional outbursts and found them emotionally abusive. We separated briefly over the issue, but in the end I relented and agreed that Kevin had to go. So back to Linda he went. Unfortunately, Linda did not have the emotional or mental resources to meet his needs effectively, and within a matter of months he was placed in an institution.

Kevin's brother Chris continued to live with us. While we had numerous disagreements over disciplinary procedures with both Chris and Jen-Ai, they were not as severe as with Kevin.

Linda continued to care for David. By the time he reached his eighth year, her binge drinking had caught up with her. Oddly enough, she never drank during the day when David was around. However, the hours when he attended school were another story. Often David went to school and returned home only to find his mother drunk. It bothered him so much that he refused to go to school. There was nothing Linda could do to make him go.

The school followed proper procedures and reported Linda to protective services. She suddenly faced the prospect of losing the last of her children. Alice and I, now in our eleventh year of marriage, agreed to take him into our home.

Predictably, Alice and I had the same disagreements over David's discipline that we had had over Kevin's. In my opinion her discipline was harsh and subject to her temper. I objected to her tone and her methods. Our disagreements about David led to a new round of arguments. Alice wanted David shipped back to Detroit, believing that his removal would solve our marital difficulties. I insisted that I would not send David back into Detroit's foster care system. Unfortunately, within a matter of months we were separated again. This time, it was she who left.

To my shock and horror, while Chris, David, and I were away one weekend, Alice packed as many possessions as she could into a trailer and left with Jen-Ai for New Mexico. We did not know their whereabouts for a month. I cannot begin to describe the pain and anguish I felt over the breakup of our marriage and the removal of my only daughter, Jen-Ai, to a place in New Mexico more than 1,500 miles away. Our household now consisted of David, Chris, and me.

Within a month I received divorce papers from Alice, and within a year she divorced me.

This was one of the most agonizing periods in my life. While I was relieved to be out of a miserable marriage, I felt like an utter failure as a husband. I viewed marriage as a sacred institution. Although I had no control over Alice's flight from our home and marriage, I held myself accountable for my part in the demise of our relationship. I felt responsible to God for all of my shortcomings that contributed to the collapse of our marriage. Added to this sense of failure was the profound grief I felt at the loss of my daughter, Jen-Ai. Although there are no words to describe the exquisite pain I felt at the loss of my daughter, I poured my heart out in an effort to express some of those feelings:

There is a hole in my heart where Jen-Ai once lived
When her laughter sang through the house.
But now only pain lives there.

The hole is neat, surgically precise.
Carved by sharp words of judge's decree
It is nine months wide
And nine months deep
And nine months long.

Time was when its edges weren't so clean
Ragged and torn

David's Story

Ripped by cruel fate's claw
As I looked to dream-clouds above.
Surprised, stunned, mortally wounded
I turned to my friends for support
Unaware of the unimaginable pain
Untouched by the untouchable
Unable to stanch the flow of invisible blood
With blind eyes they looked on.

I hoped that the surgeon
Would replace the plug
Stitch it neatly in place
So that though pained I could recover.

But with his sharp razor words
He simply trimmed the tattered edges
And made the dimensions of the wound precise
He finished the job with bright embroidered stitches
Of Christmas and Springtime and Summer

When she was born my heart doubled in size
In order to hold the new love
Now the pain is equal to the love It once held.
But for the surgeons' embroidery
I would die.

Although I felt that death would have been a relief from my suffering, I lived on. Chris, David, and I looked forward to the three times each year when Jen-Ai visited me: winter break, spring break, and for eight weeks during the summer. Between her visits I struggled as a single parent to meet Chris's and David's physical, social, emotional, and spiritual needs.

Two years after my divorce, I met Kim Meilicke, who later became my second wife.

11

Love and Marriage

BACK IN DETROIT, THINGS WERE GOING more smoothly for Brigid. She supported herself by working for the Federal Census Bureau and later for the State of Michigan while she attended college. Having enrolled in Wayne County Community College in 1970, she attended for one year, then enrolled part-time at Wayne State University. She continued to work for the state until she graduated with a liberal arts degree in 1977.

In her spare time, Brigid attended meetings of the Socialist Workers Party. She, like most of the others in the family, held the belief that our government needed to make radical changes in order to fairly represent all people. While I chose religion as an avenue for change, she chose radical politics. The Socialist Workers Party was attractive to her because it stressed racial and gender equity.

While she attended classes at Wayne State University a gentle, soft-spoken man with a slight Swedish accent attracted her attention. He roomed with one of her friends. His name was Chris Crantz, and he was extremely intelligent and well read. Although he worked on the assembly line for Chrysler at the time, he had been a political science student at Wayne State University until he ran out of money. He possessed a keen awareness of political events in this country and around the world. Although his blond hair and blue eyes sharply contrasted with my father's sepia complexion and black hair, his keen intellect was a match for anyone's, including my father's. Brigid and Chris became close friends and eventually married, bearing and raising a single daughter, Brianna.

Chris returned to school to earn his bachelor's and master's degrees in political science and eventually enrolled in a doctoral program. Brigid made a career of civil service in the welfare department and earned a promotion to become a supervisor. Brianna became a straight-A student at Liggett, a prestigious private school in Grosse Point. When she applied to colleges she was accepted at both the Massachusetts Institute of

Technology and the University of Michigan. Chris and Brigid's marriage, a close and loving relationship, remains strong to this day.

My brother Colin's marriage, in contrast, lasted only a short while. Married to his high school sweetheart in 1965, they gave birth to two beautiful children, Scott and Michelle, in the course of five years. Unfortunately, the marriage broke apart after only a few years. Colin's ex-wife, Marzieh, retained custody of their two children and moved to a small town in Ohio. Colin continued his career climb, enjoying great success as the bureau chief of *Ebony*'s New York office. Extremely confident in his writing and editing ability, he began to believe that he was irreplaceable. He started to miss deadlines and soon lost his job.

As talented as he was handsome, Colin found jobs easily. He was named the first managing editor of *Black Enterprise* magazine when it was launched in 1970. In 1981 he landed a job with the *New York Times,* where he worked as a copy editor for the "Week in Review" section and as a reporter on the metropolitan staff. His work at the *New York Times* was difficult but rewarding. Colin enjoyed the status of working there but developed few friendships with his White coworkers. His circle of friends was almost exclusively Black professionals who did not work for the *Times.* He remained an editor with the *New York Times* until his untimely death from cancer in 1992 at the age of forty-five. While working at the *Times* he was married to a woman named Mickey for a short time; however, this marriage was so short-lived that most of our family never even met her. On January 26 of 1985, the same year that Alice left me, Colin married Sheryl, his last wife.

Sheryl was well suited to Colin in many ways. Her beauty matched his good looks, and her verbal skills matched his writing ability. He was awed by her physical beauty and, love-struck, described her as having the beauty of a model. She could match him word for word and argument for argument in any debate. She, like he, had enough charisma to fill a room. In the end, the clash of strong personalities and other personal problems led to their separation and divorce. I think they loved each other to the end but could not live comfortably in the same house. Before their separation she bore him his third child, Jessica, whom they both loved dearly.

In 1987, one year after my divorce from Alice and two years after Colin's marriage to Sheryl, I met Kim Meilicke and was immediately attracted to her. We met at Louhelen Bahá'í School, a religious retreat center in Davison, Michigan, devoted to the purpose of spiritual renewal. Although Kim and I were immediately attracted to each other, we developed our relationship slowly for two years through letters, phone calls, and visits before we decided to marry.

As our relationship grew more serious we both became concerned about her parents' reaction to our relationship. Kim was a blue-eyed blond of German descent, and her parents had very little personal experience with African Americans. As members of the Bahá'í Faith, we were required to obtain the consent of all living parents in order to be married. The big question was how they would react to the prospect of having a Black son-in-law and Black grandchildren. Kim knew this would be a test for her parents. She knew that they would be concerned with what other family members, particularly Kim's grandparents, thought of interracial marriage. I knew this was the litmus test for many Americans who profess belief in brotherhood and equality.

Kim arranged for me to meet her parents. I was to go to their house for a social visit one afternoon. I was nervous as I drove through their neighborhood in Glenwood, Illinois. It was a middle-class suburban Chicago neighborhood. I presumed it was all White and encountered no evidence to the contrary. Kim told me that her dad had very negative images of African Americans—stereotypes born from hearsay and the images presented in the media. Although I was a little apprehensive about how well I would be received, I had a lot of confidence that things would go well. After all, I already had a lifetime of successful experience convincing Whites that I was their equal. The only difference was that here we weren't talking about academic excellence or professional merit—we were dealing with elusive qualities of character and issues of social equality. Nevertheless, I was confident that my charm and wit would utterly disarm them.

Kim's mother—a warm, middle-aged housewife whose quick glances and hesitant voice revealed her nervousness—greeted me at the door. She welcomed me into her living room, where Kim embraced me warmly. Kim's father, a tall man with graying sandy hair, entered the room, extending his hand cordially. The three of us spent the next two hours chatting and exchanging pleasantries. I was amazed at how well we seemed to get along together. He had a quick wit and a good sense of humor. He laughed at my jokes, and I laughed at his. We both played chess and had an interest in computers. He later commented that I was the best man Kim had ever brought home.

Kim's mother was gracious enough to accept anyone that Kim really liked. Nevertheless Kim's mom was impressed with my personal qualities. The results of the visit were so positive that I was sure we would have no problem getting consent when we reached the stage in our relationship at which we would have to seek their blessing.

Our courtship lasted about two years. Kim continued to live in Arizona, where she was finishing her master's degree, while I continued to work as a counselor in Michigan. We communicated through correspondence and long, late-night telephone calls. Some months our phone bills equaled a small car payment. I felt that I could tell her anything and she would understand.

We talked a lot about race relations and the serious degree to which our society is still afflicted with the problem of racism. She impressed me with the depth of her understanding of the nature of racism and with the activist role she took as a college student.

Kim felt outraged by some of the events on campus that displayed gross insensitivity toward African Americans. She described a university meeting in which the complaints of African American students were aired. The students described an incident in which a life-size inflatable doll in the image of an African American had been passed around in the crowd during a football game while White spectators made lewd racial comments. The incident was clearly upsetting to African American students, who felt degraded by it and were concerned that similar events would occur if strong preventive measures were not put in place. In a second occurrence, two female African American students were harassed with racial comments on campus late at night by a group of White males. When the women complained to the campus police, the police took no action. In a public meeting these officers defended their inaction by saying that the women should have been able to ignore the comments. After all, police were insulted regularly and learned to ignore it. Why couldn't African American women do the same?

Kim stood up and pointed out the obvious differences between the two situations. The women were far more vulnerable than the police. They were physically weaker than the men who were verbally assaulting them, and, unlike the police, they were unarmed. She pointedly asked if the campus police officers would have the same laissez-faire attitude had it been White women who were verbally harassed at night by a group of African American males.

Kim's response to these and other events helped me to realize that she had the compassion to see how African Americans are affected by racism and the courage to take action against it. This was an important factor in my decision to marry her. I had visions of working together with Kim to help eliminate racism in our society.

Kim's relationship with my parents was even better than my relationship with hers. From the beginning, she got along very well with my mother. They were both writers. They both loved to talk spontaneously and share their feelings about everything they were going through. They were both attracted to introverted African American males with whom they had to work to make verbal connections. They shared an understanding of the oppression of African Americans to which most Whites are almost completely oblivious. My father never said much about what he thought of Kim, but I could tell from their positive interactions that he approved.

About the time that Kim and I decided to get married, my mother experienced serious health problems. My mother, now seventy-nine, had suffered from arthritic pains in her hip for years. The pains had gotten steadily worse during the last few years and had reached the point that my mother could not walk without experiencing great pain. She decided in the spring of 1990 to undergo hip replacement surgery. Kim and I set the date for our wedding for July 28, hoping that Mom would be well enough to attend by the time our wedding came. Unfortunately, when our wedding date arrived she was not well enough to travel. My father did not want to attend without her. Indeed, he wanted to stay with her until she had recovered. Linda, always dependent upon my parents for transportation, did not attend either.

Kim and I had decided that we wanted to be married at the Bahá'í House of Worship in Wilmette, Illinois, one of the northern suburbs of Chicago. The temple held a deep spiritual significance for both of us and provided a beautiful setting for exchanging our sacred vows. It was close to her parents, grandparents, and many other relatives. She had many friends in Chicago because she grew up there and had worked for several years at the Bahá'í National Center. My brother, Colin, and his wife would fly in from New York, and my sister Brigid and her family could drive from Detroit. We planned a wedding that was small by most standards, with about one hundred guests.

Though the wedding was small, given the makeup of our two families and our friends, it was racially diverse. I suspected that this was the first time many of Kim's relatives had mixed socially with a number of African Americans. Nevertheless, they were warm and cordial to all of my relatives and to our Bahá'í friends. Our wedding demonstrated in a very tangible way the power of interracial unions to bring social change. Kim's parents and extended family had accepted me as one of their own, just as Kim had been welcomed into my family.

Although our parents and most of our extended families welcomed our marriage, my nephews David and Chris found our new household arrangement challenging. They experienced difficulty in adjusting to a new stepmother. Kim found her new role as stepmom equally challenging. The difficulties were compounded when Jen-Ai decided that she would rather live with us than with her mother. We had not been married more than a few months when she moved up from New Mexico to live with us. We had suddenly expanded from a family of three to a family of five!

By fall, when my mother had recovered almost completely from her surgery, my father was diagnosed with colon cancer. We were all devastated. He had always been such a strong, healthy man. I can't recall ever having seen him with so much as a cold. His mother had lived a healthy life to the age of ninety-six. I held expectations that he would experience similar longevity.

Following the recommendations of his doctors, he decided to pursue a course of treatment that combined radiation treatment, surgery, and chemotherapy. My brother took a leave of absence from his job at the *Times* to help both of our parents for the next several months. He was there to take my father to the hospital, to go grocery shopping for them, to help clean house, and to offer emotional support. After several weeks of radiation treatment, my father had colon surgery and a colostomy. Several weeks of chemotherapy followed. By Christmas of 1990 my father was well on the way to recovery, and my brother returned to New York.

Within the next few years Jen-Ai entered college, both Chris and David joined the military, and our daughter Aleah was born.

12

Grandmother's Legacy

DEATH OFTEN COMES BY DEGREES, signaling its onset with a series of tell-tale signs. That's how it stole upon my brother, my father, my mother, and even my father's mother. For my grandmother, the signal of its beginning was the deafening report of a gun fired point blank and a bullet ripping through her gut, followed by the gradual onslaught of the signs of inevitable death. The year was 1981. She had reached the age of eighty-nine and had been quite active before that, often traveling downtown alone almost daily by bus to a senior citizen's center where she ate lunch, socialized, and attended senior activities. Her mind was still sharp enough for her to enroll in an algebra course. She enjoyed her conversations with her senior companions even though some of them were quite racist. One even gave her some KKK literature, attempting to win her allegiance, entirely unaware that she was of African descent. She accepted it, never revealing her racial identity, hoping to find out more about the Klan and its activities.

Then one morning as she was waiting for the bus to take her downtown to the senior citizen's center, a young man approached her with a pistol. He demanded her purse, saying that he would shoot her if she didn't give it to him. She complied, but to her amazement and complete consternation, he shot her in the stomach anyway. Despite her advanced age, she had been in good physical condition, so her body slowly mended, and after several weeks in the hospital she was able to return home. The real tragedy of this incident was that the quality of her life was ruined with that shot. When she went home she was never the same. She had never been afraid of anything in her life, and now she was afraid to leave her house. Instead of taking her daily excursions to the senior citizen's center, she remained imprisoned at home. She lived alone in her home, her isolation disturbed only by the weekly visits of my father, occasional visits of other family members, or the daily visits from her neighbor and close friend, Mrs. Scott, who went shopping for her.

My parents had moved out of her house two years earlier in 1979 after getting back on their feet financially. They had lived with her since 1972 when they lost the house on Boston Boulevard. Then in 1973 their financial condition gradually began to improve after my father started working for the Michigan Employment Security Commission. The state hired him as a clerk, but he soon applied for and received a promotion to the position of employment counselor. Several years later he was earning enough money for my parents to afford to live on their own again, and they moved into a modest apartment near Wayne State University. Their small two-bedroom apartment had a magnificent view of the university campus. Linda's daughter, Elizabeth, lived with them in their apartment almost as much as she lived with her mom, who had bounced back and forth between living with our parents, at our grandmother's house, and living on her own. At the time when my grandmother was shot, Linda was living in an apartment by herself.

Grandmother, now unwilling to leave the safety of her house, lost all of the mental and physical stimulation that had kept her vital. In the course of a couple of years, she lost the ability to clean and cook meals for herself. My parents then invited her to live with them in their small apartment. Although it was uncomfortable for the three of them in that small two-bedroom apartment, she had little choice. It was either live with her son and daughter-in-law or go into a nursing home.

She lived with them for some six uncomfortable years until she had a stroke in 1988. They had never had a comfortable relationship. My grandmother had always been strong willed and independent. Some would say domineering. Yet she was the person to whom we all turned when we needed financial help. It was not easy for her to assume the role of helpless dependent. Furthermore, there had always been tensions between her and my parents. Although she always helped my parents whenever they were in need, they always felt her disapproval for having gotten into financial difficulty. There were also tensions between her and my mother, because my mother always felt that my grandmother had abandoned and abused my father during his childhood.

The stroke left her unable to swallow without choking; consequently, she spent several weeks in a nursing home, where she was tube fed before she insisted on returning to my parents' apartment. My parents agonized over their choices before deciding to bring her home again. The only way that she could survive was by staying in the nursing home. Leaving the care of nurses meant she would either choke on the food she attempted to ingest or starve to death. Yet that was what Grandmother wanted, and my parents supported her decision.

My parents tried to feed her a liquid diet, but without the ability to swallow properly, she choked and aspirated some of the liquid. My parents rushed her by ambulance to the hospital for help. When the hospital stabilized her condition she returned home, where my parents faced the same awful choices: Try to feed her and risk choking, or let her go without food and watch her starve.

Again they opted to give her small quantities of liquid food, hoping by some miracle that it would work this time, but she refused. Gradually, her condition worsened as she became weaker from lack of nourishment. One morning in 1988 my parents went to her room to check on her and found that she had died during the night. My parents were relieved both for her sake and for theirs. Her death brought an end to tensions that had lasted decades. It also brought an end to her suffering.

Although my parents' relationship with my grandmother had never been comfortable, my parents had benefited immensely from her generosity and were always grateful to her. She had helped them from the time they first met in 1942 until her death in 1988—over forty-five years of emotional and monetary support. Without her help, our lives would have been much different, and we might well have been confined to the housing project in Chicago for a much longer period of time, maybe forever. We would not have known the material comfort of our early years in Detroit when we lived in her house on Virginia Park Street. Nor would we have been relieved as quickly of the misery we felt when there wasn't enough money to pay the bills, were it not for her generous support. Following her example, my parents did what they could to help their children and grandchildren in the way that she had helped them.

Until my parents died in 1995, they did everything in their power to support their offspring. Although they never had much money, they always helped when any of their children or grandchildren ran into temporary financial difficulty. In the case of Linda, they offered long-term financial support. They supplemented Linda's meager social services check when she chronically ran short of money or food stamps at the end of the month. They stepped in for Linda, acting as surrogate parents to her children when she was unable or unwilling to meet her children's needs. They frequently provided security deposits for rent and utilities when Linda needed to move into a new apartment.

They also supported Linda's first daughter, Elizabeth, in the same way. During her childhood, Elizabeth was raised as much by my parents as by Linda. Late in her teen years Elizabeth moved in with my parents rather than go to a foster home at a time when Linda was reported to protective services for negligence.

Elizabeth gave birth to a child—a boy named Steven—shortly after she moved in with my parents. Steven was later diagnosed as autistic. Elizabeth never revealed the name of the father, and he was never there to help out, so my parents helped to supplement her welfare check in the same way that they helped to support Linda. My mother made tireless efforts to assist Elizabeth to become a good mother. She was there for Elizabeth whenever she needed advice. She fought doggedly to get Elizabeth extra help for her special-needs child. She helped force the city school system to provide the special educational programs that Steven needed. My mother seemed to have learned from her mistakes in parenting Linda; she never took over parenting for Elizabeth and only gave advice. She succeeded in teaching Elizabeth basic parenting skills. Her constant encouragement and support helped Elizabeth develop the self-confidence and knowledge to work effectively with the department of social services and various other social agencies. However, despite my mother's persistent efforts, Steven eventually wound up in a foster home. Elizabeth needed surgery to have her gall bladder removed, and Steven needed someone to care for him while she recovered. Given Steven's special needs, a foster home seemed to be the best alternative. My father, though less involved with the details of helping Elizabeth, always supported my mother in her efforts.

At one time Brigid and I naively believed that our parents helped Linda and Elizabeth in the wrong way when it came to money. We thought that instead of bailing them out of a never-ending string of emergencies, it would have been better to take a "tough love" approach. Both women could have been encouraged early in their adult lives to get jobs and better themselves instead of always relying on my parents' generosity and welfare for support. However, after talking with Linda, I have a different perspective.

Linda greatly appreciates my parents' support. Recalling the way that my parents helped her, she broke down in tears. "Mom was beautiful," she said. "She was caring, she was wonderful. It wasn't her. It was me who was doing all the wrong. They tried to help me. I got with the wrong crowd when I was sixteen years old. I lived in the streets. Mom and Dad always took me back." Linda went on to explain that she abandoned her children over and over again, but my parents always took care of them when she was gone and always took her back when she was ready to return. It got to the point that Dad was ready to kick her out of the house. But Mom intervened, saying, "If you kick her out, I'm going too."

Linda continued to pour out her heart, saying, "I had a problem, a drinking problem. I don't know what was wrong with me. I know they loved me. They wanted me to come back. My drinking and drugging almost ruined my children's lives. I let the bottle control my life. When I was sober, I took care of my kids. When I was drunk I didn't care about anything but the bottle. It was my comforter. It was my lover. It was all I cared about. I left the house, leaving her with the kids all the time. The streets are very hard. They are very cold. But the bottle had me. I didn't know what to do."

Linda explained that she had been in several treatment programs, but to no avail until after her children had been taken from her. She went to Genesis House for treatment and met a counselor named Fred Williams who helped her out. She feels enormous remorse for the choices she made and an enormous gratitude to God and to Fred Williams for helping her out.

Linda emphasized that she loved her children and that she tried to do her best to become a responsible parent. She fed and clothed them as well as she could on her limited budget. She took them to doctor's and dentist's appointments. She read to them and took them to visit the zoo and museums. Like all loving parents, she made sacrifices for them, often putting their needs in front of her own. But in the end alcohol took over. She had a problem with alcohol from the age of sixteen that she didn't overcome until her mid-fifties.

Linda made one final revelation that rocked me to my core, taking my breath away and causing us both to shed tears. She drank to cover up the pain stemming from the rejection she felt after leaving Altgeld Gardens. The Gardens had provided a warm, loving community for her. There she felt as if she were part of one large family. Ripped from the Gardens at the age of fourteen, she lost the support of her peers and her many surrogate aunts and uncles—countless adults who treated her like family. In Detroit her peers rejected her because her mother had white skin and her father black skin. She dropped out of school in part because she couldn't face a teacher who daily projected a negative attitude toward her because her parents were of different races. The people who accepted her were other alcoholics and addicts who used drugs to escape their pain and, of course, the men who used her.

Linda has enormous regrets about the path she took in life and the mistakes she made while her children were with her. Since her recovery from alcoholism she has done her best to make amends with her family.

She says, "I made amends with Mom and Dad before they died. I made amends with David. I made amends with Chris. I still have not made amends with Elizabeth. I have never been happier. Mother and Dad loved me. They cared for me. I didn't care for myself."

Unfortunately, none of us knew how to help Linda. My mother gave her complete and unconditional love, and that wasn't enough. My mother never had the capacity to take any other approach. Her greatest strength—her ability to empathize with others and see the world through their eyes—was not enough to help Linda. Her desire to see her children and grandchildren through uncomfortable situations always prompted her to help in whatever way she could. It's clear now that Linda's drinking problem was bigger than any of us had imagined, and none of us knew how to deal with it.

It's also clear to me now that Elizabeth, having been repeatedly abandoned by an alcoholic mother, is still grappling with the emotional traumas she suffered as a child. Although my parents helped both Linda and Elizabeth until they died, that was not enough. Both Linda and Elizabeth needed more than financial help. Even in death my mother continued to support them by leaving the bulk of her estate to the two of them.

Colin, on the other hand, rarely needed monetary assistance. In fact, he projected an air of independence that seemed to say that he was entirely above the need of anyone's assistance. In the twenty-five years between the time he left home and his untimely death at the age of forty-five, there were only two occasions to my knowledge when he deigned to borrow money from family members. On one occasion he borrowed money from me; on the other he borrowed from our father. Although my parents shared their financial resources, we children approached our parents individually when we looked for financial support. Linda and Elizabeth always went to Mom, because she was invariably more empathetic. My brother approached our dad, quite possibly because he didn't want to burden our mother with his problems.

Colin spent his years in New York in relative isolation from the family. If he was ever troubled by the loss of his job or his three failed marriages, I never knew it. He never shared the inner turmoil those difficulties must have caused him. As a child, when he experienced trouble he often became moody and temperamental. I suspect that he continued that pattern into adulthood. As an adult he wrote our father a few letters in which he shared some of his feelings, but I was not aware of the letters until after Dad's death. While I have not seen the letters Colin wrote to our father, the letters that Dad wrote to him reveal his concerns about Colin's drinking and its effect on his marriage. Our mother had the ability to sense when something went wrong in Colin's life and demonstrated her unconditional love for him consistently throughout his difficulties by offering him support and encouragement.

From the time Colin left home in 1967 until his death in 1992, I saw him fewer than a dozen times and spoke to him by telephone even fewer. He lived in New York and I lived in Michigan, but an even greater space separated us emotionally. A huge emotional chasm born of unresolved adolescent emotional issues grew between us. We had grown apart during our teen years and never resolved our differences. He occasionally came to visit our parents in Detroit, and I generally made a point of driving to Detroit to visit him during his stay. When he married Sheryl in 1985 the whole family went to New York for the wedding. The only other time I traveled to New York to visit him occurred in May of 1992, when doctors diagnosed him with terminal cancer.

Our parents supported Brigid and me in our adulthood during the 1980s in the same way that they supported Colin. They listened to us, encouraged us, and occasionally loaned us a few bucks when we really needed it. We always felt our parents' love, and I looked forward to the time when I could care for them in the same way that they cared for us all. It wasn't that I wanted my parents to become disabled with age; rather, I felt determined that if they ever needed care in their declining years, I would willingly provide it rather than abandon them to a nursing home. In those melancholy moments when I thought about death, I never imagined that my brother would be the next one in the family to taste its sting.

13

No Tomorrow

ON A RELAXED EVENING IN MARCH of 1992 I received a call from my parents, who were gravely concerned that my brother, Colin, was ill. They said he had been experiencing shortness of breath and that he slurred his words when he spoke. He was also having problems with his vision. Often without warning his eyes suddenly rolled back in their sockets for several seconds before returning to normal. These symptoms had been affecting him for several weeks before his ex-wife Sheryl finally convinced him to see a doctor. When he went for an examination, x-rays of his chest and head revealed cancer in his lungs and brain.

Although the doctors scheduled a series of radiation treatments, which were to be followed by radical chemotherapy, they offered little hope. They gave Colin less than six months to live.

The entire family was devastated. Colin had always seemed so strong. I couldn't remember his ever having been ill. And now without warning he was stricken with cancer and needed someone to help him while he underwent treatment.

After talking with my wife, Kim, and other family members, I decided that I would take two weeks off from work to assist Colin during the therapy. He needed help getting to and from the hospital since there was the ever-present danger of passing out as the tumor in his head consumed increasing portions of his brain. He also needed help with shopping and cooking since he could not go out by himself and had lost his former strength. At the end of the two-week period he would fly to Detroit, where he would be close to loved ones. Our parents and sisters were there along with his fiancée, Jill Foley.

When I arrived in New York's La Guardia Airport, Colin's older daughter, Michelle, now in her mid-twenties, greeted me. On the ride to Colin's apartment I discovered that she didn't know very much about her father's condition. She knew that he had cancer, and she was aware of his symptoms, but she didn't know how bad it was. My brother had told her everything that he had shared with us, but he tended to minimize the severity of the situation when talking to his daughter. At the time, I knew little more than she did, but I understood that his condition was much more serious than she seemed to think. She wanted me to convey my impressions of his health and prognosis to her after I had seen and talked to him.

When we entered Colin's apartment he greeted us warmly, giving us both a hug and a kiss. His physical appearance startled me. Instead of being thin and emaciated, as I believed most cancer victims were, he had actually put on weight. His usually thin belly had begun to protrude, as if he had swallowed a basketball. I soon discovered why. The anticonvulsant medication that he took increased his appetite dramatically. He ate almost constantly, showing a special fondness for sweets such as ice cream, cheesecake, and chocolate chip cookies.

He looked strong, and were it not for the fact that his legs were a little wobbly and his speech slightly slurred, I would not have known that there was anything wrong. I was glad to see that he was doing relatively well. Seeing his apparently robust condition cheered my heart.

The memories of the two weeks we spent together have melted into a stream of meaningful events, all charged with a bittersweet, melancholy flavor. In many ways they were the best two weeks that I ever spent with Colin. Each moment was extremely precious. I had been alienated from him since our teen years when an immeasurable gulf seemed to grow between us. As adults living in different states, we hardly saw or talked to each other, so none of our childhood differences were ever really overcome. But now, whatever resentments, jealousies, or estrangement remained from childhood seemed to vanish in light of his illness. I felt nothing but love for him and the strong desire that his body should somehow miraculously heal, even as our relationship miraculously healed.

The twinges of jealousy that I had felt throughout my life completely vanished, even though it was quite obvious that by comparison Colin was still ahead of me in many ways. He made more money than I. He had more friends than I. He still played Scrabble better than I ever could. He had more charm and wit in his little finger than I had in my entire body, and even at death's door he seemed to have more self-confidence than I ever had. All of these qualities were as ephemeral as a mirage that was about to vanish, fading forever in the heat of a deadly desert sun.

The resentment I used to feel in his domineering presence was absent, even though he continued to treat me like a child—the sixteen-year-old kid brother he had left behind when he married and left home at eighteen. When I ran errands for him during those two priceless weeks, he found it necessary to give me detailed instructions, including how to fill out a deposit slip for the bank. When he realized the absurdity of what he was doing, he apologized, and we both laughed.

In fact the entire two-week period was filled with laughter and tears from both of us. His sense of humor had grown sharper over the years, and he could make a humorous running commentary on any subject that arose, keeping me in stitches with his wit. We filled the time between bouts of laughter with grocery shopping, games of Scrabble, walks around the neighborhood, watching television programs, traveling to the hospital for radiation treatments, and mindlessly indulging in desserts between meals.

At times our discussions were serious. Although I was almost certain that Colin's religious point of view had not changed over the years since we last lived together, I brought a Bahá'í prayer book for him. Like our parents, he had been an atheist, and I assumed that he had not changed his views since I had heard no news of any conversion. Over the years, in a few brief discussions about my religious views, he had not been the least bit interested. Nevertheless, I risked rejection and offered the prayer book to him, hoping that it would be a source of comfort and healing for him.

He surprised me and accepted it very graciously, saying that it meant a lot to him. I asked him if he'd changed his mind about the existence of God.

He replied with a twinkle in his eye, "In the last two weeks, me and God have gotten real tight." He went on to explain that while he had no particular religion and accepted no one's theology, he felt that there was more to life than material existence. Without elaborating he said the only religious people with whom he identified were mystics.

I remained standing, but I was so shocked at this radical departure from his earlier beliefs that the slightest puff of air from the buzzing wings of a passing fly could have knocked me over. "I'll be damned," I thought, "you're not an atheist." This was one of many incidents during the course of that two-week period that caused me to draw closer to Colin than I ever imagined possible.

Before his first visit to the hospital, Colin asked me to do something for him.

"Hey Dave," he said in a casual offhand way, "will you do something for me?" I hate the name "Dave" when most people apply it to me. I feel in my gut that I am more of a "David" than a "Dave." Dave is just too casual. But coming from him on that occasion it felt good, almost intimate.

"Sure," I replied, "what would you like?"

"Would you shave my head?" He wanted his head shaved before the upcoming radiation treatments made his hair fall out. He always liked to do things in style, and the Michael Jordan look was in.

"If you like," I said, concealing my surprise. I didn't know exactly what to expect when he asked for a favor, but I had never imagined this particular request. "Are you sure you trust me? I've never shaved anybody's head before." I was nervous about the prospect of nicking him.

"You shave yourself, don't you? I'm sure you can handle it."

I was pleased and encouraged by his confidence in me. I felt like a little boy who had just been accepted as a man. Outwardly, this was a very small matter, but inwardly I felt what I imagined it must feel like to be a Masai warrior who has just come of age and been invited to kill his first lion. In the twenty-three years since I had reached adulthood, this was the second time that I felt my brother place a lot of confidence in me. The first had been seven years earlier when he asked me to toast his marriage to Sheryl at their wedding reception. It felt good to know that he had faith that I could do the job.

The act of shaving Colin's head was a moment and gesture of tenderness that I will cherish forever. It started in a very mundane fashion, with me very awkwardly cutting his hair in great, ungainly, uneven clumps with a pair of scissors. I cut as close to his skull as I could in order to make the job of shaving as easy as possible, taking care not to draw blood with the scissors. As I held his thick curls in my hands, I felt a wave of tenderness surge within me. This was the closest I'd been to my brother since our childhood. As I clipped his dark locks, cluster by cluster, I was hyperconscious of my desire to please him and my fear of injuring him even in the slightest way. It was as if we were both children and he had extended an invitation to be on his baseball team, and I was at bat. I didn't want to let him down. But more than that, I was aware that the loss of his hair represented the loss of his strength to a dreadful disease, and I didn't want to make his suffering any worse with a slip of my scissors.

When I had done as much work as I could with the scissors, I sighed with relief that I had not injured him. Even though he looked like a victim of the world's worst barber, with clumps of hair missing in a patchwork of uneven shearing, we were both pleased with the progress.

As I massaged his head with shaving cream, I felt another wave of tenderness surge. The act was much deeper than simply preparing his head for the razor's edge. I was, in fact, caressing his head, and in doing so, expressing my love for his entire being. I held his head gently, tenderly, delicately as I might hold the fragile head of a newborn baby and began to stroke it with the razor. While my hands and fingers went through the motions and did the work of shaving, my heart was engaged in an eternal act of love. It was if all of the love that I held for my brother throughout my entire life were compressed into those few short moments and as if this infinite love for him were expressed through the touch of my fingers and the gentle glide of the razor's edge. When I finished that simple yet timeless act of love, my eyes welled with tears. I loved him, and he was dying.

The following day I took him to the hospital for his first radiation treatment. After he received the required dose of radiation, I had the opportunity to talk to his doctor alone. He confirmed my worst fears. The conversation was brief.

"How bad is it?" I asked.

"Bad," he responded. "We're using the most aggressive therapy we can, but there are no guarantees. We don't know how effective it will be."

"How long does he have?" I asked.

"Weeks, maybe months. You never know with brain tumors. Six months at the outside."

Part of me knew with certainty that he was speaking the truth. Part of me didn't want to believe it. I clung to the hope that through some miracle Colin would recover. My brother and I were silent on the way back to his apartment.

Realizing more with each passing day the seriousness of the situation, I increased my determination to do everything in my power to improve his chances of survival. He still drank beer regularly, against the advice of his doctor, and occasionally smoked even though he had lung cancer. When I spoke with him about abandoning these harmful habits, he minimized my concerns, saying that it didn't really matter anyway. It seemed that he just didn't want to give up his beer and his nicotine.

I felt more strongly than ever that prayer offered his only hope. I prayed daily for his healing, but I yearned to do more. I wanted to do everything within my power to promote his healing. I craved the opportunity to touch him while I was praying—to somehow act as a vehicle for the spirit of God. I wanted to be a conduit for the infinite Spiritual Force that is the source of all life, all existence. At the same time, I was afraid that my brother would dismiss the idea as too hokey or nonsensical.

Nevertheless, I gathered my courage and asked if he would mind if I touched his head and his chest while I prayed for his recovery. To my surprise he agreed, saying, "It can't hurt."

There are no words to describe our experience that evening. Whatever I say about it will be inadequate because the underlying reality of the event that occurred is beyond my comprehension.

I gently placed my hand on Colin's bald head while he sat on the couch. Slowly and reverently, I began to utter words of prayer, beseeching God to heal my brother. I focused all of my attention on my desire for God to make his body well again. Tears began to flow from my eyes and down my cheeks. There was nothing in the world I wanted more than for him to recover from his illness. As I prayed I felt a subtle and mysterious flow of energy pour through my hand and into his head. Midway through my prayers I transferred my hand from his head to his chest, maintaining my concentration on healing. By the time I finished we were both in tears.

Amazed at the physical sensation of energy I felt pouring through my hand from my body to his, I wanted to know if he felt it too. I asked, tears pouring down my face, "Did you feel it?"

He responded, his voice cracking with emotion and his eyes glistening with tears, "I felt it!" We embraced each other as we silently wept, and for the next several minutes it was as if we were one. I had never felt that close to him before and haven't felt that close to him since. I hope that in the next world we will feel that close once again.

Before Colin left for Detroit, where his fiancée, Jill, would take care of him and his family would be there to support him, he gave me a glimpse of a new and unfamiliar world: his world—the world of his New York friends. The weekend before he was scheduled to leave New York forever, his friends decided to throw a going away party for him. They wanted an opportunity to say good-bye to him. It gave me a chance to meet some of his best friends. I didn't know what to expect since he rarely talked about his friends.

We walked around the corner and down the block to a nearby apartment building where we rode an elevator to one of the upper floors. He politely knocked on an apartment door. When it opened, an attractive woman greeted him warmly. They hugged and kissed each other on the cheek. When we entered the apartment, I saw a room filled with almost a score of people. They were all African American. They chatted and joked in a relaxed, comfortable way that told me they were close friends. Many greeted my brother with hugs and kisses. As the evening wore on, it was apparent to me that this was a very close-knit group of friends. They knew the details of each other's lives. They laughed and joked with each other. They cared about each other. Within the city of New York, which I had always imagined to be impersonal, was this close-knit community of friends, almost like a village. They were all professionals—writers, editors, engineers, and politicians—and they were all Black. They were all successful in their respective careers. They were all friends with each other and with my brother. This was a part of the community of middle-class Blacks of which I had never been a part. Colin, having as much self-confidence as any ten people, and so much charisma that he was immediately the center of attention in any gathering, never had any problem making friends. The number of friends did not surprise me. It was their closeness, their intimacy, and the fact that they were all Black.

Somehow when I talked to my brother about his life in New York I had not imagined that he lived in a social world of Black professionals. I had no idea that he had his own little support system in New York—a loving, supportive community of professional African Americans. He was fully integrated into a world of which I had no part. It was not as diverse as the ideal community that I had imagined a few years earlier, but it was a very attractive world nevertheless. While it made me feel good to know that friends had surrounded my brother all these years in New York, I also felt a mixture of jealousy and sadness—jealousy over this wonderful community of African American friends, and sadness at the fact that he would soon be leaving them forever. When we left the party that evening, Colin hugged, kissed, and said good-bye to all of his friends. There was an unspoken poignancy to each farewell. We all realized the tacit reality that this would be the last time many of them would see him. This small community of loving friends was losing one of its most cherished members.

A few days later I helped him pack his things for the plane ride to Detroit. He planned to complete his chemotherapy treatments in Detroit, where he would be close to his family of origin. By this time his illness had rendered him visibly weaker. He now walked with a shaky, unsteady gait. Nevertheless, he boarded the plane without assistance. Unfortunately, our flights were at different times, so I couldn't fly on the same plane as he. As I watched his plane take off, I wondered what fate awaited him in Detroit.

I left the airport and returned to my brother's apartment, where I had agreed to meet Michelle later that afternoon. My plane wasn't due to leave for another day, so I had time to help Michelle sort through the possessions he had left behind. She faced the task of packing the few things my brother thought would be essential for living in Detroit and giving away most of the things he left behind. I was there to help with the limited advice I could offer.

The atmosphere in the apartment was thick with melancholy. Every room reminded me of his powerful presence and spoke to me as if to say that my brother's life was over. His small apartment, crammed with books, reflected his love of literature. He loved books as much as he loved writing. Like many avid readers, he read a minimum of a book each week, sometimes two. My tear-filled eyes scanned the hundreds of volumes that he would never read again. On his desk sat his ancient Zenith personal computer, the main tool of his career. I remember the feeling of surprise that came over me when I first saw that he did most of his writing on a first-generation IBM clone. The year was 1992, and two generations of computers had been created since his ancient machine had rolled off the assembly line, yet he still cranked out his weekly articles on a piece of equipment that many computer buffs would regard as junk. It was painful to realize that his fingers would never touch those keys again.

Michelle and I began the work of packing his books and personal possessions. He had given her instructions about how to divide his personal effects. A few essentials were to be sent to him. Others were to be divided among his friends and family members. As we sorted through his belongings, I had the odd sensation that he was already dead and we were distributing his property according to his last will and testament: His computer was to go to his best friend, Herschel; his books to Michelle; his United Nations field jacket to me. I struggled to remind myself that he was still alive and in Detroit, at least for now.

I telephoned my parents to make sure that Colin had arrived safely. I learned from them that he had landed in Detroit without event and had been picked up by his fiancée, Jill. He had met her several years earlier when he was on assignment in Detroit. She had been working for the *Michigan Chronicle,* where Colin had won his first position as a journalist and had later worked as an editor. Jill had done a story about him during that visit and had come to know him quite well. They had become romantically attached to each other and maintained contact over the years through letters and phone calls between Detroit and New York. Deeply in love with him, she intended to care for him during his illness. She and her seven-year-old son had made a place for him in their apartment.

Knowing that he had arrived safely in Detroit and believing that he was in good hands, I felt I could return to my home in Benton Harbor.

For the next few weeks Colin lived with Jill and her son in the apartment, struggling against the disease, attempting to maintain hope until the end. They dreamed and made plans together. While Colin was still ambulatory they shopped around for an apartment that would be suitable for the three of them. They made wedding plans. Even as they planned for the future, their dreams gradually faded into the darkness of the disease. As the cancer seized control of his brain, it became harder with each passing day to decipher Colin's statements. In a few weeks, he lost his ability to speak in anything more than grunts and mumbles. He lost his ability to walk and to control his bowels. He was reduced to a state of absolute dependence.

I received a call one evening that he had been hospitalized. His breathing was labored, and my family was afraid that he would not last long. Without hesitation I drove the four hours between Benton Harbor and Detroit so that I could be with him during this crisis. When I arrived at the hospital, I found him sitting up in bed and conscious. I could see that he labored for each breath of air. Every breath was a struggle for survival. I wondered how long he would last. I attempted to talk to him, hoping that he could understand me better than I could understand him. He was obviously distressed as he tried to communicate with me. His brain had lost the ability to make his mouth form words, but it was obvious that he was trying to say something. I tried in vain to understand but only got more and more frustrated as he forcefully grunted out fragments of half-formed words. What could I do?

I stayed with him until almost midnight, hoping that my presence would offer him comfort. When I left, he seemed to be sleeping. I gently kissed his forehead, trying not to wake him, and said good-bye for what turned out to be the last time. I returned to Benton Harbor that night, planning to come back to Detroit on the weekend. Fate would have it otherwise.

I never saw Colin again. He passed away in his sleep that night with Jill sleeping on a cot nearby. He died on August 11, 1992, four days before they were to be married. The *New York Times* sent an emissary to his wake in Detroit. My parents received letters of condolence from Jackie Vaughn, III, a United States Senator for the state of Michigan; George Johnson, a writer from Santa Fe, New Mexico; Don Wycliff, the public editor of the *Chicago Tribune;* Clyde Haberman, a *New York Times* colleague residing in Israel; and from editors across the country.

Parents never wish to outlive their children, and my parents were no different. In addition to the unspeakably deep sense of personal loss they felt, my parents were struck by the tragedy of Colin's unfulfilled life. A loving and deeply caring man, he had been married three times and divorced three times. He was not able to maintain relationships with those he loved most deeply. Although he loved his two older children, he was separated from them for much of their lives because their mother, Marzieh, chose to live in Fostoria, Ohio, and he chose to pursue a career in New York. While he achieved a measure of fame and success greater than anyone else in the family did, we all felt that he had the potential for greatness that was never achieved because his life was cut short. He died as an accomplished writer and editor, with his best work unwritten.

14

Moving On

MY PARENTS SPENT THEIR LAST YEARS in isolation from all but family members and a few close friends. After my grandmother died, they moved to a smaller apartment on Jefferson Avenue, not too far from Belle Isle. Without the additional money that my grandmother paid in rent they were unable to afford the apartment they had been renting near Wayne State University. Although the new apartment was right across the street from the Jeffersonian, a large upscale apartment building with a view of the Detroit River, it was a world away in terms of status and security. On my parents' side of the street, a liquor store peddled its poisonous wares to a variety of unsavory characters. My parents' apartment was in fairly good shape, but the view from their fourth-floor window was a run-down two-story apartment building with a series of boarded up windows on the second floor. The shadows of the neighboring apartment building were the breeding ground for a number of illegal and immoral activities.

It was not unusual for me to see a van with curtained windows and dark glass parked in those shadows. Apparently, it was where one of the local prostitutes turned tricks.

One evening while visiting my parents I heard a female voice screaming in terror, "Stop! Let go of my purse!" When I looked out of the window to see what was going on, I saw a woman who had been knocked to the ground and a man fleeing around the corner with a purse in his hand.

On another occasion while walking from my parents' parking lot to their apartment, I witnessed a violent verbal encounter between two men as they walked down the street. A large man whom I guessed to be well over six feet and at least two hundred pounds was being pursued by a smaller man who stood at least half a foot shorter and a hundred pounds lighter. The smaller man thrust his hand in his pocket and threatened the larger man.

"Give me your wallet," he demanded, "or I'll shoot you." The audacity of the would-be robber to make this demand in broad daylight in the presence of a witness without the slightest hint of nervousness astonished me.

The larger man continued walking and said, "You're gonna have to shoot me, because I'm not givin' you my wallet."

The bold resistance that the larger man put up astounded me. I hurried to my parents' apartment as quickly as I could, worried that shooting might start at any second. To my relief, nothing happened. Apparently, calling the would-be robber's bluff had worked. I didn't bother to call the police because I knew from experience it would be hours before they arrived, and the incident would have been long since resolved by the time they got there.

Incidents such as these made me fearful about the safety of my parents. Before they moved into this apartment building, Brigid and I had both encouraged them to spend a little more money so they could move into the Jeffersonian, where security guards were stationed at the entrance twenty-four hours a day. My parents would be safer and more comfortable. At the Jeffersonian, they would have more conveniences: a dishwasher, a washer and dryer on the same floor as their apartment, new carpeting, and a balcony with lovely views of the Detroit River and Belle Isle. Although my mother was willing, my father declined because he didn't want to pay the extra two hundred dollars per month in rent. The money that they saved by moving to a smaller, shabbier apartment went to support Linda and Elizabeth.

My father's days consisted of working as an employment counselor for the state of Michigan. He never spoke about his work. My mother said that he was highly regarded on the job. She, for her part, spent her time reading or talking with family members on the phone. She had daily contact with Linda, Elizabeth, and Brigid. Linda and Elizabeth, beset daily with the struggles of life below the poverty line, turned to my mother for emotional support, advice, and of course financial assistance. Most of my mother's social security check went to support them. My mother, in turn, leaned on Brigid for emotional support and advice. Although the years that should have been golden were fairly spartan, my parents were reasonably content with their own lives. Even though the career my father had settled into differed greatly from his youthful dreams of becoming a college professor or a diplomat, he enjoyed the work he did and found it meaningful. My mother, unable to drive, only left the apartment when they went on errands or occasionally went for a drive to Belle Isle. Their social life had been meager since leaving the Gardens decades earlier. Mom read constantly to entertain herself and talked to family members daily on the phone.

The only visitors my parents entertained during their years in that small two-bedroom apartment were relatives or our old camping companion, Margaret, who occasionally visited. My father never brought home his coworkers, and my mother's closest friend, Theresa Haynes, had moved to New Mexico. The relationship my mother had developed with Theresa Haynes in Altgeld Gardens had lasted a lifetime. Although they seldom wrote letters to each other or talked on the phone, they maintained a deep, heartfelt connection with each other. Family assumed added importance to my parents since they had so few social connections. The Michigan branch of our family got together regularly for Christmas and Thanksgiving. However, in retrospect it seems odd that we celebrated these two holidays, since my parents still held atheistic views and had no particular feeling for the religious aspects of Christmas. They viewed Thanksgiving as one of America's most hypocritical holidays. How could Americans so piously thank God for the "gifts" they had received when the prosperity of this country was based on a trail of broken treaties with the Native Americans and the systematic exploitation of African Americans and other minorities throughout its history? For our family, these holidays were purely social occasions, opportunities afforded by days off from work for us to get together as a family.

My parents seldom left their apartment even for recreation or entertainment. Mom still enjoyed occasional trips with Dad to Belle Isle to watch the boats and dream of traveling, but they never went to movies, never dined out, and never visited any friends. My father never felt comfortable in public with my mother, even though interracial marriages became more common. As the oldest interracial couple most people had ever seen, they still attracted stares. It took the enjoyment out of entertainment for my father. My mother, on the one hand, accepted this limited existence with resignation. While she possessed great natural social skills and an innate love of people, the decades of racial discrimination she experienced in our society led her to believe that a normal social life was impossible for her and my father. My father, on the other hand, had always been introverted and seemed to be unaffected by their lack of a social life.

One exception to my parents' isolated existence arose from their attraction to the racetrack. For several years they went almost weekly to the local horseracing course in Hazel Park, a nearby suburb of Detroit. They spent hours poring over racing journals and studying the horses and jockeys before carefully picking their favorites. When they went to the racetrack they spent the entire day placing their bets and watching the races. They always hoped to win big so they would have enough money for my father to retire and so they could travel and still have money enough left over to help Linda and Elizabeth. Unfortunately, they never won the "big one." They became good enough at handicapping and betting so that they never lost much, but they never won much either.

The racetrack habit served as an escape for my parents and became almost an addiction. The excitement of the races and the hope of winning big allowed them to forget about their unfulfilled dreams of professional success and a comfortable life. It helped them to forget about the pain of Linda's tragic life. In the fervor of the race, they blended with the crowds of excitement-crazed gamblers and could even forget that outside of the racing arena, people viewed them as "different."

Vacations by car to parts of Ontario, Canada's southernmost province, offered my parents another avenue of escape. They enjoyed the acceptance they felt in Canada. Seldom did they venture outside of Michigan or Ontario, but on one occasion they ventured to New Mexico to visit my mother's friend Theresa Haynes. These trips were rare, occurring only once every few years. For the most part they stayed in their apartment, keeping to their daily routines, never leaving except when the time came to go to work, to run errands, or to go to the racetrack.

The times Kim and I spent with my parents were always happy. Our favorite pastime was Scrabble. My parents were both excellent players, having large vocabularies, creative minds, and skill with word games. Their verbal skills presented a challenge for us even when my father reached his seventies and my mother her eighties. Kim and I went to Detroit to visit them three or four times each year, and on each visit we played our ritual Scrabble game. They were both delighted to learn during the fall of 1992 that Kim was pregnant. After Aleah's birth on June 15 of 1993, our new daughter accompanied us on our visits to Detroit.

Early in our marriage, Kim and I were planning to move from Benton Harbor to Holland, Michigan, to be closer to the school district where I was starting a new job as a school counselor. As with all facets of my life from my birth, during my childhood, during my teen years, and into adulthood, race was a factor in both my job change and my move. Before this time I had been working as an elementary school counselor in a small farming community in southwestern Michigan. A few years before, the school board had been found guilty of gerrymandering the school boundary lines to keep the school's population all White. The court-ordered remedy was to invite African American students from a nearby school district. When I was hired by the school system, about 25 percent of the student population were African Americans who were bused in from outside the community. In addition, each year the school population swelled by about the same number of Mexican American students who migrated from Florida or Texas. These were the children of migrant farm laborers who came in the spring to help with planting and remained during the summer and fall to help harvest the abundance of fruits such as strawberries, blueberries, grapes, apples, peaches, and tomatoes that grew there.

This made for a very interesting and diverse group of students. While there was very little overt racism, it was always there, just beneath the surface, ready to emerge at the slightest provocation. Even to the casual observer, it was obvious that the students formed friendships largely along ethnic and cultural lines. When students were allowed to choose their own seating, they almost always formed small groups of the same ethnic or language group. The inevitable cliques that formed were almost always racially divided. Just as our nation becomes racially divided on Sundays, our school became ethnically divided at lunchtime. Except for a small group of cross-cultural students, White students sat together, Black students sat together, and Hispanic students sat together.

Following the pattern set by their parents, our students segregated themselves into separate societies, with no violent expressions of racism most of the time. Nevertheless, there was an underlying feeling of racial tension that was expressed in a variety of ways. Occasionally, when I was counseling White students I would hear the "N" word, or students would talk about how their parents would not allow them to receive phone calls from Black students or invite them into their homes. I also observed African American students who accused teachers of racism when they were disciplined for violating the school rules.

DAVID'S STORY

The ugliest moments occurred when an argument or fight erupted between students who happened to be members of different races. The fights would usually start with typical kid differences: an accidental bump in the hallway, teasing that went too far, or play-fighting that got out of control. Then voices rose, insults were hurled, crowds of students gathered, and the friends of the combatants joined in, dividing along racial or ethnic lines and adding racial epithets to the insults. Within a short time an incident that started as a minor disagreement between two students could escalate into a near race riot. In most cases teachers were on the scene in time to prevent the impending battle, but the tensions that arose from such conflicts lasted for weeks after the crisis was over.

I saw it as one of my responsibilities as a counselor to work with students to overcome the racial divisions that existed in our school. To that end I made classroom presentations in which we discussed prejudice and racism, attempting to have the students apply critical thinking skills to problems of stereotypes and discrimination. I openly encouraged friendships between members of different ethnic groups. In private counseling sessions, I attempted to help students deal with the prejudiced reactions that their parents sometimes showed toward their friends.

For the first few years I had the support of the administration in encouraging improved race relations. After all, the school was attempting to implement a court-ordered desegregation order in the most peaceful way possible. But after several years I began to get feedback from a variety of sources that my efforts were not welcomed by many community members. These misguided souls felt that by encouraging children of all races to develop friendships, I was paving the way for interracial dating as the children matured. Furthermore, my marriage to a White woman set a bad example for the children. Finally, some community members were extremely unhappy with the editorials I wrote in the local paper encouraging better relationships between Blacks and Whites.

I tried not to let this negative feedback discourage me and finished the semester, doing my best to continue to promote positive interpersonal relationships between people of all races both inside and outside of school.

In the middle of July I began to think about the next editorial I would write for the local paper. Paying no heed to the negative feedback I had received from various community members, I wrote an essay against the type of personal ads that appear in the classified columns of newspapers and magazines, asking for prospective dates and friendships by race. Typically, they read something like this: "Attractive White female who enjoys sunsets and long walks on the beach is searching for fun-loving, financially secure White male with similar interests for possible friendship or romance."

The gist of my opinion piece was that such ads were unconsciously racist because they made race a criterion for relationships. The column appeared on a Wednesday. The board of education had its regular meeting the following Monday. The next evening I received a call from my union representative saying that the board had voted to change my position. At best, if I were to stay with the district, I would be a half-time counselor and half-time special education instructor. I would receive the same pay, but I would only be doing the work I enjoyed for half of my working hours. I could not help but wonder if negative community reaction to my article had not somehow influenced the board's decision to change my position.

Fortunately, another opportunity had just developed. Two days after I wrote the editorial, I had been contacted by my former principal. She wondered if I knew of any school counselors who were looking for a job. Not knowing that my current position would soon be changed, I replied that I didn't know of any, but I promised to keep her informed if I ran across more information. Immediately after I heard from my union representative, I called her up to ask if the job was still available.

"Yes, it is, but you'll have to move fast" she replied. My local school board had acted on Monday. I heard about the action on Tuesday. I phoned on Wednesday, faxed my resume on Thursday, and interviewed on Friday. Early the following week, I was assured that I had the position.

Though my work situation was somewhat settled and I was prepared for a new position in a new school district, my family was not prepared for the trying year ahead.

15

Twilight

MY FATHER CONTINUED WORKING UNTIL his seventy-fifth birthday. He possessed amazing stamina, enjoyed work, and felt that he needed the money to continue to support my mom, my sister Linda, Elizabeth, and Elizabeth's son, Steven. For years my mother had been encouraging Dad to retire, hoping that they could enjoy the last years of their lives without having to work. But he insisted on working through the summer of 1994. As he continued to work during that summer, my mother became increasingly worried about him.

The years of hard work seemed to be taking their toll. Dad seemed to be more and more tired at the end of each working day. My parents were no longer able to go for long rides without his running out of energy. Finally, he decided that he that he had had enough of the working world and was ready to quit. He retired in October 1994.

I wasn't prepared for the conversation I had with my mom on the phone that fall shortly after he retired.

"There's something wrong with your father," she said in a strained voice. "He's tired all the time. I'm really worried about him. He went to see the doctor, and they want to do some tests."

"What kind of tests?" I asked.

"I'm not sure," she answered hesitantly. "X-rays and blood work. You know, the usual."

I didn't know what "the usual" meant, but I tried to reassure her. "It's probably nothing," I responded. "What are you worried about?"

"I'm afraid his cancer might be coming back." My mother's words brought back memories of my father's previous bout with cancer.

My mother's worst fears were confirmed—not all at once, but by degrees. The tests revealed that Dad's white blood-cell count was up, and x-rays showed a spot on his liver. Our concerns worsened when the doctors ordered a biopsy, yet we still hoped that the spot on his liver might be a benign growth. Within a couple of days the biopsy results revealed that he had cancer of the liver.

My father took the news with his usual stoicism. No tears, no anger—just resignation. My mother did her best to conceal the agony she experienced, but she broke into tears whenever Dad wasn't around. We all knew that she felt as if she couldn't live without him. It was hard to watch our mother suffer. She had sacrificed herself tirelessly throughout our lives to help us in any way that she could. Now the thought that the man who had been her partner for more than fifty years was dying tormented her. Although we all wanted to ease her suffering, we could do little to help her.

There is no experience that compares to watching your loved ones fade away. In July, my father had seemed like a strong man. Although quiet, he retained his wonderful sense of humor and his eyes sparkled. As fall came, he grew noticeably more tired. By the time he retired in October, he had lost so much of his vibrancy and energy that he came home exhausted at the end of every day. In November we received the news from his doctor that he was afflicted with liver cancer and had less than six months to live. From that point his physical decline was extremely rapid.

I had always thought that my mom would be the one to go first. More than ten years his senior, she led a sedentary lifestyle. I remember that when I was in my twenties and she was approaching sixty, I started to worry about her. She smoked about a pack of cigarettes a day, exercised very little, and was overweight. I began preparing myself for the loss of the emotional mainstay of our family. I was certain that she would die years before my father, who was a decade younger than she, a non-smoker, and not significantly overweight.

Kim and I discussed the possibility of having my parents move in with us. It seemed like the most practical way to ensure their well-being. Dad had reached seventy-four, and Mom eighty-four. We wanted to be able to care for him during his illness, and we wanted to be able to care for my mother after his death. We all realized that living together would be difficult. It is never easy for grown children to live with their parents. It's even harder when the parents reach that paradoxical point when the children become the caregivers and the parents become the dependents. Yet that seemed to be inevitable in our situation.

After a few months of commuting some fifty miles from Benton Harbor to Holland every day on my new job, I had had enough. We began looking for a house in Holland. We were hoping to find a house that would be large enough to accommodate our nuclear family of three—Kim, Aleah, and me—and both of my parents.

In late October we invited my parents to visit for the weekend. We discussed the possibility of their living with us. They reluctantly agreed to consider the possibility, not wanting to impose on us. While they were visiting we explored a variety of neighborhoods in and around Holland, looking at houses and discussing what it might be like to live there together. I was surprised to discover that there was a difference between my parents and me in our attitudes about housing.

As we drove through a variety of neighborhoods, my parents kept asking, "Where are the Black people?"

Although I tried to reassure them that there were a few here and there, it quickly became apparent that they were uncomfortable with the thought of living in neighborhoods that were mostly White. I had not thought of it before, but most of my adult years had been spent living in integrated neighborhoods that were predominantly White. Although I always felt a measure of discomfort, believing that at least some of my neighbors would prefer to have me gone, the discomfort was not enough to make me consider living somewhere else. I was willing to live in any neighborhood where I could find suitable housing. I had long ago overcome my adolescent discomfort with the negative attention I received because I had chosen a White marriage partner. I had learned to feel proud of pioneering in the field of interracial relationships regardless of the reactions of others, regardless of where I lived. My parents' experiences in life had led them to a different place. Having encountered profound rejection from the White community early in their marriage, they had spent virtually all of their married years in Black neighborhoods and apartments. They were unwilling even to consider living in a neighborhood that had only token Black membership. At the end of the weekend they reluctantly informed us that we should buy a house based on the needs of our family, with no consideration for them. They were not planning to move in with us. My parents wanted to live out their final days in an area where they felt comfortable and accepted. They would not feel that way in a White neighborhood.

Their discomfort with the prospect of moving into an all-White neighborhood was not their only brush with racism in their final days as a couple. When my father went to the hospital for tests accompanied by my mother, they both felt ill at ease. It had been years since they had spent that much time in public as a couple. They still were not used to the attention they attracted. They were a study in contrasts. He was still a door-filling hulk with his six–foot-three-inch, 220-pound frame, while she was a petite five-foot-four inches made shorter by the effects of aging. He stood, looking strong as an oak, despite his illness, while she could only stand for a few minutes with the aid of a cane. And of course there was the color difference. At seventy-four and eighty-three, they were the oldest interracial couple most people had ever seen. Naturally, they attracted attention.

But my parents felt there was something more than that. At the doctor's office my mom felt that she was treated warmly until she revealed that she was married to my father. Beyond that, there was the nagging suspicion that he was not receiving the best service. His calls were not always returned, and his questions were not always answered. More than that, the proposed treatment plan troubled my father.

He had a course of x-ray therapy followed by the traditional chemotherapy. When these treatments proved ineffective, a second treatment of chemotherapy was recommended. My father declined, believing that the quality of his life while being treated with the cancer-killing chemicals was so diminished that it was not worth the few additional months it might give him. When the doctor proposed an experimental treatment, both of my parents wondered if the doctor would have dared propose this experimental treatment to a White patient.

As their son, I thought that their fears amounted to a kind of paranoia, growing like a cancer from their experiences of the past fifty years. But I could not blame them for their fears about racism. Had they not seen enough in their fifty years of marriage to make anyone suspicious?

The dreaded call came in the early hours of the morning, less than two months after my parents' last visit. My mother's voice sounded faint and frightened.

"What's wrong, Mom?" I inquired, not wanting to reveal the cold sensation of fear her call set off in me.

"It's your father," she said, her voice cracking. I could tell that she was trying to hold back the tears. "He won't wake up."

She sounded so pitiful. My eyes welled up with tears for her. She was all alone in her apartment with the body of the man she had loved for more than half a century, unable to believe his life was gone—that their life as a couple was over.

"Is he breathing?" I asked the obvious.

"I can't tell," she responded.

"Does he have a pulse?" Even though I knew he was dead, it was easier to participate in the fantasy that he might still be living.

"I don't feel anything. He seems cold. But he looks just like he is sleeping."

"Call Brigid," I instructed. "She'll know what to do." My younger sister was only twenty minutes away in another part of the city. I was across the state, almost four hours away.

"I already have. She's on her way." I breathed an inward sigh of relief. I hated the thought of my mom's being alone in the apartment with my father's dead body. I kept talking to her until my sister arrived and confirmed that our father had gone.

When I arrived a few hours later, my father's body had already been taken to the funeral home. I was disappointed. I had hoped to see him there in the apartment, where I last saw him. I wanted to say good-bye to him in warm, familiar surroundings, not in the formal public surroundings of a funeral home. Knowing that my parents detested traditional funeral ceremonies and that there would be no wake before his body was cremated, I made arrangements for a private viewing the following day when my mother and I were there to make the funeral arrangements.

While my mother waited in the funeral home's conference room, I went to the viewing room, and the funeral director wheeled my father's body out on a stainless steel gurney similar those used in hospitals. Because there would be no funeral service and he was to be cremated, his body had not been prepared in any way. He lay there just as he must have been in bed when he died.

He lay on his side in a very natural position, with his eyes peacefully closed, almost as if he were asleep. A red velvet blanket, like him, faded and worn, covered his frail body. As in life, he maintained an attitude of dignity. His face was thinner now that the cancer had drained his life away, his cheeks sunken, and his eye sockets hollowed. There in the middle of a shabby inner-city funeral home, covered in worn red velvet, he still radiated majesty. He resembled a king in exile who had lost all of his riches and hadn't eaten for days—tired, thin, impoverished, and ill clad—yet even in death he maintained a noble and commanding presence.

I felt a mosaic of emotions: pride that he had maintained an interracial marriage for more than half a century, sorrow that there had always been a distance between us, grief that his dreams had vanished like mist in the simmering heat in the desert of racism in this country, and love for the man who had sacrificed his life for his wife and family. I grieved at the realization that I only knew glimpses of the inner workings of his soul as they were reflected dimly through my mother's eyes. I gently caressed his face in a way that I could not have done while he was living and wondered how my mom would survive without his strong presence and sustaining emotional support.

The next six, and final, months of my mom's life were a kaleidoscope of images, activities, and emotions. As my sisters and I struggled to help her build a new life, she fought to bring closure to a life that was almost over.

We helped move her from her old, run-down apartment to the upscale Jeffersonian across the street. For the first time in decades she lived in a secure middle-class setting. It felt good to know that she would now be living in a building with doormen and building security. Her new apartment had brand new carpet and a dishwasher, luxuries she had never experienced before. Brigid talked with Mom at least twice a day. In fact, Brigid, Elizabeth, and Linda frequently stayed overnight to keep her company. Brigid did her grocery shopping, and Linda and Elizabeth helped with laundry and cooking. I called once a week and visited once a month.

Helping Mom move to the Jeffersonian and seeing that she was physically cared for was the easy part. Her emotional needs were another matter. Although she held herself together during the day, the nights were very difficult. She missed the man she had slept with for the past fifty years and suffered from insomnia. She cried nearly every night.

Her only solace during the last months of her life was the book she was writing. Every day she poured herself into writing the story of her marriage and family. She wrote furiously from February to June, churning out more than forty thousand words in less than four months. She wanted the world to know how difficult her marriage had been because of the racism that exists in our society. She wanted White people in particular to know that the racism that Blacks constantly complain about is real. She hoped that her book would prick the consciences of White Americans so that they would work to reform American society and make it a comfortable place for interracial families and ethnic minorities. To our family's dismay, she told us that her only reason for living was to finish her book.

Ironically, although writing her story was her only reason for living, it was extremely painful for her. At best, remembering the tender moments she and my father had shared made her miss him all the more. At worst, she relived every insult, every disappointment, every threat, every hurt, and every rejection they had suffered together during the course of their courtship and marriage. She included many of these experiences in her memoir. Others she chose to share in private with family, choosing not to make them public. Writing about her experiences was gut-wrenching agony. In the end, I believe, it killed her.

In March my niece Elizabeth became extremely ill. She was jaundiced and went to the hospital for tests. The doctors determined that she had a gall bladder infection and that her gall bladder had to be removed. During her recovery she would move in with my mom. The two invalids would care for each other.

Early in May I got a call from Brigid. Mom had fallen in the elevator and had hurt her head. Evidently, this had happened just after one of Brigid's Saturday morning visits. Mom had gone down to get the mail and had apparently tripped while entering the elevator on her return. When she fell, she hit her head. The elevator doors automatically closed behind her, and she remained on the elevator floor, unconscious and bleeding for an unknown length of time until another tenant found her. Someone called for an ambulance, and she was taken to Detroit's receiving hospital. The apartment manager notified Elizabeth, and Elizabeth called Brigid. Brigid rushed to the hospital as soon as she received the news.

When Brigid arrived at the hospital she hurried to the registration area. Worried to tears about Mom's health, she asked the emergency registration attendant about her condition. The young woman hastened to the back of the ward to find out how Mom was doing. By this time Mom was fully conscious and told the registration clerk that she was fine. Brigid was allowed to visit her and sat with her while they stitched her forehead. She remained in the hospital overnight for observation. In addition to her head injury, she had a bruised and swollen leg. The doctor prescribed bed rest. Despite her injuries, she continued to write. Since she could not reach her typewriter, she began to write longhand. Nothing could stop her from pouring out her life in words.

During the month of June, four months after my father's death, I received another ominous call in middle of the night, this time from

Elizabeth rather than my mother. My mother was experiencing extreme shortness of breath and had been taken by ambulance to the hospital. Brigid and Chris were on vacation and could not be reached. I immediately left Holland for Detroit.

When I arrived, Mom was sitting up and in good spirits. She was feeling rather feisty and insisted that the doctor let her go home. Her doctor wanted to perform a number of tests, so she stayed an additional night and met with the doctor the following day. He broke the news that she had had a heart attack—not recently, but some time ago. A third of her heart tissue was dead, making it difficult for the organ to pump all the blood she needed. It would be necessary for her to go on medication to help her heart beat regularly. With the prescribed medications in hand, she returned to her apartment, anxious to resume work on her book.

During the last part of May and into early June, my daughter, Jen-Ai, and my nephew David's wife, Angie, stayed with Mom to help take care of her physical needs. A visiting nurse came by twice a week. When Jen-Ai and Angie had to return to their lives in Kalamazoo and Benton Harbor, Elizabeth stayed on to help.

Mom continued to work diligently on her book. Within a month she suffered another setback and was taken to the hospital in an ambulance. She had awakened in the middle of the night, complaining to Elizabeth of shortness of breath. As they put her in the ambulance she told Elizabeth, "Have them do everything they can to save me."

This time when I arrived at the hospital, I found her lying in a semiconscious state. It was difficult to tell how conscious and aware she was. The doctor informed us that she had experienced a stroke and the left side of her body was paralyzed. She could neither move nor talk. The doctor said her prognosis was not good.

When members of my family offered her a pad of paper to try to get her to write, her scrawling was hard to decipher. It seemed at times that she was trying to communicate, but we could never be sure what her eye movements and facial expressions meant, if they meant anything at all. We held her hand and tenderly tried to convey our love to her even as we wondered how much she could feel or understand.

I stayed overnight in Detroit at Brigid's house and returned to visit Mom the following morning. I had only been in the room a few minutes when the alarm from her heart monitor sounded. Glancing up at the monitor, I could easily see why. The sharp peaks that represented the beating of her heart were gone. A flat line had replaced them. She was in cardiac arrest. As I began calling for a nurse, hospital personnel began pouring into the room. As one of the nurses wheeled a cart carrying a defibrillator on it, someone ushered me out of the room. I began praying for her recovery. I recited one of my favorite Bahá'í prayers: "Is there any Remover of difficulties save God? Say: Praised be God! He is God! All are His servants, and all abide by His bidding." Miraculously, as if in answer to my prayer, her heart resumed beating before they applied the defibrillator.

Nevertheless, the doctor ordered that she be put on a ventilator to make certain that she received enough oxygen. A heart specialist informed me that her only chance of survival would be to have a pacemaker installed, and even with a pacemaker installed, so much of her heart had been destroyed by the heart attack that her chances of living more than a short time were minimal. We tried in vain to communicate the medical options to her. Sometimes we were sure that she understood, based on a squeeze of the hand, a gleam of the eye, or an expression on her face. At other times we wondered if we were merely deluding ourselves. We knew that the ventilator made her uncomfortable. We also knew that she would not wish to live if "life" meant that she would be bedridden with a mechanical breathing tube inserted into her throat forever. Her only reason for living was to finish her book. She would be unable to complete her work unless she recovered sufficiently to breathe on her own and had some means of communicating. In her current state she was more helpless than a baby. Would she recover from the effects of the stroke? Would she be able to breathe on her own? Would she regain her powers sufficiently to be able to communicate? We finally decided to have a pacemaker installed, believing that we were following her wishes and that it was her only chance of survival. We hoped that with her heart beating more strongly, she would be able to breathe on her own and that the much-hated ventilator could be removed.

The operation was successful, and indeed she did become stronger. She seemed to be fighting to recover. After a few days of recovery, we insisted that the medical technicians begin the process of weaning her from the ventilator, knowing that her only hope of living the life that she wanted was to become independent of the machine. However, it soon became apparent that she would not be able to survive without it. We were faced with the choice of warehousing her in a medical facility or taking her off the machine and allowing her to die.

There were other factors to consider as well. Her entire body was deteriorating. Her Achilles tendon was tightening from lack of use, and her feet were pulled so that her toes were pointed like those of a ballerina en pointe. The nurses placed special boots on her feet to counteract this tendency, but the boots cut off her circulation so that the outer surface of her skin died, exposing the layer of muscle underneath. Her kidneys began shutting down, yielding thick, brown urine. It seemed as if she had aged twenty years in twenty days. When she entered the hospital her face was that of a seventy-year-old, still retaining much of the beauty of her youth. She now looked old and haggard, much like my grandmother did when she was in her nineties. She had lost the gleam in her eye and stared blankly into space. Then there was the question of morphine. We had no idea how much pain she felt from the endless medical interventions the doctors put her through: the IV in her neck, the newly installed pacemaker in her chest, the catheter in her urethra, the ventilator down her throat, the boots on her feet, the straps on her arms to keep them immobilized. This was not how she would have wanted to live or die. We instructed the doctors to give her enough morphine to make her comfortable. But pain is so subjective. How can anyone know how much pain she felt?

When we ordered that she be taken off of the ventilator, the doctors and nurses thought she would die within hours. But she fooled them. God only knows how she summoned the strength in that frail body to continue to live, but she did. She had always been a strong-willed woman who refused to accept defeat. For the first time in days I had a new glimmer of hope that she would gradually recover. But my hopes were dashed as her lungs began to fill with a sickening pink fluid. The respiratory therapists would periodically suction the disgusting liquid from her lungs, only to have them fill up again. And still she fought on. How long could she last?

I hadn't seen my family in a week and decided to drive back to Benton Harbor for a brief visit. Jen-Ai would stay with Mom. No sooner did I reach my home in Holland than Kim informed me that Mom had just passed on to the next world. It was as if she had been waiting for me to leave so that she could die. I was glad that Jen-Ai had been with her as she passed from this world into the next. I prayed that my mother would be reunited with my father, the greatest love of her life. I knew that she would find peace, rest, and comfort that she had not found in this life. I believe that in the next world, all colors are merged into one color, and all are bathed in the ocean of God's love.

I recalled a dream I had had the previous year. In the summer of 1994, my parents' last good season on earth, I had awakened one morning remembering a very powerful dream. I was in the middle of a forest, watching as lumbermen began taking down a mighty oak tree. The oak was larger than any tree I'd seen while awake. Its trunk was as big as a giant redwood's, and it was at least three hundred feet tall. It was beautiful and in good health. It saddened me to see that the timber men were sawing off the limbs branch by branch and taking the oak down. I mourned its loss and awoke crying.

I felt that the tree was my mother. I have always been in awe of her courage, love, and strength. She had traveled alone to China when most American women could only dream of traveling abroad. She had earned a master's degree from a major university at a time when women were not supposed to be educated. She had been a devoted wife in an interracial marriage during decades when it was both abhorrent and illegal. And throughout her life she had been an example of self-sacrifice for her husband and family. The huge oak tree represented the strength and capacity of her soul. The branches that had protected our family for generations were now transported to another plane of existence.

We all felt the loss of her sheltering love and protection. Who would the family gather around at Christmas and Thanksgiving? Who would provide for Linda and Elizabeth in their ensuing emotional and financial crises? Who would give us the understanding we all inevitably needed in times of inner and outer turmoil?

My mother's body was cremated, as my father's had been, and her ashes were interred near my father's and my brother's in a cemetery just north of Detroit. Our family held a memorial service attended only by family members. Tearfully, we all recounted stories that illustrated the great themes of her life: her love of family, her ability to put total strangers at ease, her yearning to return to China, her voracious appetite for reading, her passion for writing, her deep appreciation of beauty, her constant self-sacrifice for all of us.

Reflecting on the lives of my parents, I realized that I had learned many things from them. From my father I learned stability and how to endure tests and difficulties with stoicism and equanimity. I learned to question everything and to think for myself. These are qualities that have served me well through the difficulties I faced in my first marriage, in challenges presented to me at work, and ultimately in my quest for spiritual truth. From my mother I learned compassion and love. She showed us all how to love completely, unselfishly, and unconditionally. She gave much to everybody and asked nothing in return. She was like the candle of which 'Abdu'l-Bahá spoke when he said, "Behold a candle how it gives its light. It weeps its life away drop by drop in order to give forth its flame of light."*

I am most grateful for the fact that my parents raised me with a heart big enough to love all mankind and a mind open enough to embrace new ideas and be free of religious bigotry. I am thankful that they prepared me with the qualities I needed to recognize the beauty of the Bahá'í Faith and to accept its truth.

---

* 'Abdu'l-Bahá, quoted in May Maxwell, *An Early Pilgrimage* (Oxford, U.K.: George Ronald, 1953), p. 42.

Afterthoughts

The well-being of mankind, its peace and security, are unattainable unless and until its unity is firmly established.

—Bahá'u'lláh

W. E. B. DU BOIS WROTE PROPHETICALLY near the beginning of the last century, "The problem of the twentieth century is the problem of the color line."[1] With that simple phrase he simultaneously foreshadowed America's perennial race riots, the growth and persistence of hate groups, and the continuing struggle of Blacks and other minorities for equal rights—in short, America's enduring racial and ethnic divisions. Applied at the international level, Du Bois's insightful words allude to the continuing series of ethnic atrocities that we have experienced in this era: the massacre of the Armenians by the Turks, the Nazi Holocaust, Africa's legacy of ethnic and tribal wars in the wake of colonialism, and the struggles for national identity on the European continent in the post-Cold War period.

On a more personal level, the words of Du Bois seem equally prophetic in relation to the problems of my parents' marriage and my own struggle for identity. From the first flicker of my parents' blameless love until my mother's fading death rattle, they were haunted by the specter of racism. The secretive nature of their romance, the reactions of their parents, their frustrated search for community, the permanently deferred dreams of my father, their struggles to raise children in an unwelcoming society were all born from the tainted stream of racism that still flows too freely through our country.

Who can tell how the members of our family might have turned out had we not been immersed in a sea of racism? Perhaps we would all have been more self-assured. Perhaps my older sister Linda would have finished high school. She would not have been forced to deal with the painful rejection of her teacher and peers. Perhaps she would not have chosen alcohol as an anesthesia for a lifetime of pain and rejection. Perhaps she would have been accepted by a loving man who could be a deserving father to her children instead falling prey to abusers of every kind. And what of my younger sister, Brigid? Would she have blossomed in her teen years instead of her twenties, enabling her to complete high school instead of dropping out as soon as she legally could? Would Colin have used his brilliance to complete his degree at the University of Michigan instead of having to work as a postal employee and freelance writer? How much of his drinking problem stemmed from the consuming desire to escape the pain of racism? How would my life have been different in a prejudice-free society? Would I have developed more friendships and had normal peer relationships during my preteen and teen years instead of becoming an introverted social isolate? Would my heart have pounded with anxiety every time I raised my hand in school between kindergarten and college had I not been conditioned to feel like an outcast? Would I have had the confidence in a thousand little ways to take the initiative in social settings, to begin and complete more challenging activities? How would my career have been different? Would I have had more opportunities for advancement? I cannot help wondering how much damage was inflicted on the children of our family by the reactions of a racist society to a family that dared to break the rules of race-mixing.

The damage to my parents was more obvious in my mother than in my father. My mom—once a sheltered, middle-class, small-town college graduate who knew nothing of Blacks or racism—was unprepared for the racist reactions to her marriage. She didn't expect the ostracism, the gunshot through her window, or the dead canary. She didn't expect to be run out of her cozy suburban Chicago home when the residents discovered that her husband was Black. The racism that permeates our society so completely and underlies most Black-White relationships totally shocked her. The stares, which bothered us all, must have hurt her more, for she had been raised as a first-class citizen and was suddenly relegated to second-class status. They must have hurt her more because she knew the hatred that was behind them. Furthermore, she always felt our pain in addition to her own. She could never bear to see her children in pain.

She suffered terribly from the treatment of those who once saw her as an equal. The burning torment of the prejudice she felt directed at her and at those she loved caused her to feel great pain and anger. Like many Blacks in America, my mother's breast was penetrated with pain and anger, causing prejudice to germinate in her heart. Although she knew intellectually that not all Whites were prejudiced, she felt in her gut that they were. Hearts are subject to conditioning by fear and pain in ways that defy the intellect. By the mid-1950s she had experienced more than a decade of rejection by White society and had faced almost daily the prejudice directed against her family. If the prejudice White Americans held toward an educated, well-adjusted adult who had experienced it only for a little more than a decade could produce such a dramatic effect, how must it affect Black Americans who suffer under its agonizing weight from birth until death?

No Black person raised in America completely escapes the negative effects of racism. This was certainly true of my father. Tragically, he was a brilliant man who could have made tremendous contributions to humanity had he not been stifled by the burden of racism. As his poetry clearly demonstrates, he held a largely unexercised capacity to express himself beautifully in words. My mom, a published author, acknowledged that he was a superior writer. Yet he was crippled by a lack of self-confidence. How much of his lack of confidence was due to the yoke of racism and how much was due to other circumstances is impossible to tell, but I believe the racist climate of America hurt him to the point of crippling him. He aspired to be a diplomat at a time when Blacks were not welcomed in high government positions in this country. What happens inside a man when he knows that his dearest dream is impossible simply because of the color of his skin?

My parents had few friends for most of their married life. Though they enjoyed a healthy social life during our years in Altgeld Gardens, you could count on one hand their really close friends during our Detroit years. When they weren't met with open hostility, they were met with veiled hostility hidden behind cold, staring eyes. Neighbors and coworkers alike shunned them. Their tentative gestures of friendship were rejected. Where were the proponents of brotherhood and equality during the fifties and sixties? Where were the champions of interracial marriage in this great melting pot of ours during the eighties and nineties? Where are they now?

For the first three decades of my life, whenever my mother and brother told me that this country was permeated by racism, I did not believe them. I knew that there were bigots, but I reasoned that they were a minority. I naively believed that the vast majority of people in America, both Black and White, were unaffected by racism. I was too inexperienced to see that the police who stopped me and my brother so frequently during our childhood were part of a ubiquitous American phenomenon that Blacks in virtually every major city and thousands of small towns have experienced. In my ignorance I thought they were just doing their job. Too self-conscious to see that the social rejection I felt from both Blacks and Whites was part of the pattern of racism in our society, I blamed myself instead of the condition of racism in our country. My parents shielded me and my siblings from the numerous painful encounters they experienced as an interracial couple throughout their married life. I believed the high levels of poverty and unemployment, the poor schools in Black communities, and the high levels of violent crime were social phenomena that sprang from social and cultural conditions unrelated to race. I couldn't understand my brother's cynicism and my mother's bitterness about race relations in America. I was in denial. My views were similar to those of many White Americans who think racism is a minor problem that only affects a few extremely bigoted Whites and with which Blacks and other people of color are obsessed.

When I reached my mid-thirties the veil gradually lifted. I began to see that the tiny threads of racism scattered throughout society were woven into a tightly knit fabric with the strength of Kevlar. Membership in the Bahá'í community helped me to understand how deeply racism is ingrained in our society. Overcoming prejudices of all kinds—religious, national, economic—is a fundamental principle of the Bahá'í Faith. Addressing the issue of racism in 1991, the National Spiritual Assembly of the Bahá'ís of the United States made the following statement:

> Racism is the most challenging issue confronting America. A nation whose ancestry includes every people on earth, whose motto is *E pluribus unum,* whose ideals of freedom under law have inspired millions throughout the world, cannot continue to harbor prejudice against any racial or ethnic group without betraying itself. Racism is an affront to human dignity, a cause of hatred and division, a disease that devastates society.[2]

Racism is described elsewhere in the Bahá'í writings as "one of the most baneful and persistent evils." The writings go so far as to say "we must pray to be protected from the contamination of society which is so diseased with prejudice."[3]

The analogy of racism as a disease became clearer to me when I studied alcoholism as part of my counseling program. Here is a physical addiction described as a disease with social, emotional, behavioral, intellectual, and spiritual components. The thought occurred to me, "What if racism could be described as a disease? Not a physical disease but a social affliction. What would it look like? What would the symptoms be? What course would it run? What would the cure be?"

These insightful questions led me to ponder the many striking similarities between racism and alcoholism. More than a physical disease, alcoholism has emotional, intellectual, behavioral, social, and spiritual dimensions. The most successful treatment programs address all of these dimensions. Similarly, racism cannot be described as a physical disease. Rather, it is more aptly described as an internal disease of the spirit, heart, and mind that manifests itself physically through acts of prejudice and discrimination. Curing racism must involve changing our values, attitudes, and thinking, and not just our behavior.

Just as alcoholism involves sick thinking and warped emotions, racism also has its roots in irrational ideas and unhealthy feelings. It begins with the commonly accepted notion of race. Everyone knows that human beings can be scientifically classified into three basic races—Caucasian, Negroid, and Mongoloid—right?

Wrong. For more than four decades scientists have known that there is no scientific justification for classifying human beings into three or four races. During these four decades scientists have attempted to find a sound alternative basis for classifying humankind into races. The number of racial categories they have hypothesized has expanded over these years into the thousands. According to S. Dale McLemore and Harriett D. Romo, authors of *Racial and Ethnic Relations in America,* scientists have argued that there may be as many as 150 different races. Recent genetic research has revealed that biological differences between so-called "races" is less than 0.2 percent. Professor Lawrence A. Hirschfeld of the University of Michigan states, "Regardless of what our senses seem to tell us, race is not a biologically coherent story about human variation simply because the races we recognize and name are not biologically coherent populations." In other words, it makes no scientific sense to divide our human family into the racial categories we currently use. According to Eliot Marshall, "Genetic diversity appears to be a continuum, with no clear breaks delineating racial groups."[4] Summarized briefly in common language, there is only one race, the human race.

Yet Americans persist in labeling themselves as Blacks and Whites as if these racial categories were real. Our governments label us, as do newspapers, magazines, pollsters, and researchers. We even label each other as if it served some positive purpose. Our very identities are wrapped up in these labels. We think of ourselves as "Black" or "White" and develop ethnic pride based on these false identities. The labels enable us to categorize our fellow human beings and separate ourselves from others based on minor or even imaginary differences. In the process, we create stereotypes and develop emotional reactions that are based on the false images we associate with racial names. If our world is ever to recover from the disease of racism, we must change the way we conceptualize race and identity.

When I realized that the concept of race is a pseudo-scientific fiction, I began to rethink my identity. Instead of calling myself "Black," "White," "mulatto," or "mixed," I began calling myself an "African American." "African American" refers to my ethnic and national identity rather than to some pseudo-scientific racial identity. However, I believe that my human identity is more important than any ethnic or national identity. My primary allegiance is to the human race rather than to African Americans or the United States of America. This broader way of identifying myself is reinforced by the universal teachings of the Bahá'í Faith, which urge all people to think of themselves as members of one human family.

This is no easy task, however. The process of changing the way we think about race is made more difficult by the emotional aspects of racism. Many of us are emotionally committed to maintaining our racial identities. We are proud of our "racial" features and identities. We feel secure in thinking and believing that we belong to a particular racial group. We may feel uncomfortable when members of a different race surround us. For some, our sense of self-esteem is tied to our racial identity. We believe that our race is better than others. We love the members of our race as a kind of extended family. In short, many of us have powerful emotional commitments to our racial identities and, therefore, to racism.

These intellectual and emotional aspects of racism are expressed in a multitude of individual behaviors. While only a fool would deny the racism inherent in slavery and segregation in America, few of us accept the possibility that racism is implied in our daily individual behavior patterns. This racism expresses itself in innumerable choices that we make consciously and unconsciously on a daily basis. Will I live in a Black, White, or mixed neighborhood? There are millions of Blacks and Whites who would never consider moving into a neighborhood that was predominantly made up of members of another race. At lunchtime, will I sit with people who are physically similar or dissimilar to me? Even in very integrated workplaces, the lunchrooms are often racially divided. Would I consider dating or marrying a person of another race? Only a very small percentage of Americans have crossed this racial barrier. According to U.S. Census statistics in 2000, only 1 in 54 marriages was interracial.[5] Ads in countless singles dating columns ask for potential dates and mates of specific races. All of these behaviors are considered normal in American society, yet they are thoroughly racist and perpetuate a divided society. Do I meet and greet people of all racial backgrounds with equal warmth and acceptance as indicated by my facial expression, words, and body language? How many of us can honestly answer yes?

These and many other individual behaviors combine to form clearly racially motivated and, therefore, racist social patterns. We live in segregated neighborhoods, attend segregated churches, and socialize almost exclusively with members of our own ethnic or racial group. While most of us believe that we are not racist, our hearts, minds, and actions reveal obvious patterns of racism.

The final component in the disease model of racism is the spiritual component. Racism is often unconscious. We unconsciously learn the concepts of race from our society. We are unconsciously conditioned to accept racial stereotypes. Our feelings toward other ethnic groups, whether positive or negative, are simultaneously conditioned by our family and friends. To a certain extent we cannot help the feelings we have toward other ethnic groups. Yet we make choices about our ideas and our feelings. These choices are moral and spiritual in nature. They involve the process of applying our values and beliefs to our actions. These choices offer the possibility of developing and using our nobler qualities of character or allowing our baser, more selfish instincts to govern.

My mother's parents, for example, actively chose to oppose the existing paradigm of racial segregation. My maternal grandmother chose to find comfortable housing for African American students who were not allowed in the university dorms. She consciously chose the values of fairness and compassion over accepting the status quo of segregation. My mother's parents made a similar choice when it came to accepting my father as a son-in-law. Although it was extremely difficult for them emotionally, when my mother married my father, her parents chose to support the marriage rather than reject it.

Similarly, when the townspeople of Woodstock discovered they had an interracial couple in their midst, some chose to support the couple and some chose to reject them violently. The townspeople made moral and spiritual choices that showed either strength or weakness of character.

We all face comparable choices in our daily lives. Will we accept the divisive racial names that have gained currency in society today, or will we choose other, less divisive terms for ourselves? Will we broaden our identity to embrace people of all ethnic groups as our family, or will we limit our allegiance to narrow national, ethnic, or color groups? Will we allow ourselves to be governed by the negative emotions we've been conditioned to feel toward people who are different from us, or will we seek out positive experiences with those people so that we can become more comfortable with the differences? Will we follow established patterns of social segregation, or will we break those patterns of housing, church attendance, and socializing?

Another dimension of the moral and spiritual choices we face is how we react to the racism displayed by those around us. Do we ignore the race-based language that others use, or do we attempt to raise awareness by engaging in productive dialogues about language? I am not suggesting discussions of political correctness. Rather than prescribing the language that people use to describe themselves, I suggest starting discussions about the meaning of race and racial language. Do we laugh at ethnic humor, or do we challenge such public displays of prejudice and racism? Do we look the other way when we see acts of racial discrimination, or do we become advocates for equity? Will we accept the race-based inequalities of our educational, criminal justice, and health care systems, or will we actively work to dismantle the racism in many of these systems? These are all questions of a spiritual nature, and our responses to them indicate our spiritual health.

When we examine the intellectual, emotional, behavioral, social, and spiritual dimensions of racism, the justification for labeling it as a disease becomes clear. It's not a physical disease, however, it's a cultural disease. Racism involves sick thinking, unhealthy feelings, destructive behaviors, dysfunctional social interactions, and harmful moral choices. Moreover, racism seems to be contagious. It is a complex set of learned behaviors that are passed from parents to children and from friend to friend. Children are not born prejudiced. They learn it from their parents, friends, and other afflicted members of society. It's so contagious that even immigrants who come here from other countries often become prejudiced against the less advantaged minorities in our society. Even recently immigrated Africans sometimes catch the disease and become prejudiced against African Americans.

How is the disease transmitted? All diseases have a vector, or means of transmission. With AIDS, the vector is contaminated body fluids that are passed from one individual to another, usually through sexual activity or through the sharing of intravenous needles. With malaria and encephalitis, it is the mosquito. In the case of racism, the deadly vector is ideas and emotions that are transmitted through social contact, from one individual to another.

Like alcoholism, racism begins as a social behavior. People share racial jokes and stories just like they share drinks. It is also similar to alcoholism in that it involves denial and rationalizations. People have a difficult time facing their own racist thoughts and feelings, so they deny them, just as alcoholics deny their addiction to alcohol. When it comes to racism all but the most blatant bigots deny their own racism. Racism is always someone else's problem, never our own.

Racism is like alcoholism in several other ways. Just as an entire family system becomes diseased when an alcoholic is present, so entire societies are affected by the introduction of racism. The relative peace of Yugoslavia was shattered with the racist political tactics used by demagogues, leading in the end to a holocaust of ethnic cleansing. In Rwanda, an uneasy coexistence between cooperating members of different tribes became a bloody attempt at genocide through the conscious cultivation of racism.

Ironically, African Americans seem to be in denial as much as European Americans are. Many African Americans persistently claim that racism is primarily a White problem. They justify their prejudice, claiming that they are exempt from racism because they do not have the power to inflict discrimination on Whites in the same way that Whites can inflict it on Blacks. In my view, African Americans are no more exempt from racism than any other group. Since the 1960s one of the popular definitions of racism among African Americans has been that racism equals prejudice plus power. The argument goes that while individual prejudice may be harmful, its evil is compounded when the dominant group in a society applies it to minorities. According to this narrow definition, only the dominant group is capable of systematically applying social and political power to subjugate minorities, and minorities have no power over the dominant group. By this definition, African Americans are exempt from racism because they have comparatively little power in our society.

This narrow definition of racism is faulty because it denies the power that African Americans have in our society. While it's true that the United

States government and its political and economic institutions are dominated by Americans of European descent, African Americans possess a considerable amount of economic, political, and social power. The combined economic strength of African Americans is greater than that of many nations in other parts of the world. African Americans do, in fact, wield political power in most large cities in this country. Furthermore, they have substantial control over the cultural and social climates of neighborhoods where they are the majority. If racism springs from a combination of prejudice plus power, African Americans have enough power to inflict a considerable amount of racism.

Furthermore, in my personal experience African Americans have demonstrated the capacity to be as prejudiced as any fellow Americans. While growing up, I often experienced emotional difficulty with many of my African American friends when they made prejudiced remarks about White people. As an adult, I've met scores of African Americans who have simply given up on all White people. Granted, the prejudice that African Americans hold springs from innumerable real experiences of discrimination, but to generalize those experiences to all White people is to stereotype. My mother's experience with discrimination demonstrates that the emotional temptation to generalize negative experiences is both natural and overwhelming. She was a White person who developed prejudice against all White people in the same way that many African Americans do. Nevertheless, as natural as the tendency for victims of racism to stereotype may be, it is still a grave injustice to the target group, regardless of color.

Let me hasten to add, however, that the stereotyping applied by relatively powerless minorities to the group that oppresses them is qualitatively and quantitatively different from discrimination by the majority. The damage that is inflicted because of the racism of light-skinned Americans (Whites) toward people of color far outweighs the damage inflicted by people of color on their lighter-skinned compatriots. Because of the overwhelming economic, social, and political power that European Americans wield in this country, the damage they inflict on people of color vastly outweighs the damage inflicted by people of color upon their paler brothers and sisters. Moreover, European Americans control the political, social, and economic systems that maintain racism in this country.

The systems of racism in the South are directly responsible for the stereotyping of light-skinned people (Whites) by African Americans. It was necessary for the survival of African Americans in the South. Not long ago, African Americans were lynched in the South if they weren't subservient. Black men were in particular danger if they demonstrated even a hint of attraction toward White women. Black men were expected to avert their gaze to avoid looking directly at White women. For the sake of safety and self-preservation, Blacks had to assume that all Whites were racist. An African American in the South who trusted Whites, giving them the benefit of the doubt, could easily end up hanging from a tree, rotting at the bottom of a lake, or missing body parts. It became necessary for parents to teach their children to act as if all White people were prejudiced just as people today teach children that all moving cars are dangerous. African Americans could not even trust Whites who acted as if they were not prejudiced because some Whites played the game of baiting and trapping Blacks into acts of "disrespect" so that the Whites would have an excuse to retaliate.

I believe, however, that the time has passed when the assumption that all Whites are prejudiced has survival value. The concerted effort made by Blacks and Whites in the Civil Rights movement gave Blacks a greater tool than subservience to survive White prejudice. We now enjoy the legal protection granted by law. Blacks no longer have to expect death when they treat Whites as equals. Yet we cling to our old prejudices as if our lives still depended upon them. Why?

African Americans are as infected with the disease of racism as Whites are. We frequently identify ourselves primarily as "Black" rather than as American or human. We sometimes regard our "Blackness" as more important than our national identity or our human identity. Emotionally, too many of us react to White people based on their skin color without giving them a chance to show us who they are. Some of us are so consumed with the anger we hold because of past wrongs that we shut out European Americans completely. We sometimes isolate ourselves socially from our European American neighbors and coworkers. We will only let them get so close emotionally. Even in communities and businesses where African Americans are the majority, we sometimes practice institutional racism against people who are not members of our group. We often fail to exercise the spiritual choices that are necessary to lift us out of the swamp of racism. When we African Americans look to remedy the problem of racism in this country, we must look to ourselves as well.

If racism is a disease, then what is the cure? Since the disease is multifaceted, the cure must be multifaceted as well; it must involve mental, emotional, behavioral, social, and spiritual remedies. If the cure is to be effective, all of these remedies must be applied. Equally important, Blacks and Whites must work as allies in the struggle to dismantle racism.

As I began to understand the depth of the problem of racism, I developed an increasing sense of responsibility to do something about it. One of the gifts of being a biracial American is feeling that my primary identity and allegiance is to humanity, not to any particular race or nation. Ironically, although my mother had high ideals, she was herself quite prejudiced against Whites, almost until the end of her life. Not until the last six months of her life did she reluctantly admit that she had, with great difficulty, learned once again to view Whites as individuals. Fortunately, I adopted her ideals and not her prejudices.

Another benefit of my biracial heritage is that I am bicultural. I have been exposed to, and identify with, both Black and White cultures in America. Although I sound White and am more fluent in White cultural circles than in Black cultural circles, I have the heart of a Black man. I identify with the feeling of swimming in a sea of prejudice that most Blacks seem to have. I feel an emotional kinship with Blacks that I feel with few Whites outside of the Bahá'í community. While I can connect with Whites, intellectually and culturally there is often something missing in the connection. With Blacks, in addition to these connections, there is a deeply rooted emotional connection. This emotional connection with my brothers and sisters of African ancestry is illustrated by my experience in Swaziland during the winter of 2000. Hosted by a warm, welcoming international Bahá'í community consisting of Iranians, Americans, and native Swazis, I had the opportunity to speak and visit with many Swazi families. One evening my host family invited me to speak briefly at a local church. I chose to speak about my reasons for coming to Africa. I spoke of my ancestors who had been kidnapped from Africa, taken across the sea, and sold into slavery in America. I told them that I had returned to be reunited with my African brothers and sisters. The story visibly moved many members of the congregation. They tearfully embraced me as a long lost brother, welcoming me to my African homeland. In their hearts they understood our connection with each other.

However deep my connection with Blacks, it will never eliminate my connection with Whites. My ancestors came from Europe as well. The difference is that most European Americans do not accept me as family, while people of African ancestry almost invariably accept our relationship. Nevertheless, I view my biracial ancestry as a priceless gift.

More important than the gift of my biracial heritage is the gift of the Bahá'í writings. The teachings of the Bahá'í Faith offer an incredibly profound solution to the problems of prejudice and racism.

Early in the 1980s it occurred to me that I had a unique contribution to make in the struggle against racism. Perhaps I could somehow help to bridge the gap between Blacks and Whites in this country. I believed at the time that there were large numbers of well-meaning Blacks and Whites who were willing to open themselves to relationships with members of other racial, ethnic, and cultural groups but remained separated because of existing social barriers. What they needed was a vehicle to bridge the social barriers—a group that was dedicated to integration. I had mixed feelings about the idea of organizing such a group. I enjoyed the thought that I might have a unique role to play in working to bridge the cultural gaps, but I shrank from the idea of taking a leadership role in organizing such a group. I felt shy and uncertain about my own capacity to act as a catalyst to organize such a group. I felt totally inadequate.

After spending weeks in a state of near depression over this conflict, in the fall of 1984 I mustered the energy to act. I called a few people I knew who were interested in improving race relations by working to eliminate prejudice and racism and increase feelings of unity among people of different races, and I invited them to form a planning committee. Our first meeting resulted in a short-lived organization called "People Together." People Together planned several public meetings to bring local residents of various backgrounds into contact with each other in a pleasant social setting. We always started with a potluck meal and followed it with a variety of activities such as games, music, and discussion. We always tried to have a broad array of cultural experiences. The organization was successful, but it lasted less than a year. It died out when I became engulfed in the turmoil that led to my divorce from my first wife. I didn't have the energy to combat racism and fight my own marital battles simultaneously.

Shortly after my divorce, I became involved with a neighborhood improvement association that incorporated race unity as part of its mission. I became chairman of the Racial Understanding Task Force. Its chief activity was a series of annual interracial picnics attended by local residents and all of the political figures we could interest, including mayors, legislators, and city commissioners. Our strategy was twofold: We wanted to strengthen social relationships between Blacks and Whites, and we wanted to give public officials the opportunity to demonstrate a positive attitude about interracial activities designed to overcome the barriers that keep people of different races apart.

Our picnics were wildly successful. We had hundreds of people attending, including the mayors of St. Joseph and Benton Harbor, United States Congressman Fred Upton, and a variety of business leaders and city officials. After the potluck picnics, we formed a line, physically linking ourselves hand-to-hand, forming a human bridge across the bridge that connects St. Joseph and Benton Harbor. I was exuberant to find that there were so many people who were willing to demonstrate publicly their belief in race unity.

Although efforts such as People Together are necessary to strengthen social relationships between Blacks and Whites, they fall short of a total solution. A complete solution requires that racism be addressed on a number of different levels: intellectual, spiritual, emotional, behavioral, and institutional. It requires that people empathize with the victims of racism so that they understand the deep wounds it inflicts. It requires that people find the spiritual inspiration to take appropriate moral stands for justice and equality. It requires that people change the way they interact with others who are culturally or ethnically different from them. Finally, a total solution requires dismantling institutional components of racism. People who would rid the world of racism must understand its complexity—that it involves sick thinking, emotional conditioning, intricate behavioral and social habits, and deeply entrenched institutional discrimination. We must understand that all of us are infected to varying degrees with the disease.

We must be willing to change the way we think of and talk about ourselves and others. We must purge from ourselves the language of racism, eschewing the very concept of race and refusing to accept the labels "Black" and "White." We must abandon our limited, illogical, and destructive racial identities in favor of our common human identity. We must take a conscious look at our thought patterns to see if they have been influenced by racial stereotypes.

We need to examine our behavior patterns to see if they are not tainted with the scent of racism. Have we made efforts to stretch our comfort zones to include people outside of our ethnic and cultural identity groups? To what extent do we participate in, or contribute to, institutional racism?

Only when we look at the complexity of racism will we have the ability to eradicate it. Only when we have the commitment to undergo scathing self-examination can we purify ourselves of its poison. Only when members of all ethnic groups actively work together to rid the world of racism will this baneful evil be eradicated from the face of the earth.

The Bahá'í Faith from its inception in 1844 has offered a surprisingly comprehensive solution to the problem of racism. It has stood uncompromisingly for the principle of the oneness of humankind from its inception until the present. The founder of the religion, Bahá'u'lláh, made it clear that unity is the spiritual imperative of the age. According to him, "The well-being of mankind, its peace and security, are unattainable unless and until its unity is firmly established." All of the tenets of the Bahá'í Faith are designed to support this central principle. The vision of the Bahá'í is a global civilization based on the spiritual principles found in all major religions. The unity of our civilization will be supported by the common understanding that people of all faiths are beginning to recognize: We are all worshiping the same common Creator. Racial, ethnic, cultural, and national boundaries will disappear as people come to realize that, in the words of Bahá'u'lláh, "The earth is but one country, and mankind its citizens."[6]

To support and achieve this vision, the Bahá'í Faith encourages its followers to rid themselves of all forms of prejudice. When 'Abdu'l-Bahá, the son of Bahá'u'lláh, visited America in 1912, racial segregation was the norm. He made it clear that members of the Bahá'í Faith must distinguish themselves from their surrounding society by eliminating racial barriers. He instructed Blacks and Whites to meet together and not separately. In a talk given at Howard University, he praised interracial meetings and expressed the hope that racial names would be eliminated, saying, "I am very happy to see you and thank God that this meeting is composed of people of both races and that both are gathered in perfect love and harmony. I hope this becomes the example of universal harmony and love until no title remains except that of humanity."[7]

'Abdu'l-Bahá made it clear, forty years before the Civil Rights movement, that words alone are not enough—action is required. Following his father's admonition "Let deeds, not words, be your adorning," he refused to stay in hotels that would not serve Blacks. He treated Black children with love and tenderness, using positive images to suggest how his contemporaries might change the way they thought about Blacks. In one meeting he held a piece of chocolate next to the skin of an African American child, comparing the child's skin to the delicious chocolate.[8] In that single gesture he was telling a world that denied the beauty and dignity of African Americans that Blacks, as members of the human family, have their own special beauty.

Since 'Abdu'l-Bahá's visit to America, the American Bahá'í community has led the nation in efforts to bring Blacks and Whites together in unity. Their efforts have included inviting ethnic minorities to participate in all levels of community life during the Jim Crow years, when segregation typified American social and religious life. Members of the Bahá'í Faith have elected, and institutions of the religion have appointed, African Americans to high-level leadership positions during the years when African Americans found few positions of leadership in the larger society. Decades before the Civil Rights movement brought Blacks and Whites together to work in unity for equality, the American Bahá'ís sponsored "race amity" conferences that brought hundreds of Blacks and Whites together in an atmosphere of equality and unity. More recently, a remarkable institution has developed within the Bahá'í community: the annual Bahá'í Black Men's Gathering. Since 1987 this unique assemblage has pioneered in understanding, developing, and honoring the special gifts that Black men have to offer. The "Gathering," as many participants affectionately call it, has helped hundreds of African American men realize their spiritual potential for positive contributions. Many have come to this unique gathering feeling beaten down and despondent because of the oppression of racism. Finding a renewed sense of their true spiritual identity, they leave with an increased commitment and an augmented capacity to serve humankind.

Although volumes can and, no doubt, will be written about the contributions of the Bahá'í Faith to the unity of our human family, these few examples suggest the breadth of the solution offered by the teachings of Bahá'u'lláh to the problems of racial prejudice.

What, then, can we expect in the twenty-first century?

The Civil Rights movement was the greatest era of cooperation between Blacks and Whites since the days when Frederick Douglass worked with the abolitionists to end slavery. It produced the greatest results since African Americans were emancipated from slavery some one hundred and fifty years ago. That wonderful, productive cooperation came to a sudden end in the 1960s with the rise of Black Nationalism and the death of Martin Luther King, Jr. Many Blacks seemed to think that the death of Martin Luther King, Jr., proved that his methods do not work. For those who were already inclined towards Black Nationalism, his death was just another proof that cooperation doesn't work and that militancy is a more successful strategy.

Tragically, there were no African American leaders of equal stature at the time who could arise and say, "Let's continue to work together in unity." The voices of militancy and Black separatism dominated, and hundreds if not thousands of European American liberals who had been allies in the Civil Rights era were alienated from the struggle. They were cut off from the opportunity to continue to work with African Americans for progress against racism. Instead of joining hands with those who were willing to work with them, many African Americans rejected the path of unity and chose a path of separatism and blame. This choice is yet another manifestation of racism.

As we move into the twenty-first century, the question of whether or not we will solve the problem of the color line remains unanswered in the world at large. The forces of racism remain strong in this country. According to a 1999 report from the Harvard Project on School Desegregation, there has been a steady increase in the level of segregation in schools since the 1980s. Most of the progress made toward integration in the preceding two decades vanished during the 1980s and 1990s. We're not back to where we were before the *Brown* v. *Board of Education* decision, but we have seen a steady increase in segregation. In the South, segregation has increased to pre-1970 levels.[9] Despite open housing laws, vast numbers of African Americans continue to live in segregated areas of our cities and towns and have little meaningful social interaction with European Americans.

Institutional racism has proven to be an almost insurmountable obstacle as affirmative action, our country's primary means of dismantling institutional racism, has come under attack. According to Susan Sturm and Lani Guinier, "We are witnessing a broad-based assault on affirmative action—in the courts, the legislatures, and the media. Opponents have defined affirmative action as a program of racial preferences that threatens fundamental American values of fairness, equality, and democratic opportunity." In 1996, Proposition 209 eliminated affirmative action programs in California, thereby reducing opportunities for Blacks to be admitted into state universities. African American children continue to receive inferior education from underfunded public schools.[10]

Our government and legal system offer only glimmerings of hope for justice to African Americans. According to a study released in the year

2000 by Human Rights Watch, on average, Black men are sent to prison on drug charges at 13 times the rate of White men. Yet, according to the U.S. Department of Health and Human Services, the percentage of Black and White drug users in the year 2000 was virtually identical. The racially disproportionate nature of the war on drugs is not just devastating to Black Americans. It contradicts faith in the principles of justice and equal protection of the laws that should be the bedrock of any constitutional democracy; it exposes and deepens the racial fault lines that continue to weaken the country and belies its promise as a land of equal opportunity; it undermines faith among all races in the fairness and efficacy of the criminal justice system. Urgent action is needed, at both state and federal levels, to address this crisis for the American nation.[11]

There also seems to be a resurgence of racism in organized groups. According to the Southern Poverty Law Center (SPLC), which tracks the activities of various hate groups, as of spring 2002 there were more than 676 hate groups in the United States, making it the second year in a row that the country has experienced a 12 percent increase in such groups during the year.[12] Further, these groups are more determined than ever to provoke racial mayhem. Many of them want nothing more than to see the country torn apart by a racially based civil war. They believe that a race war would provide an opportunity for Whites to prevail by eradicating Blacks from the North American continent for all time.

In spite of the failure of our political and traditional religious systems to remedy the disease of racism, there are promising social movements across the country. The number of interracial couples and marriages is higher than ever before. According to the U.S. Census, as of 2000 there were 1.046 million interracial couples in the United States. Christian groups such as the Promise Keepers are beginning to admit the degree of racism that exists within the church. Children such as Anisa Kintz, a member of the Bahá'í Faith who at the age of nine organized an interracial conference attended by more than four hundred children, increasingly make organized efforts to build bridges between diverse ethnic groups. Her courageous efforts have lead to the creation of dozens of Calling All Colors conferences across the country. Interracial and cross-cultural adoptions are on the rise. Advances in news media and electronic communications make it possible for us to become intimately acquainted with people from cultures and ethnic backgrounds all over the world. Finally, because of increases in travel and immigration, a mosaic of peoples from around the world are brought face to face with each other on a daily basis.

The question is which social trend will triumph? Will we allow a few thousand violent racists and the inactivity and ignorance of the majority of our countrymen to give racism a stronger foothold? Or will we acknowledge the depth of the problem and consciously choose to eradicate it? Answers to these questions can be found in the stunningly bright vision of the future that the Bahá'í Faith offers.

'Abdu'l-Bahá early in the twentieth century prophetically described it as a "century of light."[13] He explained that during this century we would achieve the universal recognition of the oneness of humankind. If we objectively survey the twentieth century it is clear that remarkable progress has been made. In this country, people of all ethnic backgrounds have the clearly established right to equal treatment before the law. As we entered the twentieth century, separate but equal was the law of the land. While African Americans still suffer from hate crimes, such crimes are no longer socially acceptable and are subject to legal prosecution. Interracial marriages are legal in all fifty states. Although our nation is still recovering from the social and emotional legacy of racism, and the struggle for equality is still necessary, the scales have tipped decidedly in favor of justice and equality. There are an increasing number of organizations dedicated to eradicating the disease of racism and helping us all heal from its debilitating effects. Institutes for the Healing of Racism, an exciting grass roots movement, have been spreading from community to community across North America, helping people of all ethnic and cultural backgrounds heal from the wounds of racism and become allies in the struggle to dismantle racism. Organizations such as the SPLC have won striking legal victories against those who commit hate crimes. The SPLC's magazine, *Teaching Tolerance,* has been delivered to thousands of teachers, who read it to learn how they can educate school children to become free of prejudice. In Holland and Grand Rapids, Michigan, hundreds of residents have met annually at Summits on Racism. In these remarkable meetings people from all sectors of society—law enforcement, education, faith communities, government, media, health care, and community organizations—gather to form and implement plans for eliminating racism from all aspects of society. Members of the American Bahá'í community have conducted hundreds of programs aimed at helping members of our nation eliminate all forms of prejudice.

AFTERTHOUGHTS

On the international level, the United Nations has become a permanent institution that addresses serious human concerns on a global scale. Agencies such as United Nations Educational, Scientific and Cultural Organization (UNESCO) work to educate the children of the world. The World Health Organization has made substantial progress in combating many of the major diseases that afflict humankind. There is an international court system that wields increasing power to bring those who dare to commit crimes against humanity to justice. All of these institutions are signs that the principle of the oneness of humanity has been firmly established on a global level. In the words of the Universal House of Justice, the international governing body of the Bahá'í Faith, "Whatever threats still hang over humanity's future, the world has been transformed by the events of the twentieth century."[14] Nevertheless, we have a lot of work to do toward making this principle a practical reality. We must work to ensure that people of all races and nations in whatever country they reside have equal access to education and economic opportunities and that their human rights are respected. We must reform all of our institutions so that they no longer discriminate against ethnic and cultural minorities. The Bahá'í Faith offers the vision that this will gradually and inevitably come to pass in the centuries to come.

It is my firm conviction that one of the greatest hopes for healing the disease of racism lies in the example my parents set of defying traditions, taboos, and laws against interracial marriage. Their relationship provided a concrete example that proves interracial marriage can work. Their marriage illustrated a very powerful principle outlined in Bahá'í scripture:

> Thou must endeavor that they [the races] intermarry. There is no greater means to bring about affection between the white and the black than the influence of the Word of God. Likewise marriage between these two races will wholly destroy and eradicate the root of enmity.[15]

My parents' marriage forced their families to confront their own racism. Their union brought into being children whose very existence called into question the concept of race. Their marriage served as a silent example to countless younger couples who in increasing numbers are crossing the line that separates Black from White in this country. Their marriage and others like it help to move our society beyond the limitations of Black and White. They are powerful beacons of hope for a promising future.

Notes

1. W. E. B. Du Bois, *The Souls of Black Folk*. Chicago: A. C. McClurg & Co.; [Cambridge]: University Press John Wilson and Son, Cambridge, U.S.A., 1903; Bartleby.com, 1999, <http://www.bartleby.com/114/>, [8 May 2002].

2. National Spiritual Assembly of the Bahá'ís of the United States, *The Vision of Race Unity: America's Most Challenging Issue* (Wilmette, IL: Bahá'í Publishing Trust, 1991), p. 1.

3. Shoghi Effendi, *The Advent of Divine Justice,* 1st pocket-size ed. (Wilmette, IL: Bahá'í Publishing Trust, 1990), p. 33; the Universal House of Justice, *The Promise of World Peace: To the Peoples of the World* (Wilmette, IL: Bahá'í Publishing Trust, 1985), p. 25; extract from a letter written on behalf of Shoghi Effendi, in *Lights of Guidance: A Bahá'í Reference File,* comp. Helen Hornby, 2d revised and enlarged ed. (New Delhi: Bahá'í Publishing Trust, 1988), no. 1347.

4. S. Dale McLemore, *Racial and ethnic relations in America,* 5th ed. (Boston: Allyn & Bacon, 1998), p. 11; J. C. Gutin, "End of the Rainbow," *Discover* (November 1994), pp. 71–75; John Woodward, "Seeing Race," Lawrence Hirschfeld, interview by John Woodford, *Michigan Today,* vol. 28, no. 2 (June 1996), pp. 2–3; Eliot Marshall, "DNA Studies Challenge the Meaning of Race," *Science,* vol. 282, no. 5389 (23 October 1998), pp. 654–55.

5. Jason Fields and Lynne M. Casper, *America's Families and Living Arrangements: March 2000,* Current Population Reports, P20-537, U.S. Census Bureau, Washington, D.C.

6. Bahá'u'lláh, *Gleanings from the Writings of Bahá'u'lláh,* trans. Shoghi Effendi, 1st pocket-size ed. (Wilmette, IL: Bahá'í Publishing Trust, 1983), pp. 286, 250.

7. 'Abdu'l-Bahá, *The Promulgation of Universal Peace: Talks Delivered by 'Abdu'l-Bahá during His Visit to the United States and Canada in 1912,* comp. Howard MacNutt, 2d ed. (Wilmette, IL: Bahá'í Publishing Trust, 1982), p. 46.

8. Bahá'u'lláh, *The Hidden Words* (Wilmette, IL: Bahá'í Publishing, 2002), Persian, no. 5; see Howard Colby Ives, *Portals to Freedom,* pp. 63–67.

9. See *Rethinking Schools Online,* vol. 16, no. 1 (Fall 2001), <http://www.rethinkingschools.org/Archives/16 01/Seg161.htm>; *Crisis,* vol. 108, no. 5 (September/October 2001), p. 9.

10. Susan Sturm and Lani Guinier, *California Law Review,* vol. 84, no. 4 (July 1996), p. 366; see Jonathan Kozol, *Savage Inequalities* (New York: Crown, 1991).

11. Amy Worden, *Is the War on Drugs a War on Blacks?* <http://www.apbnews.com/cjsystem/justicenews/2000/06/08/drugwar0608_01.html>, APBnews.com, 8 June 2000; [Jamie Fellner], "United States Punishment and Prejudice: Racial Disparities in the War on Drugs," *Human Rights Watch Report June 2000,* May 2000, <http://www.hrw.org/reports/2000/usa/>, (11 September 2002).

12. *Intelligence Project,* published by the Southern Poverty Law Center, Spring 2002, <http://www.klanwatch.com/intelligenceproject/ip-index.html>.

13. 'Abdu'l-Bahá, *Promulgation of Universal Peace,* p. 65.

14. [Universal House of Justice], *Century of Light* ([n.p.]: Bahá'í World Centre, 2001), p. 129.

15. 'Abdu'l-Bahá, in *The Power of Unity, Beyond Prejudice and Racism: Selections from the Writings of Bahá'u'lláh, the Báb, 'Abdu'l-Bahá, Shoghi Effendi, and the Universal House of Justice,* compiled by Bonnie J. Taylor, National Race Unity Committee, Bahá'í Publishing Trust (Wilmette, IL: Bahá'í Publishing Trust, 1986), p. 55.

Index

I

J

About the Bahá'í Faith

In just over one hundred years the Bahá'í Faith has grown from an obscure movement in the Middle East to the second-most widespread independent world religion after Christianity. With some 5 million adherents in virtually every corner of the globe—including people from every nation, ethnic group, culture, profession, and social or economic class—it is probably the most diverse organized body of people on the planet today.

Its founder, Bahá'u'lláh, teaches that there is only one God, that there is only one human race, and that all the world's religions have been stages in the progressive revelation of God's purpose for humankind. Bahá'ís believe that the unity of the entire human race is not only necessary for human progress but also inevitable. The Bahá'í Faith teaches, among other things, that religion should be a source of unity; condemns all forms of prejudice and racism; upholds the equality of women and men; confirms the importance and value of marriage and the family; establishes the need for the independent investigation of the truth; insists on access to education for all; asserts the essential harmony between science and religion; declares the need to eliminate extremes of wealth and poverty; and exalts work done in a spirit of service to the level of worship.

Bahá'ís believe that religion should be a dynamic force that raises the individual, family, and community to new spiritual heights. To this end Bahá'ís all around the world work to create an atmosphere of love and unity in their own lives, in their families, and in their communities.

For more information about the Bahá'í Faith, visit http://www.us.bahai.org/ or call 1-800-22-UNITE.

About Bahá'í Publishing

Bahá'í Publishing produces books based on the teachings of the Bahá'í Faith, a worldwide religious community united by the belief that there is one God, one human race, and one evolving religion.

For more than a century, Bahá'í communities around the globe have been working to break down barriers of prejudice between peoples and have collaborated with other like-minded groups to promote the model of a global society. At the heart of Bahá'í teachings is the conviction that humanity is a single people with a common destiny. In the words of Bahá'u'lláh, the Founder of the Bahá'í Faith, "The earth is but one country, and mankind its citizens."

Bahá'í Publishing is an imprint of the Bahá'í Publishing Trust of the United States.

Other Books Available from Bahá'í Publishing

THE HIDDEN WORDS
by Bahá'u'lláh

A collection of lyrical, gem-like verses of scripture that convey timeless spiritual wisdom "clothed in the garment of brevity," *The Hidden Words* is one of the most important and cherished scriptural works of the Bahá'í Faith.

Revealed by Bahá'u'lláh, the founder of the religion, the verses are a perfect guidebook to walking a spiritual path and drawing closer to God. They address themes such as turning to God, humility, detachment, love, to name but a few. These verses are among Bahá'u'lláh's earliest and best known works, having been translated into more than seventy languages and read by millions worldwide. This edition will offer many American readers their first introduction to the vast collection of Bahá'í scripture.

THE BAHÁ'Í FAITH:
THE EMERGING GLOBAL RELIGION
by William S. Hatcher and J. Douglas Martin

Explore the history, teachings, structure, and community life of the worldwide Bahá'í community—what may well be the most diverse organized body of people on earth—through this revised and updated comprehensive introduction (2002).

Named by the *Encylopaedia Britannica* as a book that has made "significant contributions to knowledge and understanding" of religious thought, *The Bahá'í Faith* covers the most recent developments in a Faith that, in just over 150 years, has grown to become the second most widespread of the independent world religions.

"An excellent introduction. [*The Bahá'í Faith*] offers a clear analysis of the religious and ethical values on which Bahá'ism is based (such as all-embracing peace, world harmony, the important role of women, to mention only a few)."—Annemarie Schimmel, past president, International Association for the History of Religions

"Provide[s] non-Bahá'í readers with an excellent introduction to the history, beliefs, and sociopolitical structure of a religion that originated in Persia in the mid-1800s and has since blossomed into an international organization with . . . adherents from almost every country on earth."—*Montreal Gazette*

REFRESH AND GLADDEN MY SPIRIT:
PRAYERS AND MEDITATIONS
FROM BAHÁ'Í SCRIPTURE
Introduction by Pamela Brode

Discover the Bahá'í approach to prayer with this uplifting collection of prayers and short, inspirational extracts from Bahá'í scripture. More than 120 prayers in *Refresh and Gladden My Spirit* offer solace and inspiration on themes including spiritual growth, nearness to God, comfort, contentment, happiness, difficult times, healing, material needs, praise and gratitude, and strength, to name only a few. An introduction by Pamela Brode examines the powerful effects of prayer and meditation in daily life, outlines the Bahá'í approach to prayer, and considers questions such as "What is prayer?" "Why pray?" "Are our prayers answered?" and "Does prayer benefit the world?"

SEEKING FAITH:
IS RELIGION REALLY WHAT YOU THINK IT IS?
by Nathan Rutstein

What's your concept of religion? A 2001 Gallup Poll on religion in America found that while nearly two out of three Americans claim to be a member of a church or synagogue, more than half of those polled believe that religion is losing its influence on society. *Seeking Faith* examines today's concepts of religion and the various reasons why people are searching in new directions for hope and spiritual guidance. Author Nathan Rutstein explores the need for a sense of purpose, direction, and meaning in life, and the need for spiritual solutions to global problems in the social, economic, environmental, and political realms. Rutstein also discusses the concept of the Spiritual Guide, or Divine Educator, and introduces the teachings of Bahá'u'lláh and the beliefs of the Bahá'í Faith.

366

A Wayfarer's Guide
to Bringing the Sacred Home
by Joseph Sheppherd

What's the spiritual connection between self, family, and community? Why is it so important that we understand and cultivate these key relationships? *Bringing the Sacred Home* offers a Bahá'í perspective on issues that shape our lives and the lives of those around us: the vital role of spirituality in personal transformation, the divine nature of child-rearing and unity in the family, and the importance of overcoming barriers to building strong communities—each offering joy, hope, and confidence to a challenged world. Inspiring extracts and prayers from Bahá'í scripture are included. This is an enlightening read for anyone seeking to bring spirituality into their daily lives.

Visit your favorite bookstore today to find or request these titles from Bahá'í Publishing.

DATE DUE

OCT 2 2 2004			
GAYLORD			PRINTED IN U.S.A.